WHY THE
COLD WAR ENDED

Electoral Systems in Comparative Perspective: Their Impact on Women and Minorities
Wilma Rule and Joseph F. Zimmerman, editors

Central Asia and Transcaucasia: Ethnicity and Conflict
Vitaly V. Naumkin, editor

Consumer Politics: Protecting Public Interests on Capitol Hill
Ardith Maney and Loree Bykerk

African Americans and the New Policy Consensus: Retreat of the Liberal State?
Marilyn E. Lashley and Melanie Njeri Jackson, editors

The Deadly Sin of Terrorism: Its Effects on Democracy and Civil Liberty in Six Countries
David A. Charters, editor

The European Union and Its Citizens: The Social Agenda
Beverly Springer

Curbing Unethical Behavior in Government
Joseph Zimmerman

How to Think About Social Problems: American Pragmatism and the Idea of Planning
Hilda Blanco

The Origins of the Twelfth Amendment: The Electoral College in the Early Republic, 1787–1804
Tadahisa Kuroda

Environmental Policies in the Third World: A Comparative Analysis
O. P. Dwivedi and Dhirendra K. Vajpeyi, editors

Social Justice in the Ancient World
K. D. Irani and Morris Silver, editors

Securing the Covenant: United States-Israel Relations After the Cold War
Bernard Reich

WHY THE COLD WAR ENDED

A Range of Interpretations

Edited by
Ralph Summy
and
Michael E. Salla

Foreword by
David Lange

CONTRIBUTIONS IN POLITICAL SCIENCE, NUMBER 353

GREENWOOD PRESS
Westport, Connecticut • London

Library of Congress Cataloging-in-Publication Data

Why the cold war ended : a range of interpretations / edited by Ralph
  Summy and Michael E. Salla ; foreword by David Lange.
      p.   cm. — (Contributions in political science, ISSN 0147–1066
  ; no. 353)
    Includes bibliographical references and index.
    ISBN 0–313–29569–7 (alk. paper)
    1. Europe—Politics and government—1989– 2. Cold War.
  I. Summy, Ralph. II. Salla, Michael E. III. Series.
  D2009.W49 1995
  940.559—dc20   94–47428

British Library Cataloguing in Publication Data is available.

Library of Congress Catalog Card Number: 94–47428
ISBN: 0–313–29569–7
ISSN: 1047–1066

First published in 1995

Greenwood Press, 88 Post Road West, Westport, CT 06881
An imprint of Greenwood Publishing Group, Inc.

Printed in the United States of America

The paper used in this book complies with the
Permanent Paper Standard issued by the National
Information Standards Organization (Z39.48–1984).

10 9 8 7 6 5 4 3 2 1

Contents

Foreword

David Lange

The world has not been short of seminal events of late. The end of the Cold War (most often symbolized by the fall of the Berlin Wall) has been followed by a variety of Middle Eastern accords and the advent of democracy in South Africa. It is inevitable that each will be analyzed to death. Each should be. For a Westerner or New Zealander of my years, the Cold War and its aftermath, which bodes fair to be a cold peace, is of immediate personal moment.

There was induced in each of us a mind-set which owed more to programmed Pavlovian visceral response than intelligent assessment. Unhappily the populist view of our immediate past is similarly reflexive. The Cold War ended "when capitalism triumphed over communism." "Godless atheistic communism" felt the warm balm of God's grace. The vigor of the West's economies brought the Soviet economy "to its knees."

This publication is a compendium of papers written by scholars who go beyond the trite and who will, in some cases, perplex. The Middle East and South Africa are seen by us as complex. We allow multifactoral explanations to be advanced as to the genesis of the much praised outcomes. But the Cold War is still seen in black-and-white terms.

These scholars introduce illuminating shades of grey. Of particular satisfaction is the acknowledgment in some of the papers of the role of intellectuals, peace groupies, dissenters, writers, and the media in hastening the emancipation of millions, which, to my mind, is the best and most enduring outcome of the collapse of the old order.

This release is timely. We need to develop a more sophisticated view of our past so that we might not fall prey to reckless optimism about our future. Things aren't always what they seem to be. This book makes that point rather well.

Acknowledgments

This collection of articles comprises most of the papers originally presented at a University of Queensland symposium on the weekend of September 24–25, 1993. The two exceptions are the chapters by David Cortright and Johan Galtung. The former was presented *in absentia*, on November 2, 1994, to a session of the Peace History Commission at the 15th General Conference of the International Peace Research Association in Malta. The Galtung chapter represents the revised form of a paper first delivered at a ceremony opening the University of Queensland's interdisciplinary Peace and Conflict Studies program in July 1991. All of the papers have subsequently been updated and subjected to a long process of revision before reaching their present publishable form.

Many people have been involved in the various steps contributing to the final output—indeed, far too many for them all to be credited. However, in the spirit of a cooperative venture, we would like to single out the efforts of a few whose assistance went far beyond anything we might reasonably have expected. We begin with expressions of thanks to the two heads of the institutions that funded the symposium. To Ken McPherson of the Indian Ocean Centre for Peace Studies at the University of Western Australia and to Don Fletcher of the Department of Government at the University of Queensland, we are indebted for their faith in the project so that it could become a reality. Their support was sustained from beginning to end. While the funds that they helped generate were greatly appreciated, their contributions also took the form of personal encouragement. That same note of appreciation is extended to other members of the Department of Government for their collegial support. It was truly a departmental project.

We wish to acknowledge the efforts of Kashonia Carnegie, Monica Hilse, Gay Mason, Linda Buckham, and John Leonard in helping us organize and conduct the symposium. For her assistance in the indexing, thanks to Sue Fraser. For his computer expertise, on which we constantly had to call, we are indebted to Tony Bunney. He somehow managed to resolve an unending stream of "system problems." And for their exceptional efficiency and cheerful mien—sometimes under what could only be called "stressful conditions"—our boundless gratitude goes to the secretarial trio of Karen Davis, Alison Kessels, and Sue Gordon. Thanks a million!

We also appreciate the fine reception and constructive support we have received from the staff at Greenwood Press, especially from the Executive Editor, Cynthia Harris. It is a pleasure working with all of you.

Finally—but certainly not least—for the encouragement, indeed inspiration, we received from our respective "best mates," Georgina Murray and Jenny Salla-Lowe, simple words of thanks would never be sufficient. You kept our spirits high and our humor and sanity intact whenever the project bogged down in the countless setbacks that appear to be endemic to the business of book editing. To do that, you must have woven some magic.

This book is dedicated to our children: Gil and Cielle, and Sebastian and Kalinda. Our fervent hope is that in their futures they may never have to experience the terror and agony of either a cold or hot war.

Introduction

Challenging the Emergent Orthodoxy

Ralph Summy

This collection of essays on the ending of the Cold War has been designed to investigate a number of questions, to open them up for debate—not to reach fixed, immutable answers. Indeed, it is because the answers currently pervading society on this topic are beginning to acquire the status of unassailable orthodoxy that it becomes necessary to go back and pose the original questions, as well as some new ones, and subject them to rigorous examination. Challenging the emergent orthodoxy does not call for the development of a revisionist orthodoxy but the demonstration of a range of counterinterpretations, each based on cogent argument and free of self-serving interest.

The book's contributors, who initially exchanged their findings at a University of Queensland symposium,[1] were carefully selected on these grounds. They were expected to provide qualities of independence, imagination, and critical analysis, focus on different perspectives, and bring to their findings a wealth of subtle variety. Despite the diversity of their approaches, however, they can be seen to start from a common set of principles. In joining the book's project they share an acknowledgment—either tacit or articulated—that debate on the Cold War's ending should *not* dissolve into orthodoxy. Their presence confirms that, far from being part of a closed debate whose answers can be assumed, questions surrounding the Cold War's termination continue to demand our attention. How we deal with these critical, unsettled questions, and the directions we give to the answers, will

My thanks to coeditor Michael E. Salla for his research assistance as well as his useful comments before the preparation of this introduction's final draft.

greatly determine the course of future conflict resolution—the way we handle the next cold wars, not to mention the hot ones.

While our main focus is directed at the question Why did the Cold War end? some of the contributors address a range of other, but related, questions such as Did the West win the Cold War? Has the Cold War even ended? Could it have ended sooner? Why were the experts surprised? What does its ending mean? How does our conception of its beginning affect our interpretation of the events of 1989 and 1990? What was the Cold War's nature? Was it a genuine conflict or was it contrived? In what way might its lessons shape the future? and Did the Cold War have a fundamentally different meaning to the Chinese than it did to the other antagonists? As Joseph A. Camilleri argues in Chapter 15, "the full significance of these events [the ending of the Cold War] cannot be grasped unless they are placed within a wider historical context, which means taking full account of the continuities as well as discontinuities between the Cold War and post–Cold War periods."[2] In his analysis, he even goes one step further—as do some of the other authors—and identifies political and economic trends that had their origins in circumstances predating 1945 and extending as far back as the nineteenth century. The contributors, therefore, approach the title question of the book not only from the different perspectives categorized under the book's main sectional headings, but from a variety of time-frames. Their different approaches are then given added meaning in the concluding chapter by means of a macroanalytical framework constructed by Michael E. Salla. His integrative analysis provides an overall focus enabling the reader to do more than pick and choose from a menu of explanations *the* "right" or "preferred" answer. Instead, each of the separate explanations can be seen to interweave and illuminate one area of an expanding total picture about this highly complex event.

Not that any of the book's authors would claim a monopoly of truth for his or her specific contribution. As was evident from the lively but amicable discussions at the symposium, each presentation was offered more in the nature of a point of view—albeit a carefully researched and reasoned one. Such an attitude stands in marked contrast to the factor that gave rise to the symposium—and now the book—in the first place. What motivated the project, of course, was a perception that a unitary, pervasive, and rigid explanation was enveloping Western thinking about the Cold War's ending and that, while every orthodoxy is potentially dangerous and should be subject to constant examination, this one has particularly pernicious implications.

Without wanting to overstate their role, I believe social scientists have an obligation to ensure that an absence of thought does not degenerate into an end of thought and, in this case, literally presage the possible ending of all thought. To borrow from Robert Browning, I dread the prospect of this orthodoxy becoming "our master, famous, calm and dead . . . Bourne on our shoulders" into oblivion.[3] In the spirit of helping to prevent such a catastrophe, it is hoped this book can at least make a modest contribution toward unmasking the emergent orthodoxy. The method resorted to by my fellow contributors has been to concentrate on the positive side—to create a comprehensive body of alternative outlooks rather than to dwell on criticizing the entrenched position. Only in this introductory chapter does the investigation focus exclusively on the orthodoxy itself. Four questions that I consider essential to the general inquiry are posed: Why is it so vitally important to challenge the orthodox view? How has a point of view been transformed into an orthodoxy? Who are the major transmitters of this orthodoxy? and What precisely is its content?

DEFINING THE ORTHODOXY

I propose to take these questions in reverse order. The orthodoxy can be spelled out quite clearly and unambiguously, and its leading exponents can be identified. Throughout virtually the entire West it takes two slightly different forms—one advanced by a right-wing camp associated with the majorities of the Reagan-Thatcher years, and the other linked to the Democratic party in the United States and some of the world's social democratic parties. The two positions are not mutually exclusive, and some of the foremost champions of the orthodoxy tend to straddle both camps. This is because both variants are essentially proclaiming the same message—namely, that the Soviet Union's capitulation and the Cold War victory for the forces of freedom and democracy were ultimately due to the relentless application of the West's military superiority and the dynamism of its ideas and economic system. These factors revealed communism's moral illegitimacy and highlighted its economic stagnation.[4]

The right-wing strand stresses that the ideological offensive and arms build-up of the Reagan era forced an intrinsically doomed system of centralized planning into penury and submission. During the 1980s the Soviets were simply unable to match the West in military hardware and consumer goods. Western superiority, especially in the field of weapons technology and productive capacity, paved the way for a peace "negotiated from strength" and exposed the hollowness of the socialist utopia. The more centrist line insists that it was the unbending determination and persistent strategy of military vigilance exerted over the long haul that wore down the Soviet Union, thwarting its expansion of empire and triggering the internal reforms that led to the denouement of 1989–90. This second strand commends the West for its resoluteness of action—maintained as it were for a period of over forty years with only rare and fleeting moments of pusillanimity—and attributes success basically to the strategy of nuclear deterrence and the old Roman maxim *si vis pacem, para bellum* (if you want peace, prepare for war). Thanks to this formula, it is claimed, not only was major war prevented but, in due course, victory was gained. Of the two versions the second, with its near universal acceptance, poses the greater challenge for critical scholarship.

SOME LEADING ADVOCATES

The rightist position is reflected in the views of a leading Republican on the U.S. Senate Foreign Relations Committee, Senator Richard G. Lugar, who credits Ronald Reagan with administering the coup de grâce: "He advocated increased defense spending and advanced research projects, including the Strategic Defense Initiative. These programs backed up Reagan's startling foreign policy goals, such as rolling back Soviet-style communism, negotiating the destruction of intermediate range nuclear weapons in Europe, and tearing down the Berlin Wall."[5]

According to Senator Lugar's line of reasoning, "the achievement of Reagan's goals demonstrated the undeniable wisdom of his policies."[6] A long list of former Reagan administration officials, as well as nongovernmental members of the "new right," subscribe to this explanation of the Soviet collapse. Not surprisingly, the list includes such prominent figures as ex-Pentagon officials Caspar Weinberger and Richard Perle, columnist George Will, and neoconservative intellectual Irving Kristol. Somewhat less predictable is the appearance of a former U.S. government Kremlinologist who was the editor of *Foreign Affairs*, William Hyland.[7] He depicts Mikhail Gorbachev succumbing to the pressures of Western military initiatives, with the delegitimation of the Soviet system occurring when *glasnost* enabled the citizenry to make comparisons with the prosperity and freedom of the West. In Hyland's account the Western offensive is also to be found in Reagan's conversion, by the mid to late 1980s, from a Cold War cowboy to a full-fledged peacemaker.[8]

Hyland's slightly more nuanced account incorporates elements of both the hardline right and centrist positions. Like the orthodox centrist, he sees containment, military strength, and confrontation from the Truman Doctrine onward securing the eventual victory. Yet he also recognizes that Reagan's (and earlier Jimmy Carter's) stepped-up military and ideological response to Leonid Brezhnev's mockery of detente in Europe and the Third World brought confrontation to a head and resolved the struggle in the West's favor.

This is also the type of broadly conceived orthodoxy advanced by former secretary of state Zbigniew Brzezinski. He argues: "The Cold War eventually ended because the West succeeded in combining firm containment with an active offensive on human rights and a strategic buildup of its own, while aiding the resistance in Afghanistan and Poland."[9] He gives historical credit for putting this winning strategy into place to Harry Truman. However, the final accolade is bestowed on Carter and Reagan, who responded to, and aggravated, the crisis of communism with a multifrontal assault. In particular, they did not hesitate to raise the military stakes. "[T]he final phase of the Cold War . . . was marked by the West's gradual recapture of the ideological initiative, by the eruption of a philosophical and political crisis in the adversary's camp and by the final and decisive push by the United States in the arms race."[10] According to the Brzezinski analysis, when the United States countered the Soviet deployment of SS-20 missiles with an accelerated military program of its own, it strengthened the resolve of its European allies and sent Soviet leaders reeling. "The massive US defense build-up of the early 1980s—including the decision to proceed with the Strategic Defense Initiative—both shocked the Soviets and then strained their resources."[11]

Kremlin leaders, he claims, began to contemplate by 1983 that the United States might be bent on a military solution, which by the middle of the decade they knew they could not match. Hence when Gorbachev came to power in 1985, he and his advisers "eagerly seized the olive branch extended by the Reagan administration . . . in the hope of gaining relief from the arms race."[12] They believed that with a respite in the Cold War, they could correct all those failed domestic and foreign policies and generally overhaul a system that had been allowed to run down. But Gorbachev and his aides badly miscalculated. Brzezinski even refers to the Russian leader as "the Grand Miscalculator and historically a tragic figure."[13] For in the Cold War's final chapter he was shrewdly outmaneuvered by star performers President George Bush and Chancellor Helmut Kohl.[14]

The role of Western elites effecting the end of the Cold War features in the mythology of both orthodox strands.[15] Such an interpretation serves to consolidate the elites' command position. Not only is their record vindicated and all the sacrifices justified, but their right to make decisions on society's behalf is further legitimated. Everyone's welfare becomes identified with that of the key policymakers. This subtle sense of co-identification comes through in President George Bush's explanation as to how "we" won the Cold War. He avows:

> Soviet communism provided no match for free enterprise. . . . [I]ts rulers [could not] deny their people the truth . . . about us. . . . Kremlin

leaders found that our alliance would not crack when they threatened America's allies with the infamous SS-20 nuclear missile. . . . [T]hey could not divide our alliance. . . . [T]he Soviet Union did not simply lose the Cold War, the western democracies won it. . . . [B]y the grit of our people and the grace of God, the Cold War is over. Freedom has carried the day.[16]

Echoing Bush's triumphalism (but without the help of the deity), James Schlesinger expresses the orthodox case in centrist terms.[17] The previous holder of numerous Washington posts (including those of secretary of defense and head of the CIA) considers the ending of the Cold War "a moment of triumph for the United States—a triumph of foresight, national resolve and tenacity stretching over 40 years." It should not be forgotten, he notes, that "[f]or a generation American military forces have been indispensable for deterring Soviet expansion—and as a glue to hold together the coalition of Free World nations."

This longer-term version of the orthodoxy is implicitly endorsed in the remarks of Democratic Senator Harris Wofford who, prior to his defeat in the November 1994 elections, was a member of the Senate Foreign Relations Committee and once a special assistant to President John Kennedy.[18] He praises his former chief for calling the American people to "pay any price, bear any burden, meet any hardship, support any friend, oppose any foe" in order to protect liberty against the encroachment of the Soviet empire and communism. Due to "the threat of Soviet military expansion and possible nuclear attack," he deems the decision to have been wise at that time for "Congress and the majority of Americans to spend trillions of dollars on systems of nuclear deterrence, large conventional forces stationed around the world, and the subsidization of a global network of allied states." In the present situation, he contends, since "with the collapse of the Soviet state, the aim of containment has been achieved," a massive military outlay is no longer required and other, nonmilitary dimensions of security need to be addressed. However, behind an argument for a "peace dividend" lies his military rationale of the orthodoxy as to why the West triumphed. Such an outlook is also what has justified the Australian Labor Party's promotion of the "joint facilities" for communication and intelligence at North West Cape, Pine Gap and Nurrungar, the visits of nuclear-armed vessels, and general endorsement of the U.S. strategic doctrine. Its most recent form seems to be reflected in a more independent military response to the nation's security needs, featuring a strategic shift to what Peter King calls "solo forward defense."[19]

DEVELOPMENT OF THE ORTHODOXY

On one level, President Bush's self-congratulatory message served his cause well. It confirmed his credentials as an exceptional statesman and strategist and it helped to rally popular support behind military solutions to the intransigence of other enemies of the United States—for example, former clients General Manuel Noriega of Panama and Saddam Hussein of Iraq. In the area of foreign affairs, it left Bush as the undisputed leader among all the other contenders in the 1992 U.S. presidential race. None of his challengers dared to question his interpretation of a Cold War victory which, almost as soon as the communist regimes in the Eastern bloc had collapsed, crystallized into *the* interpretation.

Ironically, however, Bush also suffered from a surfeit of perceived success in foreign affairs. Despite trying during the presidential election to exploit the orthodoxy to his advantage, he soon discovered that its universal acceptance precluded it from appearing on a political agenda that formed exclusively around contentious domestic issues. Of overriding concern were the state of the economy, problems of mounting social dislocation, and a conflict raised between images of trust and change. Indeed, his presidential rivals even managed to turn his identification with uncontested orthodoxy into a political liability. The theme was constantly hammered into the American voter—where it found a receptive note—that the president spent too much time overseeing the nation's foreign portfolio to the detriment of pressing problems directly affecting people's lives. Victory abroad was not an issue to promote (especially since it meant the loss of hundreds of thousands of jobs in the defense industry); nor was it an issue to contest (due to the strength of the orthodoxy).

The country was so locked into a nonpartisan endorsement of past and present defense thinking that the only remotely related issues to gain prominence concerned Bush's involvement in the Iran-Contra scandal and the so-called wedge issue of Bill Clinton's patriotism at the time of the Vietnam War. Bush repeatedly tried to insert the latter issue into the debate, contrasting Clinton's behavior with his own record as a heroic navy flyer during World War II. Apart from these sorts of character issues, the three nationally televised debates of ninety minutes each never seriously inquired into a single foreign policy question.[20]

By their silence, the print media also confirmed the orthodox view of the Cold War's ending. No debate was generated, because the answer was already known. *Time* magazine, for instance, covered a full year of the election with only one reference to the question. Amid all its election verbiage appeared just this single sentence, and it affirmed the conventional wisdom: "Reagan-

Bush policies hastened the collapse of communism."[21] Admittedly, following the election, this leading weekly did present a guest essayist, Gary Wills, who injected a note of somber reflection into the Western victory thesis.[22] Though confirming a Cold War victory, Wills greatly decried its cost. "The hard question no one in the US dared raise was whether, in bringing down the shell of the USSR, the country had been hollowing itself out economically. . . . Had Americans outspent not only the enemy but also themselves in battle with a phantom, becoming a debtor nation to accommodate a victory without spoils."[23] Such reservations—questioning the wisdom of the massive military build-up (as Keith Suter does in the first part of his chapter)—have not filtered through to the politicians and general public. To repeat Wills's observation: it is "[t]he hard question no one in the US dared raise." If the colossal debt is deplored, its causes are attributed to bureaucratic profligacy or corruption or to the failure of America's allies, particularly Japan and Germany, to pay their fair share of the Cold War burdens and subsequent U.N.-sponsored actions. Furthermore, there is little, if any, appreciation of how the diversion of resources to the military has undermined American society in various indirect, but critical, ways (again, see the chapter by Suter).

Noticeable in its failure to contest the orthodoxy is a political force one might normally expect to find promoting a counterview—indeed, claiming a role in the victory. That is the peace movement. But apart from a few peace researchers/peace activists of the caliber of the late E. P. Thompson,[24] the late Petra Kelly,[25] Louis Kriesberg,[26] Johan Galtung,[27] Mary Kaldor,[28] and especially scholars like David Cortright[29] and Paul Joseph,[30] together with the occasional reference in a peace movement publication, there has been a surprising silence. One explanation might be the invisibility of the movement since its members have drastically declined in numbers or moved temporarily into other social causes (especially those involving survival politics). The outcome of the Gulf War had a demoralizing effect. Moreover, those activists that have remained in specific peace work have taken up new issues. The dangers of superpower nuclear confrontation have been replaced by issues such as the arms trade, ethnic/religious repression, war toys, television violence, and the promotion of peace studies. Finally, throughout their history, peace movements have always tended to be issue-oriented rather than to focus on broad analysis.

Thus reasons can readily be mounted to explain the silence. On the other hand, it is a well-known principle in movement politics that protesters need victories to celebrate. The celebratory dimension is crucial to future success, as it helps to foster morale, build personal relationships, and create the necessary group cohesion. When I suggested in early 1992 to a group of Melbourne peace representatives, who wanted to recapture the halcyon days of the mid-1980s, that they might consider commemorating the peace movement's role in bringing down the Berlin Wall and therefore proclaim November 9 Peace Day, they responded quite enthusiastically. Their attitude seemed to be saying: "Yes, here, for a change, is a positive event to celebrate." Yet when the day arrived, nothing happened. Significantly, a popular world peace diary and directory, the *Housmans Peace Diary* of 1993, overlooked nonviolence's great triumph and instead singled out November 9 as the day in 1943 that the United Nations Relief and Rehabilitation Administration (UNRRA) was founded. No mention appeared anywhere during the months of October and November of the peaceful collapse of authoritarianism in East Europe in 1989.[31]

Among a handful of academics, intellectuals, and ex-Soviet officials, however, the topic of the Cold War's ending is attracting some attention. One can detect the first rumblings of the orthodoxy's critique. While the bibliography appended to this book contains some items that only tangentially explore the question at hand and many that actually affirm the orthodoxy, a gathering voice of criticism is also recorded (e.g., the entries of Charlton, Chernoff, Deudney and Ikenberry, Nissani, Gorbachev, Risse-Kappen, Venturelli, Gaddis, Allen and Schurmann, Ilukhina, and Sturua). Their analyses point to the problematic nature of the question; they find the orthodoxy to be wanting and simplistic, and they offer alternative, more sophisticated explanations for consideration. Nonetheless, at this juncture, their studies tend to be buried in specialized journals, a few books, and papers presented at closed academic gatherings. An imperative exists to extend the debate, to bring it into the main arena of citizen discourse and public policy formulation.

THE NEED TO CHALLENGE THE ORTHODOXY

The way we construct our histories, to a large extent, prefigures our options. Interpretations of both our failures and successes echo into the future. If the lesson to be gained from the demise of Soviet communism is to be found in "peace through strength," then future conflicts will be approached with the same confrontational and competitive mind-set. Superior military force or the threat of it applied at the right time, at the right place, and in the right way will be seen to be the decisive factor in state relations based on a win/lose outcome. Alternative modes of cooperatively striving to resolve underlying grievances and meet basic human needs (see the chapters by John W. Burton and Kevin P. Clements) will be automatically dismissed as irrelevant or utopian fantasies, because they do not conform to methods believed to have "worked" in the past.

By taking a one-eyed perception of events, as well as concentrating on short-term surface considerations, we fail to detect the underground forces shaping the modern world and to formulate strategies attuned to new challenges. J. L. Gaddis speaks of "historical tectonics," comparing them to the concealed tectonic plates beneath the crust of the earth which build up pressures and suddenly erupt in earthquakes.[32] While these eruptions may appear to be random and capricious, the seismologist, who studies the strains that build up along geologic fault lines, has not been caught totally unawares. Similarly, the social scientist who delves beneath the surface of immediate events is not surprised when supposedly stable social structures suddenly fly apart. He or she is aware of the social forces acting beyond our normal range of perception. These tectonics of history, explains Gaddis, have not been set in motion by a single nation or group of individuals. "[T]hey result, rather, from the interaction of events, conditions, policies, beliefs, and even accidents. They operate over long periods of time, and across the boundaries we use to define place. Once set in motion, they are not easily reversible; they therefore give us one of the few reasonably reliable means of predicting, in very broad terms at least, what is to come."[33]

If we understand the broad historical tectonics of our age, we can begin to recognize the fault lines and coordinate policies that will avert disaster; we can fashion a world that will conform more closely to the interdependent needs of all. We will not be surprised by shocks like the one in 1989 (which Gaddis admits surprised him) because we can expect the possible convergence of certain postindustrial trends. One of the most crucial trends to grasp is the fact that a combination of economic capacity and military prowess no longer ensures world domination.[34] Due to a "juxtaposition of technology with ecology," explains Gaddis, "[t]he scale of violence had outstripped—exponentially—the scale of the arena in which the violence was to be employed; this made it difficult for any nation that had accumulated such military power to see how it might use it against any comparably equipped nation without risking escalation that could lead to the destruction of both of them."[35] This fact—and its appreciation—he contends, was *one* important factor in the calculus ending the Cold War. In the modern era the Clausewitzian notion of military force being an extension of rational statecraft has become outmoded. The gladiatorial sport of war ceases to be productive in every sense of the term when the outcome is death for all the combatants and the persons they are supposedly defending, not to mention the destruction of the fighting arena and all its surroundings. From a militarist perspective, there is no purpose in waging war if it destroys the institution of war itself and wipes out the prospect of future combatants to carry on a warrior tradition. The institution of slavery met a similar kind of fate when, among other things, it ceased to be "productive."

During the Cold War military security for the superpowers assumed priority over economic solvency, but the pursuit of the former proved to be counterproductive. The real victors turned out to be the defeated powers of World War II, Japan and Germany, who pursued a nontraditional route to great-power status—one that synthesized with the new shifting conditions.

By perceiving the end of the Cold War through the lens of one of Gaddis's tectonic forces, one comes to a very different understanding and assessment of its outcome than that advanced by the orthodox view. The prescriptions that follow also take a different tack. Concepts such as common security, sufficient defense, social defense, preventive diplomacy, confidence building, global interdependence—all of which denote peace building and mutual recognition of human rights—prevail over the old thinking of *si vis pacem, para bellum*, military victory, and balance of power. While there is nothing sacrosanct about the assumptions upon which the new prescriptions are based,[36] they do pose a challenge to the dangers of thinking within narrow and fixed parameters.

To avert the likely disaster rooted in distorted and closed thinking, qualities of flexibility and imagination—the antithesis of orthodoxy—are demanded. I am inclined to think that the undermining of orthodoxy will not emanate from the ranks of politicians and diplomats, who are too engrossed in the detailed problems of immediate cases to see the larger picture and too programmed into set ways of acting. The impetus for change will probably come from independent sources and the pressures of an informed public. How these sources can widen the debate and reach their representatives in government—whether it can occur by reformist means or will require fundamental structural changes—constitutes the subject of another important debate. However, that debate should not be allowed to divert attention from the immediate, urgent goal of challenging an orthodoxy that has implications of unprecedented catastrophe when that orthodoxy precludes open inquiry.

History is replete with the misuse of history. It is strewn with disasters that can be traced to diplomats yearning to avoid the repetition of perceived past mistakes, combined with the hope of repeating the perceived successes. The United States, with its relatively limited experience in world affairs, is probably more susceptible to drawing wrong lessons than some of the great powers with longer and mixed historical memories. However, generally I believe it is the case for all state officials that the more recent the event, the more likely it is to be salient in their memory and therefore to have a disproportionate and misleading effect. As Robert Jervis once noted, "If generals are prepared to fight the last war, diplomats may be prepared to avoid the last war."[37]

An alleged principal cause of World War II dominated much of the West's thinking during the Cold War. The policy of appeasement, which at the Munich conference in 1938 allowed Hitler to annex the Czech Sudetenland, was to be avoided at all costs. Appeasement, which formerly had meant reasonable acquiescence, now was equated with surrender and even cowardice. The lesson of Munich was that the new dictators, Stalin and his successors, must be dealt with firmly, no quarter given. Clearly announced intentions, backed by hard-nosed military preparations, would avoid making a catastrophic mistake similar to that preceding World War II. Ironically, Neville Chamberlain took his Munich position, in part, because he hoped to avoid the belligerent and short-sighted diplomacy that preceded the ghastly slaughter of World War I. By evaluating the Cold War situation in terms of the Munich lesson, one wonders about the degree to which the so-called realistic skepticism of U.S. "security managers" prolonged and intensified the Cold War rivalry. Could agreements, especially in the area of arms control and disarmament, have been reached before the Gorbachev era?

Since we cannot rerun history (thank goodness!), we shall never know. However, we do know that the lesson of Munich competed against a number of other lessons explaining World War II. In designing a strategy against the Soviets we chose not to focus on the mistakes that were made at Versailles, or the consequences of the Allies' post–World War I indemnity and loan programs ("Uncle Shylock"),[38] or the major weaknesses inherent in the structures of the League of Nations, or the repercussions in blocking off economic markets to the Japanese, or the power games played by the Western nations in jockeying for advantageous disarmament ratios. Those lessons would have led to approaches more oriented to what John Burton calls "provention," the way to peace building.

CONCLUSION

The collapse of the communist regimes of Eastern Europe at the end of 1989, followed by the breakup of the Soviet Union itself, and then the fall from power of two of the three main pillars of communist rule—the party and the KGB (with the third, the military, gravely demoralized)—ushered in a new world the politicians and analysts are now grasping to understand. After the West's immediate exhilaration that nearly fifty years of nuclear confrontation and massive military build-up had ended, new uncertainties appeared, generating far more fears than expectations of opportunities for positive peace. Ethnic and religious conflicts of frenzied proportions erupted in parts of the former Soviet and Russian empire and on the glacis of its western flank. The long-dreaded problem of nuclear horizontal proliferation gained a new urgency. Terrible violence, both direct and structural, pervaded the entire globe. As this bleak situation continues, relieved only by some favorable signs in South Africa and perhaps in Cambodia and the Middle East, it is almost as if the comparative peace and certainties of the Cold War era are able to resonate a nostalgic irony of better days.

Not surprisingly, quickly following the unwarranted optimism accompanying a "new world order," our statesmen found themselves floundering, instead, in a "new world disorder." Today, they seem uncertain as to what configuration of a world order they should be proclaiming. Old notions of superior military power and competitive market economics as the solutions to problems confronting the world community continue to dominate global thinking. Such views become particularly difficult to discard—indeed, are reinforced—when one believes that this is what essentially "won" the Cold War.

However, the Cold War's ending—if that is what occurred—is much more complex, and it needs to be understood on a range of levels and not in terms of self-serving interests if its meaning is to have any positive relevance for the post–Cold War world. Even the question of relevance is problematic. What a sophisticated understanding of an epochal event like the Cold War's ending can do is not so much provide direct lessons but rather widen our horizon so that we can imagine more proficient ways to face the future. Since the goal is to institute positive and flexible approaches to international relations— leading to the kind of proposals Kevin P. Clements spells out in his concluding section on policy implications—the experiences of the past must be carefully weighed so that they assist, if possible, and at the very least not obfuscate, the process of future decision making. It can only be hoped that this book, in challenging the emergent orthodoxy, has contributed, however modestly, to a refinement of our knowledge to that end.

NOTES

1. The four overseas contributors, Jennifer Turpin, David Cortright, Robert Elias, and Johan Galtung, were unable to attend. The chapter by Galtung is a revised and updated version of an address he delivered at the University of Queensland on July 10, 1991, when he inaugurated the university's interdisciplinary Peace and Conflict Studies program.

2. Joseph A. Camilleri, "The Cold War . . . and After," Chapter 15 of this volume, p. 233.

3. Robert Browning, "A Grammarian's Funeral," in *Browning: Poetical Works, 1833–1864*, ed. Ian Jack (London: Oxford University Press, 1970), p. 760.

4. This analysis contrasts sharply with the predictions of these same commentators, who during the Cold War warned against the growing Soviet danger and its cataclysmic consequences. To his credit, James Schlesinger, who helped form the Committee on the Present Danger, now admits that respect for the Soviet Union was "based on inflated perceptions of its military power" ("New Instabilities, New Priorities," *Foreign Policy* 85 [1991–92]: 21), but other Cold War warriors are not so forthcoming in confessing their miscalculations.

5. Richard G. Lugar, "The Republican Course," *Foreign Policy* 86 (1992): 86–87.

6. Ibid., p. 87.

7. William Hyland, *The Cold War Is Over* (New York: Random House, 1990).

8. This view of a significant volte-face is also argued by two critics of the orthodoxy, Daniel Deudney and G. John Ikenberry. They depict long-time Cold War warrior Reagan, by the beginning of his second term, showing "commitment to anti-nuclearism and its potential for transforming the U.S.-Soviet confrontation." "Who Won the Cold War?" *Foreign Policy* 87 (1992): 125–28.

9. Zbigniew Brzezinski, "The Cold War and Its Aftermath," *Foreign Affairs* 71, no. 4 (1992): 45.

10. Ibid., p. 41.

11. Ibid., p. 42.

12. Ibid., p. 43.

13. Ibid., p. 46.

14. Ibid., p. 44.

15. As used here, "mythology" does not necessarily imply falsity, but rather conveys the meaning of a traditional discourse embodying popular views about a social phenomenon.

16. George Bush, "America—The Last Best Hope for Man on Earth: A World in Which the Rule of Law Prevails" (speech delivered at Texas A & M University, December 15, 1992), *Vital Speeches of the Day* 59, no. 7 (1993): 194–95.

17. Schlesinger, "New Instabilities," 3, 17.

18. Harris Wofford, "The Democratic Challenge," *Foreign Policy* 86 (1992): 99, 100.

19. Peter King, "Australia, Regional Threats and the Arms Race: Everybody Else Out of Step?" in *The New Australian Militarism: Undermining Our Future Security*, eds. Graeme Cheeseman and St John Kettle (Sydney: Pluto Press, 1990), p. 135.

20. During the first TV debate, President Bush did boast that the Cold War would never have been won "if we'd gone for the nuclear freeze crowd," but this view was not contested by either of his two rivals. See "The 1992 Campaign: Transcript of First TV Debate Among Bush, Clinton and Perot," *New York Times*, October 12, 1992.

21. Michael Kramer, "Eyes on the Prize," *Time*, October 19, 1992, p. 38.

22. It should be noted that *Time* earlier had promoted a more rounded interpretation of the Cold War's ending. "Gorbachev," it reported, "is responding primarily to internal pressures, not external ones. The Soviet system has gone into meltdown because of inadequacies and defects at its core, not because of anything the outside world has done or not done or threatened to do. Gorbachev has been far more appalled by what he has seen out his limousine window and in reports brought to him by long-faced ministers than by satellite photographs of American missiles aimed at Moscow. He has been discouraged and radicalized by what he has heard from his own constituents during his walkabouts in Krasnodar, Sverdlovsk and Leningrad—not by the exhortations, remonstrations or sanctions of foreigners." Strobe Talbott, "Rethinking the Red Menace," *Time*, January 1, 1990, p. 33.

23. Gary Wills, "The End of Reaganism," *Time*, September 16, 1992, p. 62.

24. E. P. Thompson, "Comments—The Ends of Cold War," *New Left Review* 182 (1990): 139–46.

25. Petra K. Kelly, "A Green View of German Reunification and Europe's Future," in *Nonviolence Speaks to Power*, eds. Glenn D. Paige and Sarah Gilliatt (Honolulu: University of Hawaii, Center for Global Nonviolence, 1992), 87–112.

26. Louis Kriesberg, "Explaining the End of the Cold War," in *New Views of International Security*, Occasional Paper Series No. 2 (Syracuse, NY: Syracuse University Press, 1990), pp. 4–15 (cited at length in the chapter by Kevin P. Clements).

27. Johan Galtung, keynote address, Australian Peace Education and Research Association Conference, Brisbane, June 30, 1991. See also his chapter in this book.

28. Mary Kaldor, "After the Cold War," *New Left Review* 180 (1990): 25–37.

29. David Cortright, *Peace Works: The Citizen's Role in Ending the Cold War* (Boulder, CO: Westview, 1993). See also his chapter in this book.

30. Paul Joseph, *Peace Politics: The United States Between the Old and New World Orders* (Philadelphia: Temple University Press, 1993).

31. The 1992 diary also failed to mark the November 9 anniversary. The omission of these two years, however, must have been drawn to the editors' attention since the oversight is rectified in the 1994 and 1995 editions.

32. John Lewis Gaddis, *The United States and the End of the Cold War: Implications, Reconsiderations, Provocations* (New York: Oxford University Press, 1992), pp. 155–67.

33. Ibid., p. 156.

34. Gaddis designates three converging trends that produced the shocks of 1989. Besides the emergence of new criteria for defining great powers, brought on by the "juxtaposition of technology with ecology," there occurred (with the need to move on to a new stage of economic development) the collapse of authoritarian alternatives to liberalism and (with the victory inscribed in the United Nations Universal Declaration on Human Rights) the beginnings of a decline in brutality.

35. Gaddis, p. 158.

36. One can, of course, also reach the same policy recommendations from different sets of assumptions.

37. Robert Jervis, "Hypotheses on Misperception," *World Politics* 20, no. 3 (1968): 24.

38. Although the Marshall Plan was introduced in 1947 to prevent an economic collapse in Europe, it is highly doubtful if the United States would have demonstrated such largesse without the confrontation with the U.S.S.R. The famous "long telegram" of George Kennan spelled out how the United States had to support the states of Europe and especially their economies if it hoped to compete successfully with the pressures of the Soviets in a postwar world.

I

POLITICAL LEADERS
AND THEIR POLICIES

1

Did Reagan "Win" the Cold War?

April F. Carter

When Ronald Reagan left the White House in January 1989 and was asked what had been his greatest achievement, he answered, "People tell me that I won the Cold War."[1] During the election of 1992 George Bush claimed an even more dramatic victory in the Cold War for the Republican presidencies of 1981 to 1992. Other members of these administrations and a number of analysts have made similar claims, which are becoming—as Ralph Summy notes in his introduction—an "emergent orthodoxy." The purpose of this chapter is to examine the logical status of such claims and to comment briefly on the adequacy of the historical evidence for them.

There are considerable difficulties involved in the formula "winning the Cold War." The first is ambiguity about the scope of the claim, as the references to Reagan and Bush indicate, since winning in early 1989 meant something different from winning in late 1992, when the Soviet Union had collapsed and Gorbachev had been ousted from power. The second and related problem is uncertainty about the actual definition of the Cold War. Both these issues are examined in more detail as the argument of this chapter develops.

"Winning the Cold War" is a highly contentious formula because it can be interpreted as a moral justification for all of Reagan's defense and foreign policies—for example, military intervention in Nicaragua under the Reagan Doctrine, a strategy which envisaged possibly fighting and winning a nuclear war and unprecedented peacetime military budgets. The notion of "victory" also appears to vindicate the policies of seeking military superiority and "negotiations from strength," which could be disastrous as precedents. It is important to explore these connotations of celebrating victory in the Cold War, but this chapter engages in the narrower task of trying to clarify what role the Reagan administration really played.

DEFINING THE COLD WAR

The Cold War can be defined in three different ways, and each formulation has differing implications. In its broadest sense the term denotes the ideological conflict between Western capitalism and Soviet Marxism-Leninism, which began in October 1917 and involved competition for world dominance between two opposing economic and political systems. This meaning has been analyzed by Fred Halliday and is adopted in this volume by Rick Kuhn.[2] In its narrowest sense Cold War has been used to denote the period of acute tension between the U.S.S.R. and the West between 1947 and 1953, which involved extreme ideological hostility, a major arms build-up with both sides developing nuclear weapons, acute fear of external attack and internal subversion, and no serious negotiations between the antagonists. It was in this sense that commentators began to identify the Second Cold War of 1979 to 1984, although the comparison was not of course exact.[3] Cold War in this narrow sense contrasted with detente between the United States and the U.S.S.R., when ideology became less prominent and the two superpowers recognized a degree of mutual interest. The third meaning of Cold War, which is the most common usage, denotes the military and ideological confrontation between the United States and the U.S.S.R. and their respective allies between 1946 and 1990. Although this period can be divided into various phases, the basic structure of international relations from 1949 to 1989 remained unchanged. It is this usage which is adopted here.

The Cold War in this third sense involved four interrelated features. First, the two superpowers controlled two opposing military and political blocs, and directly or indirectly their confrontation dominated world politics. Second, the struggle between the two blocs depended on both military power and economic power; the military power was the most visible, but the economic power was ultimately more decisive. Third, both blocs proclaimed the superiority of their political values and types of society and tried to propagate these beliefs among people on the other side. Fourth, the United States and the U.S.S.R. were engaged in a struggle for influence or control in the Third World, and military, economic, and ideological forms of power were all invoked. Whereas Europe was firmly divided into two camps, the position in the Third World was more fluid and spheres of influence less clear, which led both sides to engage in continuing rivalry even during periods of detente. The competition between the United States and the Soviet Union was complicated by the role of China, which engaged in its own ideological struggle with both superpowers in the 1960s and effectively switched to the Western side in the 1970s.

A systematic analysis of the Cold War invites us to consider whether either the United States or the U.S.S.R. had a built-in and permanent advantage. After 1949, when the Cold War seemed irrevocable, it was clear that the West had two major advantages. First, the United States had much greater economic power and was able to promote capitalist regeneration in Western Europe and Japan at a time when the U.S.S.R. was taking economic resources out of Eastern Europe. Although both sides enjoyed economic growth in the next two decades, Western capitalism proved permanently stronger and better able to generate technological growth.

The second advantage which the United States had over the U.S.S.R. was that the Western bloc was much more genuinely cohesive than the Soviet bloc. There was, of course, West European opposition to the dominant role of the United States, based both on some popular resistance to U.S. foreign and defense policies and on nationalism. But only the French government openly defied Washington to break partly with NATO, and despite continuing tensions within the alliance, the majority of people in most West European countries supported NATO even when they strongly opposed certain nuclear weapons policies.[4] (For specific historical reasons Greece and Spain were in various periods more inclined to hostility to the United States.) Therefore, although the United States was always nervous of the U.S.S.R. detaching Western Europe, there was never a very serious likelihood that NATO would disintegrate. The economic links between the United States and Western Europe, initially fostered by the Marshall Plan, were also close despite a degree of trade rivalry.

The Soviet Union, however, faced the continuing problem that in almost all East European countries Communist party rule was resented as a foreign imposition, so minority dissent could potentially spark mass nationalist rebellion. Even where there was some popular sympathy for socialism, as in Czechoslovakia, the experience of Soviet-style party rule prompted desire for change. The uprisings of 1953 and 1956 marked a rejection of Stalinism. The more moderate regimes in most of Eastern Europe of the 1960s and 1970s were able to offer their people some economic advantages, but their economic weakness was also apparent and they became indebted to the West. Popular unrest in Poland in the 1970s culminated in the Solidarity movement of 1980 to 1981 and demonstrated that Soviet control still ultimately relied on use of domestic or Soviet military force. The 1968 Prague Spring had shown earlier that the Soviet leadership was unable to allow any significant autonomy to East European states for fear the bloc would fall apart, and that

Moscow was committed to retaining Eastern Europe as a buffer zone against the West.[5]

Where the Soviet Union did have at least a potential advantage was in the Third World, where a legacy of Western colonialism and continuing economic dependence on the West made capitalism and Western ideology unattractive to many (though by no means all) countries. The Soviet Union fully recognized this potential in its own theoretical evaluation of the struggle with the West. However, despite some Marxist governments coming to power, the Soviet Union did not achieve significant and sustained support in the Third World. Many countries showed in their endorsement of nonalignment a desire to be independent of both blocs, and some military allies of the Soviet Union in the Middle East (for example, Egypt and Syria) did not hesitate to change sides or to defy the Soviet Union when it suited their national purposes.[6] The struggle with China also reduced the Soviet Union's potential influence in the Third World.

The Soviet Union did have a solid military advantage in certain spheres and was taken very seriously as a military power by the West. The most obvious advantage enjoyed by the U.S.S.R. in Europe was in military manpower. The Soviet Union consolidated its potential advantage in a land war by keeping large numbers of Soviet troops and tanks in Eastern Europe, backed by other Warsaw Pact divisions, where they created the specter of a Soviet blitzkrieg overwhelming Western Europe. Although for a long time the Soviet Union was well behind the United States in nuclear weapons and nuclear missile technology (despite the alarm caused in Washington in 1957 by Sputnik), it was generally agreed that by the 1970s the Soviet Union had achieved approximate parity at the strategic nuclear level.[7] Opponents of arms control in the United States began to argue that the Soviet land-based intercontinental ballistic missiles (ICBMs) with multiple warheads threatened U.S. land-based missiles, made the United States vulnerable, and created potential Soviet nuclear superiority.[8] In retrospect, however, it seems clear that despite its arsenal of sophisticated missiles, the growth of the Soviet navy, and improved conventional forces in Europe, the U.S.S.R. was by the end of the 1970s beginning to suffer from its fundamental technological and economic inferiority. William Odom has argued that the Soviet Union, when faced with the "third military revolution" of microelectronics and lasers in the 1970s, began to fall inexorably behind.[9] Moreover, in the 1980s the priority given to military research and development and the high proportion of Soviet gross domestic product devoted to military uses had created a crisis in the U.S.S.R.'s domestic economy.

Therefore, any convincing explanation of the end of the Cold War has to refer primarily to the inherent weaknesses of the Soviet system. These weaknesses derived initially from the economic and political organization of the Soviet Union itself, the limitations of a centrally controlled economy, and the repressive nature of its style of one-party rule. Ironically, the Soviet Union's two main claims to great-power status, its military might and its control over the East European bloc, were also the sources of its greatest weaknesses. Military investment placed a cumulatively intolerable burden on the Soviet economy, while Eastern Europe—which also began to be a drain on the Soviet Union by the 1970s, for example, as the recipient of cheap Soviet oil—was potentially unstable. Both aspects of Soviet great-power status created fear and hostility in the West and promoted the Cold War. The very structure of the Cold War confrontation therefore in the short run tended to enhance Soviet power, but also to create the conditions for its eventual erosion. If the built-in vulnerability of the Soviet bloc is accepted, then the key question about the role played by Reagan in ending the Cold War is how far he precipitated recognition of this weakness inside the Soviet Union.

DEFINING THE END OF THE COLD WAR

Before trying to assess the impact of the Reagan administration, we need to clarify what was entailed in the end of the Cold War, by identifying the key elements in Gorbachev's approach after 1985 and the unexpected outcomes of the process of external and internal reform. Gorbachev's policy changes took place in four main areas; in each case the policy gained momentum and became more radical beginning around 1987.

First, the Soviet government began after 1985 to modify aspects of its military policy seen as especially threatening by the West, and concurrently to change its approach to arms control. Gorbachev began to reevaluate military doctrine, introducing the concept of "reasonable sufficiency" at the nuclear level (which suggested that lower nuclear weapons levels would be required) and moving toward "defensive defense" at the conventional level, in an attempt to quell Western concerns about surprise attack.[10] The major switch in arms control policy was suggested by the dramatic proposals made at the Reykjavik summit meeting in October 1986 and confirmed during the Intermediate Nuclear Forces (INF) negotiations in 1987, when the Soviet side indicated an unprecedented willingness to accept detailed on-site verification and larger cuts in its missiles than those required of the United States.[11] Gorbachev's speech at the United Nations in December 1988, when he promised significant unilateral reductions in Soviet troops and armaments in East Germany and European Russia, indicated the seriousness of his commitment to scale down military forces.

Second, Gorbachev signaled a change in the ideological content and declared goals of Soviet foreign policy, moving away from a concept of international class war toward a more liberal vision of peace and cooperation. Peace propaganda had played a role in Soviet policy in the past, but Gorbachev laid a new stress on "human values" and on the importance of the United Nations.[12] The U.S.S.R. accompanied a new ideological style with practical indications of a real change in policy, for example, paying up its contributions to U.N. peacekeeping operations and cooperating with the International Atomic Energy Agency over Chernobyl.[13]

Third, Gorbachev began to withdraw Soviet military and political support from Marxist regimes in the Third World as part of his fundamental rethinking of foreign policy. Cuban troops were withdrawn from Angola and the government was encouraged to negotiate with its internal enemies; Moscow encouraged Vietnam to withdraw from Cambodia; and, most crucially, the Soviet Union agreed to end its long war in Afghanistan and brought all its troops home by early 1989.[14]

The fourth and most dramatic move by Gorbachev was to alter Soviet policy toward the East European states. In his December 1988 U.N. speech he indicated that the Brezhnev Doctrine, claiming the right of the Soviet Union to invade Eastern Europe under the banner of socialist internationalism, had been abandoned. During 1989 Solidarity reached an agreement with the (Communist) Polish United Workers' party and joined the government in August; in Hungary a new constitution and multiparty elections were announced in September. In both cases the move away from Communist party rule was the result of a long process of internal pressure and the emergence of flexible party leaders, but change was clearly sanctioned by the Soviet Union. Gorbachev hoped to influence the more recalcitrant leadership of the German Democratic Republic (GDR) on his visit in early October 1989. The Brezhnev Doctrine was formally renounced by the Warsaw Pact when foreign ministers, meeting at the end of October 1989, stressed the right of each country to go its own way.[15] Despite Gorbachev's endorsement of significant change in Eastern Europe, it is doubtful if he anticipated, or wished for, the dissolution of the bloc which occurred after the revolutions at the end of 1989.

The final stage in the ending of the Cold War—the gradual breakup of the Soviet Union itself and the sweeping away of Communist party rule after the abortive coup of August 1991—was obviously a wholly unintended consequence of a reform process which had run out of control.

The Reagan administration could have been directly responsible only for the first three areas of policy change which denoted the ending of the Cold War: Gorbachev's rethinking of military, ideological, and Third World goals and strategies. There is no evidence that the Reagan administration tried to promote dissolution of the East European bloc, or even took significant steps to support East European dissent, apart from imposing sanctions after the crushing of Solidarity. Rhetorical stress on human rights (directed only against communist or socialist states) only served to sharpen the rift with Moscow. If we incorporate the Bush administration into the analysis, then it appears that, as Michael Mandelbaum has argued, Bush's main contribution to the momentous events in Eastern Europe in 1989 was to stay quietly on the sidelines.[16]

It is even less plausible to suggest that the Reagan administration foresaw or aimed to achieve the overthrow of Communist party rule in the U.S.S.R., or the country's disintegration into independent nation-states. Richard Pipes, the best-known advocate of putting pressure on the Soviet economy, told audiences in Europe in October 1982: "Now no responsible persons can have any illusions that it is in the power of the West to alter the Soviet system or to 'bring the Soviet economy to its knees.' These are spurious objectives. What one can and ought to strive for is compelling the Soviet regime to bear the consequences of its own priorities."[17] Bush's claims in 1992 to have won the Cold War cannot therefore be sustained by any serious historical evidence that the Reagan-Bush administrations were directly instrumental in bringing about the collapse of Soviet communism. But the argument that Reagan directly influenced Soviet policy changes between 1985 and 1988 is worth examining.

DID REAGAN FORCE GORBACHEV TO CHANGE?

One possible counterargument against the claim that Reagan forced change upon the Soviet Union is that Gorbachev's domestic reforms and his complementary reformulation of external policies stemmed solely from internal pressures. If so, they had very little to do with who was in the White House. There is clear evidence that there was awareness at the top of the Soviet hierarchy in the early 1980s that significant changes were needed. Marshal Nikolai Ogarkov, chief of the Soviet General Staff, called in 1981 for the restructuring of economic and political institutions, as well as reorganization of the armed forces in order to ensure greater military efficiency. His article in *Kommunist* in July 1981 has been widely cited by Western commentators.[18] When Yuri Andropov came to power, his first address to the Central Committee Plenum in November 1982 stressed the problems of the economy and the need for reform.[19] It is therefore arguable that only the prolonged immobilism of the Brezhnev period, and the subsequent illness of both Andropov and Constantin Chernenko, delayed changes in domestic policy. Gorbachev inherited an agenda and sought to create an international environment favorable to his domestic reforms.

Given the logic of the superpower confrontation in the Cold War, it does, however, seem more probable that the White House had some direct impact. One reason why it is plausible that Reagan prompted Gorbachev's rethinking of defense and foreign policy is simply the timing. The initiatives by the Soviet government after 1985 could be a direct response to the first Reagan administration. *Post hoc* is not necessarily *propter hoc*, but there is a *prima facie* case that the Reagan administration forced the Soviet leadership to confront internal weakness and narrowed the options open to them. The Reagan administration, when it came to power, openly proclaimed it was altering the rules of the game with the Soviet Union after a decade of detente. U.S. policy toward the U.S.S.R. had been becoming more intransigent in the late 1970s, partly due to internal right-wing pressures and partly due to perceptions of the Soviet threat, especially after the invasion of Afghanistan. But there was a decisive change both in rhetoric and in military and arms control policy under Reagan. It can therefore be argued that Reagan forced a reevaluation of the previous Brezhnev strategy, which combined the pursuit of military parity, enshrined in arms control agreements, and of economic and technological aid from the West through detente with an active attempt to extend Soviet power in the Third World. Brezhnev himself recognized in October 1982, just before his death, that the United States had "launched a political, economic and ideological offensive" against the Soviet Union and had begun an "unprecedented arms race."[20]

What is much more debatable is exactly *how* the Reagan strategy impinged on the U.S.S.R. A theory about the dynamics of arms races would suggest that Moscow was likely to respond to the Reagan rhetoric and military program by becoming more intransigent and increasing its own weapons; indeed, there was some evidence of this response, especially in 1984. In that case Gorbachev's diplomacy might need to be explained not as a result of Washington's actions, but *despite* them.

A welcome attempt to frame and test a precise hypothesis has been made by Fred Chernoff.[21] He examines the claim put forward by Dan Quayle and others that the rapid military build-up under Reagan forced the Kremlin to respond by increased military spending. As a result the Soviet Union, it is posited, encountered such extreme economic difficulties that it had to give up the arms race and make substantial arms control concessions. It is very hard to find reliable statistics on Soviet military spending, but by using CIA estimates Chernoff demonstrates that there is no convincing evidence that the Soviet military budget increased in reaction to U.S. military spending.

There is a possible weaker hypothesis that, although the Soviet leadership did not try to match the Reagan arms program, the perceived costs of continuing the military confrontation by 1985 forced a drastic reevaluation of Soviet foreign and military policies. Chernoff notes this alternative formulation and concedes that it has rather more plausibility, though it contradicts the premises of the "strong build-up" argument that the U.S.S.R. would inevitably respond in military terms. This second hypothesis is put forward by a number of commentators on Gorbachev. One version is proposed by Allen Lynch: "Reagan's more aggressive tack deeply unnerved the Kremlin and discredited the prevailing paradigm of Soviet-American relations among the political class at large. This proved to be a necessary, though by no means sufficient, condition for the sea change in Gorbachev's foreign policy."[22] Lynch suggests that the sufficient condition was the conjunction of Reagan's mounting pressure with the dwindling viability of Soviet foreign and security strategies, which resulted in a foreclosing of options. If this hypothesis is correct, then it would imply that any Soviet government coming to power in 1985 would have had to follow Gorbachev's policies. Lynch does in fact claim that almost any leadership facing the same internal and external crises would have followed similar policies.

If this were true, one might posit that there would be unanimity—or at least very substantial agreement—on the course to be followed. But the evidence adduced by Western analysts strongly suggests that there was not. Gorbachev faced opposition to his policies both in the top echelons of the party and among sections of the military. Gorbachev is reported to have met with the military high command in July 1985 (after ousting Grigory Romanov, a key Politburo opponent) and to have told them that there would be strict limits on the military budget. During 1985 and 1986, Defense Minister Sergei Sokolov apparently pressed for higher military expenditure.[23] The full radicalism of Gorbachev's arms control and foreign policies did not become apparent until 1987, after he had managed to oust many of his key military opponents.

The requirement of agreement on new policies might be deemed an unsatisfactory test of the hypothesis on the grounds that perceptions are skewed by dogmatism, habitual modes of thought, and other elements of irrationality or personal motivation. In that case the relevant question to ask might be whether the Soviet leadership had, on any objective calculation, any real options in foreign and defense policy. A key issue here is the impact of the Strategic Defense Initiative (SDI) or Star Wars, which is frequently cited as having had a decisive impact on Soviet policy because it threatened a major technological arms race in which the U.S.S.R. could not hope to compete. It is indeed very doubtful if the U.S.S.R. could have directly matched SDI by seeking to develop an equivalent space-based shield against ballistic missiles (although it was engaged in some space and antisatellite research). Marshal Sergei Akhromeyev did threaten in October 1985 that the U.S.S.R. would match SDI, but Gorbachev was careful not to make similar threats. A number of articles published in the Soviet Union shortly after the Geneva summit in late 1985 stressed the limits of SDI and suggested strategies of jamming or overwhelming the system or pursuing forms of attack (e.g., cruise missiles) which could bypass it.[24]

It is arguable that SDI posed Moscow with starker choices. Even though Gorbachev himself indicated well-founded skepticism about the technological feasibility of Reagan's personal vision of a shield for the United States, even more modest antiballistic missile projects would increase strategic uncertainty. But it is far from clear that Gorbachev's radical approach to arms control was the only possible response. Indeed, any attempt to formulate a hypothesis that Reagan's pressure directly brought about Gorbachev's policies fails—as Chernoff and various contributors to this volume have noted—to account for the imaginativeness and radicalism of Gorbachev's international agenda.

WAS THERE A COHERENT REAGAN STRATEGY?

The complexities of the real decision-making process in the Soviet Union point to another set of questions which need to be raised about the thesis that Reagan dictated the nature of Gorbachev's response. This thesis makes sense only if it is assumed there was a coherent Reagan strategy. There are a number of obvious objections which can be made to this proposition.

One objection is that no American administration can really pursue a coherent strategy because of the conflicting requirements of pressure groups and Congress and above all because of the internecine bureaucratic warfare which precedes any official policy decision. Where the president takes an active role these problems can be mitigated, but Reagan was notorious for his lack of interest in details and lack of understanding of key issues of, for example, nuclear strategy. Strobe Talbott's *Deadly Gambits* depicts the conflicts and muddle involved in elaborating an arms control policy.[25]

Nevertheless, it can be argued that the broad lines of Reagan's strategy were clear enough. The aim was to build up U.S. military power to attain clear superiority over the Soviet Union, to abandon the Strategic Arms Limitations Treaty (SALT) model of arms control, and to weaken the Soviet Union by denying it access to Western technology or economic support. These aims were enshrined in the military budgets, the launching of Star Wars, the fact that (despite internal confusion) the administration sabotaged the Geneva arms control talks between 1981 and 1983, and the attempts to prevent cooperation on the Soviet natural gas pipeline. It has been noted that Reagan sometimes diverged from this strategy—for example, by lifting in April 1981 the grain embargo on the U.S.S.R. which had been imposed by Carter after the invasion of Afghanistan. Alexander Haig in his memoirs lamented this decision, which he saw as sending the wrong signals to the U.S.S.R. over Poland at a time when the future of the Solidarity movement was uncertain.[26] But this decision might be seen as an exception made to placate domestic farming interests.

A central problem in establishing consistency in the Reagan strategy is the switch in policy between his first and second administrations. Reagan, the archenemy of the "evil empire," the proponent of U.S. military power, and the critic of arms control, discussed at Reykjavik the possibility of eliminating all nuclear weapons and began to negotiate seriously on cutting the U.S. arsenal. It is possible to find quotes which suggest that Reagan always favored genuine arms cuts (though these statements may at the time have been an electorally acceptable way of damning SALT).[27] But the contradiction between the thrust of the first Reagan administration and the second is illustrated by the fact that Weinberger and Richard Perle—who appeared to represent quintessential Reaganism up to 1984—opposed serious arms control negotiations after 1985 and left in 1987. Some commentators have suggested that Reagan always harbored radical hopes of abolishing nuclear weapons—hopes Gorbachev apparently shared—and that therefore Reagan was always to some extent detached from his own administration.[28] Certainly some of Reagan's more utopian dreams linked to the launching of Star Wars—such as the possibility of sharing the technology with the Soviet Union—were never entertained for one second by the Pentagon.

It is not necessary here to pursue the question of whether Reagan personally had a reasonably clear set of goals. The central point is that the Reagan administration was never monolithic and was open to pressure from Congress and public opinion. When Gorbachev came to power in 1985, he began to stress in public that despite the dangerous military plans of some extreme groups in the United States, there were also more encouraging signals from the administration. Gorbachev also singled out the positive influence of the Western peace movements and argued that Soviet diplomacy could alter Western policy.[29] Whereas proponents of the "Reagan victory" perceive a triumphant White House which had imposed its vision on internal opponents and could impose it upon the Kremlin, the perception from Moscow was more nuanced.

CONCLUSION

Has this examination of the role of the Reagan administration led to any clear conclusions? This chapter has concurred with analysts who claim that the Soviet Union was approaching an economic and technological crisis by the 1980s, and that maintaining its military power and global ambitions was seriously overstretching its resources. This analysis, of course, formed part of the rationale for the Reagan strategy, but it was also the basis of Gorbachev's "new thinking." It has also accepted that the policies of the first Reagan administration did increase pressure on the Soviet leadership and therefore tended to encourage a reevaluation of the Brezhnev approach.

This chapter has, however, rejected the proposition that the Reagan policies *necessarily* led to Gorbachev's reconstruction of defense and foreign policy, because the U.S.S.R. was left with no alternative. Any such claim is unsustainable because there is always scope for differing interpretations of power relationships and always some disagreement within governments about the choice of policies. Moreover, the nature of politics implies there is room for choice, initiative, and the unexpected.

In addition, this chapter has rejected suggestions that Reagan's arms build-up and his economic pressure on the U.S.S.R. directly influenced the *content* of Gorbachev's policies, for example, the new Soviet approach to arms control. There is a good deal of evidence that Gorbachev fundamentally reevaluated Soviet military strategy and, in the case of INF, saw the intermediate-range missiles as unnecessary and counterproductive. The guidelines for Gorbachev's thinking were totally opposed to those the first Reagan administration had endorsed, and were certainly not understood by Gorbachev as simple capitulation to superior strength.

NOTES   •

1. Nigel Hawkes, "The Dawn of a New Age," *The Observer* (London), March 5, 1989, p. 21.

2. Fred Halliday, "The Ends of the Cold War," *New Left Review* 180 (March-April 1990): 5–23.

3. Fred Halliday, *The Making of the Second World War* (London: Verso, 1983).

4. Bruce Russett and Donald R. Deluca, "Theatre Nuclear Forces: Public Opinion in Western Europe," *Political Science Quarterly* 98 (1983): 185–87.

5. Zdenek Mlynar, *Night Frost in Prague* (London: C. Hurst, 1980), pp. 238–41.

6. Galia Golan, "The Middle East," in *The Soviet Union in World Politics*, ed. Kurt London (Boulder, CO: Westview, 1980); and Seweryn Bialer, " 'New Thinking' and Soviet Foreign Policy," *Survival* 30, no. 4 (1988): 293.

7. Strobe Talbott, *Deadly Gambits: The Reagan Administration and the Stalemate in Nuclear Arms Control* (New York: Alfred Knopf, 1984), pp. 210–11.

8. Ibid., pp. 212–13.

9. William E. Odom, "The Soviet Military in Transition," *Problems of Communism* 39, no. 3 (May-June 1990): 55.

10. Robert Levgold, "The Revolution in Soviet Foreign Policy," *Foreign Affairs* 68, no. 1 (1989): 87–88.

11. April F. Carter, *Success and Failure in Arms Control Negotiations*, Stockholm International Peace Research Institute (Oxford: Oxford University Press, 1989), pp. 205–27.

12. David Holloway, "Gorbachev's New Thinking," *Foreign Affairs* 62, no. 1 (1989): 70–71.

13. Levgold, "The Revolution in Soviet Foreign Policy," p. 94.

14. Michael Mandelbaum, "Ending the Cold War," *Foreign Affairs* 68, no. 2 (1989): 19–20.

15. Adam Roberts, *Civil Resistance in the East European and Soviet Revolutions*, Monograph Series No. 4 (Cambridge, MA: Albert Einstein Institution, 1991), p. 10.

16. Michael Mandelbaum, "The Bush Foreign Policy," *Foreign Affairs* 70, no. 1 (1991): 5.

17. Cited in Laurence Barrett, *Gambling with History: Ronald Reagan in the White House* (New York: Doubleday, 1983), p. 294.

18. Ilana Kass, "The U.S.-Soviet Strategic Relationship," *Annals of the American Academy of Political and Social Science* 517 (September 1991): 32. See also William E. Odom, "Choice and Change in Soviet Politics," *Problems of Communism* 32, no. 3 (May-June 1983): 11.

19. Boris Rumer, "Structural Imbalance in the Soviet Economy," *Problems of Communism* 33, no. 4 (July-August 1984): 24.

20. Holloway, "Gorbachev's New Thinking," p. 68.

21. Fred Chernoff, "Ending the Cold War: The Soviet Retreat and the US Military Buildup," *International Affairs* 67, no. 1 (1991): 111–26.

22. Allen Lynch, "Does Gorbachev Matter Anymore?" *Foreign Affairs* 69, no. 3 (1990): 23.

23. Bruce Parrott, "Soviet National Security under Gorbachev," *Problems of Communism* 37, no. 6 (November-December 1988): 7, 14.

24. Honore M. Catudal, *Soviet Nuclear Strategy from Stalin to Gorbachev* (London: Mansell, 1988), pp. 209–39. See also Parrott, "Soviet National Security under Gorbachev."

25. Talbott, *Deadly Gambits*.

26. Alexander Haig, *Caveat: Realism, Reagan and Foreign Policy* (London: Weidenfeld and Nicholson, 1984), pp. 110–11.

27. Reagan promised at the end of his 1980 electoral campaign: "As President, I will make immediate preparations for negotiations on a SALT III Treaty. My goal is to begin arms reductions." Talbott, *Deadly Gambits*, p. 221.

28. Robert W. Tucker, "Reagan's Foreign Policy," *Foreign Affairs* 68, no. 1 (1989): 23; Daniel Deudney and G. John Ikenberry, "Who Won the Cold War?" *Foreign Policy* 87 (1992): 123–38.

29. Parrott, "Soviet National Security under Gorbachev," p. 3.

2

Ronald Reaganism
Ended the Cold War—in the 1960s

Robert Elias

"If there's going to be a bloodbath,
then let's get it over with."

—Ronald Reagan, 1960s[1]

"We've decided to destroy the Soviet Union,
bombing begins in five minutes."

—Ronald Reagan, 1980s[2]

No one thing caused the now apparent demise of the Cold War. But among the things to which that end has been attributed, some influences have been relatively neglected. Other ingredients have perhaps been only narrowly understood.

It has been argued, especially by Cold War hawks (see the introduction by Ralph Summy in this volume), that Ronald Reagan ended the Cold War in the 1980s, by launching a calculated, massive escalation of U.S. destructive power and by promoting the fantastic scenario of Star Wars—a Strategic Defense Initiative system. This, as the argument goes, beat the Soviets into economic and strategic submission, and then Reagan turned dove, welcoming peaceful relations with his Soviet counterpart, Mikhail Gorbachev.

This view is exaggerated at best (see the chapter by April Carter in this volume), and selective not only in ignoring the multiple pressures on the Cold War but also in blurring the history leading up to its demise. Ronald Reagan did more to escalate and perpetuate the Cold War, beginning with his fervent anticommunism in the 1960s. He did the same thing while president in the

1980s, repeatedly shunning opportunities to lessen tensions with the Soviets.[3] In fact, a much better case could be made for Mikhail Gorbachev having ended the Cold War (see the chapter by Jennifer Turpin in this volume). But if Ronald Reagan had any role in ending the Cold War, then it was entirely indirect and unintentional: arguably, his longstanding fanaticism had the greatest impact.

Reaganism (more than simply Reagan) helped end the Cold War only because it significantly motivated the global forces that more directly produced the changes we have seen in the last few years. In particular, Reaganism—the extremist and wholly reprehensible use of public power (from repression to invasions to nuclear proliferation)—helped create, rejuvenate, and launch the social and political movements—both in the East and the West—that deserve far more credit for the Cold War's decline. Reaganism had its effects not merely in the 1980s and the years immediately preceding the revolutions of 1989, but even more so back in the 1960s when Reagan began his hysterical anticommunist crusade as a prelude to being elected governor of California, where his initial targets were the 1960s political movements both on and off U.S. college campuses.

Reagan and Reaganism in the 1960s turned the initially mild calls for reforming the U.S. system into the revolutionary movements of the latter part of that decade. By targeting, even violently attacking, groups such as students, blacks, and civil libertarians, Reaganism made activists realize that they were now enemies in their own society and that social change was not merely a matter of persuading supposedly well-meaning politicians to see the light. Rather, Reaganism taught activists that nothing short of fundamentally restructuring U.S. domestic and foreign policy would save the country from disaster both at home and abroad.

Reagan's response in the 1960s, quoted at the beginning of this chapter, shows the same extremism and irresponsibility that he again demonstrated as president in the 1980s. That response embodied attitudes and policies that escalated the Cold War and also helped provoke a massive antiwar movement in the 1960s in the United States and elsewhere around the world. That movement opposed not merely the Vietnam War but also the unconscionable militarism, imperialism, and nuclear build-up being practiced by both superpowers.

While that movement was counted as dead by the early 1970s, its legacy lived on, and it reemerged—sometimes in unexpected ways—in the 1980s. A new antiwar and antinuclear movement arose in response to the Reaganism of the 1980s. But more hidden was the long-term impact of the 1960s movements on U.S. activism in the 1980s and, more important, on the budding revolutions in the Soviet Union and Eastern Europe.

When we consider the political and intellectual development of leaders and activists such as Václav Havel, Mikhail Gorbachev, and George Konrad, for example, we can see that the revolutions of 1989 were substantially—although obviously not completely—motivated by the political movements of the 1960s—especially those of 1968.[4] Arguably, the revolutions ending the Cold War were a long-term response to the Reaganism of the 1960s even more so than to Reagan in the 1980s.

REAGANISM IN THE 1960s

The year is 1965. The previous few years have been filled with social turmoil—a prelude to the escalating unrest that would follow, in the United States and elsewhere abroad. The civil rights movement is becoming increasingly active, from the freedom riders and the freedom summer to the march on Washington and the march from Selma to Montgomery. Urban violence has erupted in Watts, and Malcolm X and John Kennedy have been assassinated. Lyndon Johnson has won the presidency and launched a War on Poverty.

The Cold War has heated up: Cuba becomes the setting for the failed Bay of Pigs invasion and the U.S.-Soviet missile crisis. The Berlin Wall is built. The Gulf of Tonkin resolution gives Johnson a blank check to escalate U.S. bombing and troops in Vietnam. Nuclear testing resumes. The antiwar movement makes increasing protests against the Vietnam War, and thousands of young men begin burning their draft cards.

On the heels of Betty Friedan's *Feminine Mystique*, women begin asserting their rights. Bob Dylan sings about the winds of change in America. The Students for a Democratic Society is launched, calling for genuine participatory democracy. The Free Speech Movement begins in Berkeley, and student activism begins to blossom. The hippie counterculture emerges, promoting alternative life-styles, and thousands of young people flock to San Francisco.

Amid this turmoil, Ronald Reagan emerges as a serious political figure. Having collaborated, as head of the Screen Actors Guild, in developing the Hollywood blacklist and in fueling the congressional anticommunist witch hunts of the 1950s, Reagan has, by 1965, switched parties and suddenly emerged as a viable Republican candidate for governor of California.

Reagan's political campaign declares war on dissent and anti-Americanism. But unlike in the 1950s when the targets were mostly die-hard communists, in the 1960s the war would be waged against much of America's youth and against other Americans from all walks of life. The United States had always been polarized between whites and blacks, between the rich and the poor. But now, middle-class whites began breaking ranks, becoming increasingly critical of their society and its domestic and foreign policies. Ronald Reagan was determined to cut this short.

Helping to generate an antiblack, antisex, and antistudent backlash, Reagan's gubernatorial campaign asked "decent," white, law-abiding Californians to fight back against forces that Reagan claimed were ruining their state and their nation.[5] He called for law, order, and authority. He opposed free speech for those who criticized the American system. He called for stronger police and military forces. He equated antiwar and civil rights activism with anti-American violence. He challenged the emerging hippie life-style and the stereotypes he associated with it.

On the strength of this backlash, Reagan was swept easily into the governor's office in 1966, unseating a once popular Democratic incumbent.[6] Reagan promptly chastised and then fired University of California administration officials for their leniency toward protesters even while students bitterly decried their harshness.[7] Reagan lashed out against the "excess" of democracy in the university and in the broader society. Reagan collaborated in the surveillance and repression of the Black Panthers, which had recently been formed in Oakland. Reagan unleashed his aide Edwin Meese (later to become attorney general during the Reagan presidency) and a law enforcement campaign against antiwar activists and civil libertarians. Reagan launched a moral crusade against youth life-styles, harking back to a mythical past of American purity and chastity.

Even more, he sent National Guard troops to University of California campuses and tear-gassed antiwar students in Berkeley. He had the police close down Berkeley's People's Park and impose martial law.[8] The ensuing protest was greeted by hours of police gunfire, leaving a hundred people wounded, one blinded, and one dead. Reagan had turned a small part of his state into a war zone, bringing the Vietnam War home in dramatic fashion.[9]

Reagan's repression taught a valuable lesson to many of the best and brightest student activists: their clashes with authorities reflected more than merely the generation gap that exists perennially between young people and their elders. This was war, declared not against foreign enemies, but rather against them, dissenting Americans. One of the protest slogans that began emerging thereafter talked about the need to move "from dissent to resistance." Protesters began realizing that "we were not all in this together," despite what American mythology had so fervently taught them.

Reaganism not only came to California but also spread around the nation. Remarkably, Reagan's backlash made him a serious candidate for the U.S. presidency only two years later, in 1968. But rather than quell the protests, Reaganism helped foment them all the more. The irony of political organizing is that bad news often rallies political protest better than good news.[10] Ronald

Reagan provided that bad news, first in the mid-1960s and then again in the early 1980s. If those who disagreed with mainstream policies and those who sought to exercise their democratic rights were the enemies of the "establishment," then what was needed was change much more drastic than first imagined.

If Ronald Reagan had any impact on the Cold War, it was entirely negative. Reaganism intensified tensions, helping to perpetuate the Cold War. Reagan provided no positive vision of peace and democracy for the East and West. On the contrary, his vision so thoroughly contradicted those objectives that rather than using his power as a political leader to end the Cold War, it was only by checking his power, by checking Reaganism, that the Cold War was given any chance at all to subside.

The reckless, violent, and antidemocratic policies of Reaganism were met by countervailing militancy for the rest of the 1960s. Activists were "churning in a sea of rage."[11] The call in the early 1960s for real democracy clashed ever more loudly with the growing repression and imperialism of official U.S. policy—now in the hands of another long-term cold warrior: Richard Nixon. But while the peace and other movements of the 1960s were beaten back, perhaps most symbolically by the National Guard killings of Kent State students in 1970, the values of the 1960s did not go unheeded, either at home or abroad. In particular, the ideals of the Port Huron Statement, which questioned both capitalism and communism and which called for an open, nonbureaucratic society, cultural activism, and participatory democracy, showed up in surprising places later on.

VÁCLAV HAVEL: CHILD OF THE SIXTIES?

Several studies have traced the peace and human rights movements that emerged in the United States against Reaganism.[12] Other studies have examined the internal factors that produced the various revolutions in Eastern Europe in 1989.[13] Less well known, however, is the story of how, beginning in the 1960s, Reaganism (and the opposition it engendered) influenced those revolutions abroad. Let's take, for example, the role of Václav Havel in Czechoslovakia's Velvet Revolution.[14]

Václav Havel, the playwright, is also the president of the Czech Republic. He was born, in 1936, into the family of a wealthy engineer and entrepreneur. By the early 1950s, he and his family were being punished, at least implicitly, for their patrician roots. Havel was denied, for example, access to higher education.

He drifted accidentally into theater in his travels through the Czechoslovak underground culture of the late 1950s and early 1960s, during which time he wrote his first of many plays. By the end of the 1960s he had become head of the Balustrade Theater, Prague's leading avant-garde drama company. His work flourished briefly during the Prague Spring of 1968—the reform movement led by then secretary Alexander Dubcek to promote "socialism with a human face." While supporting the movement, Havel also criticized Dubcek for not moving far enough away from communism toward real socialism. The Soviet invasion of Czechoslovakia ended the debate and forcibly repressed the movement.

While a particularly harsh, new repression arose in Czechoslovakia thereafter, socialism with a human face did not completely die. Arguably, it was the direct antecedent for what subsequently emerged as *glasnost* and *perestroika* in the Soviet sphere. For example, the Czechoslovak Zdenek Mlynar, one of the Prague Spring's chief engineers, studied at Moscow State University. While there, he laid out his ideas on how to reform communism in a kind of ongoing seminar, for five years, with his roommate, who was none other than Mikhail Gorbachev. When Gorbachev visited Czechoslovakia in the late 1980s and was asked the difference between the Prague Spring of 1968 and Soviet *glasnost* of 1987, Gorbachev said simply, "Nineteen years." Were these the origins of Gorbachev's "new thinking"?

Socialism with a human face lived on in other ways, at least in spirit, in Czechoslovakia. Like many other artists and writers who had not come to some "accommodation" with the Czechoslovak government, Havel and his work were repressed: his job was taken, his plays banned. While Havel remained motivated by the reform movement—even turning down opportunities to emigrate from Czechoslovakia—he was not a particularly active dissident until the mid-1970s. In 1975, he wrote his "Letter to Dr. Gustáv Husák" (the Czechoslovak dictator), where he described Czechoslovak society as an "order without real life."[15]

Even though he was arrested briefly for this letter, the real turning point for Havel's activism came a bit later, around an unlikely incident: the arrest of the Plastic People of the Universe, a leading Czechoslovak underground rock band, detained not for political acts but rather for cultural actions—that is, for playing rock and roll.

Václav Havel regards himself as a child of the 1960s counterculture. He is a rock aficionado, attracted particularly to American rock of the 1960s. The movement Havel eventually led, in 1989, to topple the Czechoslovak government became known as the Velvet Revolution, named not just for the little blood it shed, but also for the 1960s U.S. rock band called the Velvet Underground. The Velvet Underground inspired the creation of the Plastic People of the Universe, which took its name from a song off *Mothermania,* a 1969 album by the U.S. singer Frank Zappa and his Mothers of Invention.

Zappa has long been wildly popular in Czechoslovakia. Rock music, according to Czechoslovak authorities, was a symptom of cultural rot, an offense to decent-minded folk, and a disturbance of the peace—sort of what the Allan Blooms and Jesse Helmses of contemporary America have been telling the public.

Havel reacted very sharply to the trial of Plastic People, since he views attacks on artists as attacks on life itself (something the U.S. Moral Majority might learn from). Indeed, the little real life left in Czechoslovakia was its cultural underground. The conviction of Plastic People convinced Havel to leave what he viewed as his relatively comfortable situation amid what he called the "world of cunning shits" (the Czechoslovak authorities and their collaborators), and he soon afterward took the lead in creating Charter 77, the Czechoslovak human rights movement which recaptured the spirit of socialism with a human face.

Havel's inspiration by rock and roll remains to this day. He considers it, like certain kinds of literature, as an expression of "a haunted, battered humanity, carrying the force of political action." He regards *John* Lennon and his counterculture as one of the major movements of this century, more so than *Vladimir* Lenin and his communist movement.[16] Joan Baez and the Rolling Stones now entertain at official Czech functions. The late Frank Zappa was a cultural emissary to the Czechoslovak government. Several of Havel's top advisers were prominent musicians in the Czechoslovak underground.

Because of a purge campaign begun by President Reagan in the early 1980s, it is now fashionable in the United States to discredit the 1960s countercultural values.[17] In contrast, Havel has embraced them. Like the 1960s hippies, he saw the Czechoslovak resistance as reacting to a world run by fearful old men protecting a corrupt power structure, whose chief enemies were youth and love. An admirer of Thomas Jefferson, Havel saw the counterculture as an inheritor of Jeffersonian principles—ideals which Havel found largely abandoned in the United States but perhaps still useful for rejuvenating his country.

Havel sees a link, in 1968, between the simultaneous smashing of the U.S. counterculture at the Chicago Democratic convention and the smashing of the Czechoslovak counterculture of the Prague Spring. He claims his own activism in Czechoslovakia was largely inspired by the student uprisings of 1968. He writes:

There are numerous parallels between the 60s in America and Czecho-slovakia in the 80s. I could illustrate with hundreds of cases. . . . The soul of the 60s is being revived by us here today . . . in a different form, more articulately. I was in the US for six months in 1968 and experienced such things as the impressive student strikes. Our revolution here had a number of preparatory steps. One of these was the Joan Baez concert in Bratislava. She invited us there and spoke from the stage about Charter 77, and the spirit of the 60s was somehow revived there with Baez, a symbol for the nonviolent 60s peace movement.[18]

Havel's production of new essays and plays escalated in the 1970s, bringing him new recognition, many awards, and increased official repression. In 1979, Havel was convicted of criminal subversion of the Czechoslovak republic for being a founder and member of VONS, the Committee for the Defense of the Unjustly Accused. He was sentenced to a term of four and one half years, the majority of which he served until a grave illness forced his release. Severely limited in his writing, Havel managed to write only one short letter per week to his wife; these letters collectively have been published as *Letters to Olga*.[19] He soon recovered and resumed his writing and also his Charter 77 work, for which he was several more times arrested. In 1986, he was awarded the Erasmus Prize from the Netherlands, which prompted the publication of *Living in Truth*, a collection of his essays. In these years, his plays accumulated: all were banned from performance in Czechoslovakia, but they circulated widely and were even occasionally performed underground.

In 1989, Havel helped found Civic Forum, the movement launched in the basement of Prague's Magic Lantern Theater, which would, a short time later, overthrow the Czechoslovak government. Rather than merely the result of Soviet nonintervention, it was a movement that had been percolating and gaining power in Czechoslovakia for at least twenty years. Within four months, Havel was propelled from his latest prison term to the provisional head of the new Czechoslovak government. In 1990 he was chosen, in free elections, to be Czechoslovakia's first postrevolutionary president. After the Czechs and Slovaks split, Havel remained as president of the Czech Republic.

HAVEL'S POLITICAL STRATEGY: CULTURAL ACTIVISM

Havel developed a provocative and prophetic theory of political resistance against repressive regimes. His clearest statement of these views comes in his essay "The Power of the Powerless."[20] Here again we can see the influence of 1960s manifestos such as the New Left's Port Huron Statement.[21]

Havel argues that the overthrow of repression is prepared in the souls of those who are repressed. For example, despite the Charter 77 activists' isolation within an apparently indifferent Czechoslovak society, Havel claimed that a timid consensus was emerging—constrained by fear and self-censorship, but which nevertheless constituted innumerable pockets of resistance, creating what he called the "unknown life" of the society. Havel believed that the moral economy of civil society would be regenerated invisibly by "antipolitics"—a series of small resistances, perhaps more cultural than political.

Czechoslovaks must, Havel argued, throw off official disinformation and the petty lies of their own lives in favor of "living in truth," a faith in truth which "operates in the existential hidden sphere, working like a bacteriological weapon of incalculable political power." Turning conventional wisdom on its head, Havel argued that violence was *not a radical enough* resistance: a resistance stronger than violence "requires a profound spiritual renewal—an existential revolution." Words, speaking the truth, would have a "heightened radioactivity," especially in conditions where speech is suppressed, which— paradoxically—gives it a special weight and power when it *is* used.[22] Havel's argument is hauntingly similar to Mario Savio's appeals as he led the Berkeley Free Speech Movement of the 1960s.

Havel wanted Czechoslovaks to expose all hypocrisy, to adopt strong principles, and to speak difficult truths without fear—a theme, by the way, of the U.S. feminist movement that rose again at the end of the 1960s. Fear must be used positively; moments of profound doubt can give birth to new certainties. Czechoslovakia needed the self-confidence of those who were not afraid of looking beyond the horizon of their narrow personal interests.

Havel tells us that *self*-transformation underlies *national* transformation. Things as personal as even our own sexual liberation can profoundly threaten repressive regimes. It is a mistake to believe that history exists only outside us or beyond us. True change cannot come from the top, but rather only from an honest, grass-roots spirit. Thus, activities flourishing underground and on the fringes of official culture are crucial. Totalitarian conditions can produce a mysterious ambiguity of human behavior: passivity and acquiescence on the one hand, but also implicit resistance and lessons learned on the other. Havel urged Czechoslovaks to have hope, even against the odds. He wrote: "Hope is not prognostication, it is an orientation of the spirit, an orientation of the heart. It is not the conviction that something will turn out well but the certainty that something makes sense, regardless of how it turns out. It's the ability to work for something because it's good, not just because it stands a good chance of succeeding."[23]

Challenging the cynical view of history as a vast, impersonal juggernaut largely unaffected by people, Havel argued for the historic importance of individual resistance and for the writer's role in creating psychic space for political or cultural activism. With the accumulation of enough small resistances, Havel predicted that the lid of totalitarianism would no longer hold;

the system would begin to crack, and perhaps the lid would blow off completely, and unexpectedly—which is very similar to what happened in 1989.

LESSONS FOR THE UNITED STATES

Havel believes the United States needs *glasnost* and *perestroika* as much as the former Soviet Union did. While it is convenient for conventional Cold War explanations, and for those in power, to simply divide the world into us and them, reality is more complex. When "they" in the Soviet sphere began questioning and abandoning the faults of their system, we were told in the West that naturally they must want to embrace the only other possible system: in our strictly black-and-white world, it was our system, of course. It may shock Westerners dutifully trained to think this way when they discover that someone like Václav Havel is far from convinced that capitalism will solve the failures of communism.

Havel argues, for example, that "the superficial variety of one system (capitalism), or the repulsive grayness of the other (communism), should not hide the same deep emptiness of life, devoid of meaning, *in both*" (emphasis added).[24] He warns us about both Orwellian and Huxleyan nightmares, and about bureaucracies both public and private. Consumerism and profiteering pervade Western cultural, religious, and educational institutions, in his view, producing a sophisticated totalitarianism of their own: one that provides the illusion of freedom and individuality while actually controlling the parameters and contours of people's lives.

Havel claims that people in the West are "manipulated in ways that are infinitely more subtle and refined than the brutal methods used in Soviet-style societies." These methods include "rigid political parties run by professional machines barring citizens from all concrete and personal responsibility; capital accumulation engaged in secret manipulations and expansions; the omnipresent dictatorship of production, advertising, commerce and consumer culture; and the flood of trivial information."[25]

Havel says that the repression of expression can occur through Soviet-style, direct censorship, but may occur "even more so in the West through the systematic trivializing, distorting and overloading of our speech, rendering it meaningless and politically powerless." Western, especially U.S., culture, with its "atomization, the commodification of every aspect of people's lives and the vulgarizing of politics has wrought not watchfulness and participation but rather cynicism and passivity, an indifference to public affairs. Instead of real freedoms, people only get distractions." For Havel, politics transcends government, and to be apolitical is to be less than human. But that politics

must be a "politics from below, a politics of humans not of the apparatus
. . . politics growing from the heart not from propaganda."[26]

RECOVERING THE SPIRIT

Havel's appeals emphasize, more than anything else, the need to "recover
our spirit" in the modern world: not religion, but rather a "deeper connect-
edness, a more human scale of organizing societies, in which individuals can
recapture their meaning." Although as president he has been severely limited
in fulfilling his visions, his view of an alternative system for his nation and
the world differs considerably from conventional Western media assumptions. That he wants real political democracy goes without saying. Like the
1960s New Left (which was more democratic than socialist), the Civic Forum
was a democracy movement. The end of the Cold War was propelled
primarily by a quest for democracy, not for capitalism. As Havel tells us: "I
have never said that we should build capitalism in our country."[27]

But if not capitalism, what then would replace communism? Havel says
he would like

> An economic system of decentralized, small enterprises . . . maintaining
> a plurality of modes of ownership and economic decisionmaking,
> including various types of cooperatives and collective ownership with
> self-management schemes, some small private enterprise, and state
> ownership of the most important public services. . . . The only way of
> saving this civilization is to liberate the human being from manipulation
> by all megastructures, East and West, which modern man has created,
> and which are now in the process of destroying him.[28]

> It really is not all that important whether, by accident of domicile, we
> confront a Western manager or an Eastern bureaucrat in this globally
> crucial struggle against the momentum of impersonal power.[29]

With socialism—often equated with communism—now a dirty word in
Eastern Europe, Havel refuses to be labeled by such ideologies, but he has
admitted that "God created me in such a way that my heart is on the *left* side
of my chest."[30]

As a revolutionary, Havel sought peace in his nation and the world. Yet
like many other Eastern European activists, he was often skeptical of peace
movements. In the Eastern bloc, "peace" was often an empty term of
propaganda, another "utopia" offered up to the masses.[31] Havel also sometimes criticized the European and U.S. peace movements for defining peace

too narrowly, sometimes as merely the control of nuclear weapons. Movements calling for "democracy" and "human rights" were more likely to motivate Eastern Europeans. Nevertheless, Havel claimed that "I feel deep down inside that . . . the young people [in the West] who do this [protest] and whom I am able to see almost every day on television are my brothers and sisters, which is a new experience for me; moreover, during my visit to the USA in 1968 I rarely felt so much at ease as in the company of the revolutionary youth."[32]

Havel's prescriptions for local participatory democracy and democratic socialism were drawn, in part, from the Czechoslovak Charter 77 movement and from the Prague Spring's socialism with a human face. But his vision came just as clearly from the influence exerted on him by 1960s American New Left manifestos like the Port Huron Statement. The ideals and language are remarkably similar; indeed, the Port Huron Statement retains a surprising timeliness for both East and West, even today.[33]

CONCLUSION

Havel and others in Eastern Europe were strongly influenced by the counterculture and radical politics of the 1960s.[34] These were precisely the values that Ronald Reagan so violently despised and that, ironically, were only further nurtured by Reagan's fervent opposition.[35] These visions did not apparently succeed back then, yet more than we knew, they influenced American culture[36]—even in the face of one political victory after another by the political Right—and influenced other cultures as well. It was not the culture of capitalism that triumphed, but rather the culture of democracy— not American culture, but rather American counterculture.

Arguably, the peace and human rights movements in the East and the West did the most to end the Cold War.[37] But in many ways they were fueled by Reagan's alarming and longstanding threats to democracy and peace at home and abroad. Reaganism led to the end of the Cold War only in the sense that it made the peace and democracy movements all the more necessary.

NOTES

1. Edward P. Morgan, *The 60s Experience: Hard Lessons About America* (Philadelphia: Temple University Press, 1991) p. 77.

2. David Cortright, *Peace Works: The Citizen's Role in Ending the Cold War* (Boulder, CO: Westview, 1993), p. 107.

3. For example, Alexander Haig's memoirs indicate that the Soviet ambassador to the United States, Anatoly Dobrynin, persistently sought serious arms control talks with the

United States from the very beginning of the Reagan administration. Each time he was turned down. See Cortright, *Peace Works.*

4. David Caute, *The Year of the Barricades: A Journey Through 1968* (New York: Harper & Row, 1988); Robert V. Daniels, *Year of the Heroic Guerrilla: World Revolution and Counterrevolution in 1968* (New York: Basic Books, 1989).

5. Todd Gitlin, *The Sixties: Years of Hope, Days of Rage* (New York: Bantam Books, 1989), p. 217.

6. Ibid., p. 247.

7. Morgan, *The 60s Experience,* p. 112.

8. Gitlin, *The Sixties*, p. 357.

9. Stewart Burns, *Social Movements of the 1960s* (Boston: Twayne Publishers, 1990), p. 96; Morgan, *The 60s Experience*, p. 186.

10. David S. Meyer, *The Winter of Discontent* (Westport, CT: Praeger, 1993).

11. Gitlin, *The Sixties*, p. 318.

12. Paul Joseph, *Peace Politics: The United States Between the Old and New World Orders* (Philadelphia: Temple University Press, 1993); Cortright, *Peace Works.*

13. Bernard Wheaton and Zdenek Kavan, *The Velvet Revolution* (Boulder, CO: Westview, 1992).

14. Eva Kriseova, *Václav Havel*, a biography edited by Jan Vladislav (New York: St. Martin's, 1993).

15. Václav Havel, *Living In Truth*, ed. Jan Vladislav (London: Faber & Faber, 1987), pp. 3–35.

16. Václav Havel, *Disturbing the Peace* (New York: Alfred Knopf, 1990), p. 119.

17. Morgan, *The 60s Experience*, p. 265.

18. Havel, *Disturbing the Peace*, pp. 115–16.

19. Václav Havel, *Letters to Olga* (New York: Henry Holt, 1989).

20. Václav Havel et al., "The Power of the Powerless," in *The Power of the Powerless*, ed. John Keane (Armonk, NY: M. E. Sharpe, 1990), pp. 23–96.

21. George Katsiaficas, *The Imagination of the New Left* (Armonk, NY: M. E. Sharpe, 1983); James Miller, *Democracy Is in the Streets* (New York: Simon & Schuster, 1987).

22. Havel, "The Power of the Powerless," p. 42.

23. Havel, *Disturbing the Peace*, p. 181.

24. Dominic Lawson, "Inside the Castle," *The Spectator*, September 15, 1990, p. 366.

25. Havel, *Disturbing the Peace*, p. 181.

26. Václav Havel in Margaret O'Brien Steinfels, "Rediscovering Politics," *Commonweal*, February 9, 1990, p. 68.

27. Václav Havel, "The Great Moral Stake of the Moment," *Newsweek*, January 15, 1990, p. 42.

28. Lawson, "Inside the Castle," p. 367.

29. Havel, *Living in Truth*, p. 150.

30. Lawson, "Inside the Castle," p. 367.

31. Havel, *Living in Truth*, p. 177.

32. Ibid., p. 212.

33. Miller, *Democracy Is in the Streets*, pp. 14, 321.

34. See Peter Wicke, "The Times They Are A-Changin,' " *Peace Review* 5, no. 2 (1993): 199–208, for a discussion of the role of 1960s U.S. rock music on the fall of the Berlin Wall in East Germany.

35. Morgan, *The 60s Experience*, p. 264.

36. Jack Whalen and Richard Flacks, *Beyond the Barricades: The Sixties Generation Grows Up* (Philadelphia: Temple University Press, 1989).

37. Cortright, *Peace Works*; Joseph, *Peace Politics*.

3

The End of the Cold War:
The Brezhnev Doctrine

Joanne Wright

The Cold War was certainly a unique period in history. It was characterized by ideological, economic, and military competition between the United States and the Soviet Union, and its effects were felt in all parts of the globe. On the basis of this definition, the Cold War is most definitely over, even if many of its legacies remain. Probably the most obvious manifestation of the Cold War's end came when the Soviet Union demonstrated that it no longer regarded Eastern Europe as vital to its national security and was thus unwilling to maintain its hegemonic position there. Why or how the Soviet Union found itself in this position is a complex question and one, like that of what caused the Cold War, that is probably impossible to answer in a universally acceptable manner. However, concentrating on Soviet relations with Eastern Europe can be justified on two grounds. First, for many people, the Cold War began in Europe and was most overtly manifested in Europe.[1] Even more specifically, Soviet behavior in Eastern Europe was both the ultimate symbol of its brutality and one of the most reliable barometers of Soviet intentions. Second, it is doubtful that all the necessary information is yet available to answer more holistic and theoretical questions about the demise of the Cold War. If we were all so wrong about predicting its end, then we should be very cautious about assuming that we understand what made the Cold War end. The best we can perhaps hope for is, by exploring specific aspects or smaller questions, to contribute to the larger picture that will at some point emerge.

I would like to acknowledge the assistance of Chris Black and Simon Lutton in the preparation of this chapter.

The question with which this chapter will be concerned is why did the East European regimes act either with such caution toward Gorbachev or try to ignore him altogether? The answer postulated is that none of the East European regimes could be sure about the status of the Brezhnev Doctrine. It was not until the end of 1988 that Gorbachev finally took steps to renounce unambiguously the Brezhnev Doctrine. In other words, the realization by both East European governments and peoples that the Soviets would not be sending in the tanks is an important part of any explanation as to why the Cold War ended.

This is not to deny a role to long-term structural factors such as economic difficulties or shorter-term trigger factors such as individual bravery or leadership in ending the Cold War.[2] However, if the threat of force was a prominent feature of the Cold War and its continuance, then it seems logical to assume that the withdrawal of the threat of force on the part of at least one of the major protagonists played a major role in ending the Cold War. Evidence for this proposition comes from two major sources: first, in the initial refusal of the Soviets, and especially Gorbachev, to renounce the Brezhnev Doctrine, together with the very mixed signals that were sent to the East Europeans throughout 1986 and 1987; and second, in the speed with which events happened in Eastern Europe once Gorbachev did make it clear, during his speech to the United Nations in December 1988, that the Brezhnev Doctrine was no longer in operation.

This chapter begins by examining the Soviet view of Eastern Europe as primarily a vital part of its national security zone. Then it outlines the various components of the Brezhnev Doctrine, which, although it was only "codified" in 1968, formed the basis of Soviet policy toward Eastern Europe for over forty years. The Gorbachev era is divided into three chronological phases: 1985, 1986–87, and 1988. Finally, the speed with which radical change occurred in all the East European countries is considered.

THE SOVIET UNION AND EASTERN EUROPE

Brown suggests that there are at least six aspects to the Soviet view of Eastern Europe.[3] The aspect that underwent a complete reversal between 1945 and 1985 was the economic one. There is no doubt that immediately after World War II, the Soviet Union saw Eastern Europe as a target of economic exploitation. Items of industrial and technological value were removed to the Soviet Union from eastern Germany and Czechoslovakia in particular. In addition, early economic relations were structured to be over-whelmingly favorable to the Soviet Union.[4] However, even in the mid-1950s, it was already apparent that Eastern Europe would not be able to continue to play a subservient but boosting role to the Soviet economy. By the 1980s, not only was Eastern Europe a considerable drain on Soviet resources, but it also represented considerable opportunity costs in terms of lost hard currency in world markets.[5] Therefore, although the Soviet Union was undoubtedly correct in its initial postwar view that Eastern Europe could be a boost to its economy, by the time Gorbachev came to power this view had completely changed and one of Gorbachev's primary concerns was how to reduce the burden to the Soviet economy that Eastern Europe had come to represent.

The second aspect of how the Soviet Union viewed Eastern Europe was as a sound basis of support in international relations and particularly in international organizations such as the United Nations. For the most part, the Soviet Union could rely on solid bloc support for its positions and proposals in international organizations. This view of Eastern Europe as the basis of a bloc in international relations is related to the third aspect of the overall picture. As Brown states: "There was evidently a Soviet conviction that the continuing allegiance of Eastern Europe and the preservation there of a system basically similar to its own was essential, not only for the Soviet system's domestic legitimacy, but for its overall standing and reputation."[6] Thus the Soviets also viewed Eastern Europe as an important source of political and ideological legitimization of the Soviet social, economic, and political system.

A fourth aspect of the Soviet view of Eastern Europe, and one especially prominent in the West, was as a springboard for offensive actions in Western Europe at the most, and a base of forward defense at the least. Western analyses stress a range of topics from the aggressive posture of Soviet and East European troop deployments and modernization programs to Soviet policies designed to force divisions within the Western allies.[7] This latter view has some substance to it and can be clearly illustrated in Soviet maneuverings in exploiting tensions between NATO members over intermediate-range nuclear weapons.[8] There is little doubt that the Soviets were capable of viewing Eastern Europe as a basis for offensive action, but this was probably mostly opportunistic.

The last two aspects of the Soviet view of Eastern Europe—as a source of Soviet heroic mythology and as a vital part of Soviet national security—have much greater explanatory power in terms of both the origins of the brutality of Soviet behavior toward Eastern Europe and the consistency of Soviet policy. In other words, they help illustrate how important the Brezhnev Doctrine was to the Soviets, and how important its removal was to the East Europeans.

Stalin had made it clear to all who would listen that whichever country's army occupied a territory had the right to impose upon that territory its political and economic system.[9] However, perhaps the best expression of the combination of Soviet heroism and the need to protect Soviet national security came from Brezhnev. An observer of some of the meetings between the Soviet and Czechoslovakian leaders at the height of the 1968 crisis recorded Brezhnev as saying:

> We in the Kremlin came to the conclusion that we could not depend on you any longer. You do what you feel like in domestic policies, even things that displease us, and you are not open to positive suggestion. But your country lies on territory where the Soviet soldier trod in the Second World War. We bought that territory at the cost of enormous sacrifices, and we shall never leave it. The borders of that area are our borders as well. Because you do not listen to us, we feel threatened. In the name of the dead of World War Two who laid down their lives for your freedom as well, we are therefore fully justified in sending our soldiers into your country, so that we may feel truly secure within our common borders.[10]

Certainly the Soviet Union justified its huge presence on East European soil as defensive—defensive against the hegemonic aspirations of the United States and its European allies and, on occasion, defensive against possible West German militarism and revanchism. A fear of German revanchism was certainly part of what prompted the Soviet-led invasion of Czechoslovakia in 1968 and the subsequent expression of the Brezhnev Doctrine.

THE BREZHNEV DOCTRINE

Karen Dawisha suggests that the relationship between Eastern Europe and the Soviet Union rested essentially on East European acceptance of three principles, all of which enabled the Soviets to exercise control and supervision over Eastern Europe.[11] The first of these was the leading role of the party; the second, democratic centralism; and the third, socialist internationalism. Although the first two principles should not be discounted, it is really the third, socialist internationalism, that is encoded in the Brezhnev Doctrine.

The leading, or vanguard, role of the Communist party was enshrined as part of the constitution in all the "people's democracies" of Eastern Europe. This gave the Communist parties two great advantages in terms of controlling the activities of their populations. It meant that any organization within the society, be it a minuscule musicians' collective or a large government department, understood that it was to the party that it was ultimately responsible. It also gave the Communist parties the legal base to organize at all levels of work and recreation. The information-gathering and monitoring potential of this was immense. As Dawisha argues, it provided a "horizontal" means of control.[12]

The "vertical" means of control through which the Soviets made their wishes known was provided by democratic centralism. Outlined by Lenin and modified and abused by Stalin, democratic centralism stifled all opposition to the Communist parties throughout the entire bloc.[13] Not only did this principle enable indigenous Communist parties to nullify dissent within their borders, but it also enabled the Soviet Union to limit any opposition within the bloc by virtue of the Soviet Communist party's leading role. Underlying both these principles, however, was socialist internationalism and the might of the Red Army.

As argued above, while the Soviet Union may have had several views of Eastern Europe and its role in Soviet policy, the primary Soviet concern was that Eastern Europe was part of the Soviet national security zone. Obviously, then, stability within Eastern Europe was considered a vital contributing factor to Soviet national security. However, given traditional hostility toward the Soviets and Russians in the region, this created a particular problem. Even well before the 1968 invasion of Czechoslovakia, the militaries in several East European countries had demonstrated themselves to be unreliable upholders of the Soviet-imposed order.

For example, in 1953 Czechoslovakian troops refused to suppress riots, and in the same year some East German army units refused to leave their barracks to prevent widespread demonstrations in East Berlin. In 1956, army units in both Poland and Hungary refused to move against their own citizens; indeed, in the case of Hungary some army units sided with Imre Nagy. This left the Soviets with two options. One was to cultivate and structure the secret police forces. This was certainly an option vigorously pursued by the Soviets, and it provided them with valuable intelligence and a means of exercising day-to-day control. However, the secret police forces were unlikely to be able to contain large-scale public-order problems. The second option then, was to have the Soviet military as the last guarantor of stability in Eastern Europe.

Stationing Soviet troops in Eastern Europe was a relatively simple task in the immediate postwar years, when Allied agreements provided the Soviets with a legal basis for leaving their troops in most East European countries. For example, the Soviets were able to maintain troops in Poland, Czechoslovakia, Hungary, and Romania on the grounds of keeping continuous supply lines to Soviet troops stationed in East Germany and Austria. Difficulties in this arrangement first arose as a postwar settlement for Austria was being negotiated. This settlement provided for the withdrawal of all foreign troops from Austrian territory, thus removing the justification the Soviets had used for maintaining troops in other East European countries. A new justification was found, however, in the form of the Warsaw Pact, which came into existence just as the Austrian treaty became operative.

Several, mostly Western, authors maintain that the Warsaw Pact was not really externally oriented as a defense against NATO, as the Soviets claimed, but rather was more internally oriented to maintain order and stability in Eastern Europe. As Kolkowicz puts it, "[t]he Warsaw Pact's primary purpose is to contain a turbulent and eruptive group of countries under Moscow's influence. Consequently, the central uses of the Warsaw Pact are internal; to contain, to police and to maintain stability."[14] Even though consultations did take place between pact leaders during the Hungarian crisis of 1956, its forces were not utilized in the subsequent Soviet invasion. The Hungarian invasion, though, remains significant as further evidence of how important the Soviets viewed Eastern Europe to their national security and to the evolution of the Brezhnev Doctrine.

A fairly common explanation for the Soviet invasion of Hungary is the trigger provided by the Nagy government's announcement that Hungary was becoming a neutral country and thereby leaving the Warsaw Pact.[15] While this explanation would certainly concur with the image of Eastern Europe as part of the Soviet national security zone, as Gati points out the timing of the announcement presents problems for this thesis.[16] Nonetheless, Gati's explanation still rests essentially on Soviet national security considerations. Gati quotes Nikita Khrushchev as justifying the invasion to the Yugoslav leadership in the following terms: "If we let things take their course, the West would say we are either stupid or weak. . . . We cannot possibly permit it."[17]

According to Gati, then, the invasion was justified on the basis of what might happen. The Soviets acted out of insecurity and fear of losing control over the bloc since the West would then perceive them as weak and foolish.[18] In Eastern Europe, the Soviet invasion of Hungary was interpreted as anything but weak and foolish, and expectations of a loosening of control in the wake of Stalin were dashed. While some of the more extreme mechanisms of Stalinist control were modified, the bottom line remained that the Soviets would use their armed forces to intervene should they deem it necessary. A year after the Hungarian invasion, an international meeting of Communist parties organized by the Communist Party of the Soviet Union (CPSU) declared:

> The socialist countries base their relations on principles of equality, respect for territorial integrity, state independence and sovereignty, and noninterference in one another's internal affairs. These are vital principles. However, they do not exhaust the essence of relations between them. Fraternal mutual aid is part and parcel of these relations. This aid is a striking expression of socialist internationalism.[19]

The most striking expression of socialist internationalism, however, was to occur twelve years later in Czechoslovakia. Although technically the invasion of Czechoslovakia was a multilateral operation on the part of the members of the Warsaw Pact, the most important military objectives were fulfilled by Soviet troops. The numbers of Soviet troops stationed in Czechoslovakia were also increased after the invasion. It is the attempted reconciliation of Soviet, bloc, and national interests in the aftermath of the invasion that provides the best-known exposition of the Brezhnev Doctrine:

> There is no doubt that the peoples of the socialist countries and the Communist parties have and must have freedom to determine their country's path of development. However, any decision of theirs must damage neither socialism in their own country nor the fundamental interests of the other socialist countries nor the worldwide workers' movement, which is waging a struggle for socialism. This means that every communist party is responsible not only to its own people but also to all the socialist countries and to the entire communist movement. Whoever forgets this in placing sole emphasis on the autonomy and independence of communist parties lapses into one-sidedness, shirking his [*sic*] internationalist obligations.[20]

The ideological justification used by the Soviets for the invasion of Czechoslovakia and the subsequent codification of the Brezhnev Doctrine had two interrelated strands; one was the general stability of Europe, and the other was the advancement of class-based, rather than national, interests. Kolkowicz quotes several Soviet media outlets stressing the vital role of the Warsaw Pact in European security as "an insuperable barrier to all those who would revise the results of the second war."[21] Class interests meant that national interests had to be subordinated to the more progressive forces of socialism. It also meant that when any difficulties or hostilities arose anywhere within the socialist commonwealth, it was the duty of other socialist countries to intervene to protect the advances of socialism.

However, when stripped of its ideological jargon, the Brezhnev Doctrine was simply saying that the Soviets would not respect the sovereignty and independence of East European countries when they judged the actions of those countries to be against their vital national security interests. In ensuring their national security interests in Eastern Europe, the Soviets' most potent weapon was the presence and threat of the Soviet army—and this presence and threat was most effectively communicated through the Warsaw Pact. Further, as Kusin argues, "[b]y having to sign the joint political platforms promulgated periodically through the Pact's Political Consultative Committee, the Soviet Union's 'allies' commit themselves to postures from which later deviation can be easily censured."[22]

It could perhaps be suggested that the mutual force reductions and confidence-building measures agreed to by the Soviets as part of the Helsinki process further complicated Soviet deployments in Eastern Europe and any ability to invoke the Brezhnev Doctrine. However, Sheehan, Buzan, and Hart point out that all the provisions agreed to by the Soviets were weak and could equally well be used to convey aggressive intentions.[23] Some evidence in support of this latter proposition can be seen in Soviet behavior during the Polish crisis of the early 1980s. Confidence-building measures did not prevent Warsaw Pact forces from conducting intimidating exercises on Poland's frontiers during the spring of 1981. The effectiveness of these intimidating measures can be demonstrated by the merely token resistance General Wojciech Jaruzelski met when he moved to arrest Solidarity leaders and other "unreliable elements."[24]

Even though the Soviets' intervention in Poland was not as direct as it had been in East Germany in 1953, Hungary in 1956, or Czechoslovakia in 1968, their behavior, nonetheless, still seemed to be predicated on the principle of socialist internationalism and the instrument of the Warsaw Pact. Coincidentally, conducting negotiations for the renewal of the Warsaw Pact was one of the first tasks for the new general secretary of the CPSU in 1985. There was very little in these negotiations that would have led the East Europeans to believe that the Soviets had revised their image of Eastern Europe as vital to Soviet national security interests.

GORBACHEV AND THE BREZHNEV DOCTRINE

Several authors note that Gorbachev seems to have gone through several different stages in his attitudes toward reform.[25] Specifically in relation to reforming the Brezhnev Doctrine, Gorbachev went through three phases of thinking and reform. The first of these, from 1985 to 1986, is characterized by a reaffirmation of the status quo including the Brezhnev Doctrine. During the second phase, which goes from 1986 to early 1988, the signals Gorbachev gave his East European colleagues about the Brezhnev Doctrine were mixed, but not sufficient to convince East Europeans that a fundamental change in attitude had yet occurred. The final phase comprises the last nine months or so of 1988, when actions finally backed up verbal assurances that the Brezhnev Doctrine was no longer operative.

Although there were some divergences from previous patterns, Gorbachev's first speech as general secretary in March 1985 was still notable for its continuities toward Eastern Europe. He pledged that the first priority of

Soviet foreign policy would be "to protect and strengthen in all ways the fraternal friendship with our closest comrades-in-arms and allies, the countries of the great socialist commonwealth."[26] Continuity was also evident in Gorbachev's funeral oration for his predecessor, Constantin Chernenko: "Faithful to the principles of socialist internationalism, our party will continue to do everything for broader interaction between the fraternal countries and for the enhancement of their position in international affairs."[27] The following month, Gorbachev's views were under scrutiny in negotiations surrounding the renewal of the Warsaw Pact.

Although Gorbachev's assumption of the general secretaryship of the CPSU may have raised East European expectations of change, his speech marking the signing of a thirty-year renewal of the Warsaw Pact gave very little cause for hope. Gorbachev chose to reemphasize that relations between socialist countries "are based on the full equality and comradely mutual assistance of sovereign states" who uphold "the principle of socialist internationalism."[28] An even stronger reaffirmation of the Brezhnev Doctrine appeared in *Pravda* in June 1985.

This article, which was signed by O. Vladimirov, contained both criticisms of "new" trends in socialist life and an appeal for loyalty to "old" values. "Revisionist, nationalistic and clerical concepts" were sharply criticized as agents of imperialism trying to drive a wedge between the Soviet Union and its socialist allies. "National models" of socialism were also vigorously condemned. Instead, all Communist parties were urged to maintain their loyalty to the "principles of proletarian internationalism and their readiness to defend socialist gains" in the interests of world socialism. Other "old" themes stressed were the "common responsibility of all the socialist countries for the fate of world socialism" and the harmony of the "foreign policy of the USSR and of the world marxist-leninist core of world socialism."[29]

The appearance of the Vladimirov article, which was reprinted in several East European newspapers, did cause concern in East European capitals that Gorbachev was, after all, going to impose rigid discipline on Soviet–East European relations. This impression was, to some extent, strengthened by Gorbachev's continued insistence on closer bloc political, economic, and military integration. Toward the end of 1985, for example, Gorbachev pushed through COMECON, a "Comprehensive Program for Scientific and Technical Progress." In language very reminiscent of earlier eras, Gorbachev claimed that the program was necessary to ensure "technological independence from, and vulnerability [*sic*; should be "invulnerability"] to, pressure and blackmail on the part of the imperialists."[30]

By the end of 1985, there were very few indications of a fundamental change in the basis of Soviet–East European relations. Soviet troops would

G. Europe

remain stationed on East European soil under the renegotiated Warsaw Pact, and socialist internationalism remained the principle underlying bloc relations. However, in early 1986, Gorbachev clearly entered a more reforming phase, although his statements on the Brezhnev Doctrine remained ambiguous.

The first signs of Gorbachev's more open, radical approach came during the Twenty-seventh Party Congress in February/March 1986, although just weeks later Gorbachev seemed to confirm the Brezhnev Doctrine in a speech made to the East German Socialist Unity Party (SED). Three major pronouncements by Gorbachev during the course of 1987 also reveal that while changes may have been in the air, so were some consistencies. Gorbachev's visit to Prague, his speech on the seventieth anniversary of the Bolshevik revolution, and his book *Perestroika* all failed to effectively renounce the Brezhnev Doctrine. Perhaps the most encouraging signs of a fundamental change in attitude toward Eastern Europe and its place in Soviet national security were the institutional and personnel changes that took place in the decision-making bureaucracy from 1986 onwards. However, even this was insufficient to convince most East Europeans that the Soviet tanks would not intervene—indeed, some East European leaders clearly believed that the tanks would intervene and used this to maintain their own positions and resistance to reform.

Gorbachev's speeches to the twenty-seventh congress of the CPSU are significant for what they do not say as well as what they do say.[31] Gorbachev's admissions that mistakes had been made in the past, that the socialist model of development had not delivered all that it could, and that reform was necessary did trigger much freer and open debate not only in the Soviet Union but also in parts of Eastern Europe, even though he actually had very little to say about Eastern Europe at all. This lack of reference to Eastern Europe and especially to the principles of socialist internationalism and common class interests has been interpreted as a significant break with the past.[32] However, as Kramer points out, Gorbachev did not really say much more than what Khrushchev had done thirty years earlier.[33] This interpretation is confirmed by Gorbachev's speech at the close of the SED's congress just weeks later in April 1986.

In addition to stressing the need for further integration and cooperation among COMECON members, Gorbachev mentioned two things that were sharp reminders of the Brezhnev Doctrine. First, he made favorable references to the crushing of "the internal enemies of socialist Poland." But perhaps more important, he also warned that "socialist gains are irreversible" and that any attempt by internal or external forces to "wrench a country away from the socialist commonwealth would mean encroaching not only on the will of the people, but also on the entire postwar arrangement and, in the final analysis, on peace."[34] The inference was clearly that Eastern Europe was still very much part of the Soviet Union's perceived vital national security interests.

In April 1987, Gorbachev visited Prague and again gave out very mixed messages about the applicability of the Brezhnev Doctrine. On the one hand, he insisted: "No one has the right to claim a special position in the socialist world. The independence of each party, its responsibility to its people, the right to resolve questions of the country's development in a sovereign way—for us, these are indisputable principles." Yet the very next sentence appears to contain a reaffirmation of the principles behind the Brezhnev Doctrine: "At the same time, we are profoundly convinced that the successes of the socialist commonwealth are impossible without concern on the part of each party and country not only for its own interests but for the general interests, without a respectful attitude toward friends and allies and the mandatory consideration of their interests."[35] Similarly, although it seems that Gorbachev tried to avoid discussing the 1968 invasion, he did endorse it in the following terms: "We have bravely thought about what happened. . . . We came to the right conclusions. Look how far Czechoslovakia has advanced since 1968."[36] The decision to subjugate Czechoslovakia's right to decide its own future and the solution to its own problems to the interests of the Soviet Union was still considered "right" by Gorbachev.

The end of 1987 saw the seventieth anniversary of the Bolshevik revolution and a chance for Gorbachev to clarify any ambiguities about the Brezhnev Doctrine. However, what emerged from speeches surrounding the marking of this anniversary was the same mixture of hints at reform and threats of continuity. A new basis to Soviet–East European relations seemed to be implied by Gorbachev's statement that "all parties are fully and irreversibly independent. We said that as long ago as the 20th Congress. True, it took time to free ourselves of the old habits. Now, however, this is an immutable reality."[37] But at the same time Gorbachev stressed that "we also know what damage can be done by weakening the internationalist principle in mutual relations of socialist states, by deviation from the principles of mutual benefit and mutual aid, and by a lack of attention to the general interests of socialism in action on the world arena."[38] Thus, while the Communist parties of Eastern Europe were supposedly independent, they must still be aware of the "damage" that could be done to Soviet interests, and therefore their own, from too much independence.

Also in 1987, Gorbachev published his best-selling book, *Perestroika*. Although it must be remembered that this book was aimed primarily at a Western market, it was quite widely available in Eastern Europe.[39] In addition to stressing that "political relations between socialist countries must be strictly based on absolute independence," Gorbachev wrote: "We are also firmly convinced that the socialist community will be successful only if every party and state cares for both its own and common interests, if it respects its friends and allies, heeds their interests and pays attention to the experience of others."[40] Again, this is really not much different from Khrushchev's "many paths to socialism."

One area that does furnish more concrete evidence of change in Soviet attitudes toward Eastern Europe was in the bureaucratic restructuring in Soviet policy-making circles that began after 1986. Prior to 1988, the important decisions in Soviet–East European relations were made by the Politburo, and most of the research and recommendations came from the Department for Liaison with Communist and Workers' Parties in Socialist Countries. During 1986, two important and reform-minded individuals, Vadim Medvedev and Georgii Shakhnazarov, were appointed to important positions in relation to East European policy. Nonetheless, this was still not enough to persuade the East Europeans that the threat of Soviet tanks had been completely removed, even if their room for maneuver had increased in certain areas and their Communist parties could exercise new degrees of autonomy.

By the end of 1987, East Europeans still could not be sure of the limits of Soviet tolerance of their independence. Brown goes as far as to suggest that up until the end of 1987, and even well into 1988, Soviet–East European relations were based on a Gorbachev Doctrine which had the following three characteristics:

1. The East European states should abide by their existing bilateral and multilateral treaty obligations—COMECON and especially the Warsaw Pact.

2. Though within the framework of the multiparty system a noncommunist government could emerge, the "decisive" ministries, defense and interior, should remain with the communists or their trusted allies.

3. However much "bourgeois-democratic" any East European state became in form, its "nature," "character," or "content" should remain "socialist."[41]

The East Europeans, then, could expect to exercise new degrees of independence and even include noncommunists in their governments, as long as the security-sensitive portfolios remained with people acceptable to Moscow. Should this not happen, Gorbachev was offering no guarantees that the Soviet armed forces would respect the sovereignty or independence of any East European state.

The following year, though, Gorbachev began to make some more unequivocal statements about the demise of the Brezhnev Doctrine, and, what is more, he began to back these statements with actions. Further evidence of a shift in Soviet attitudes comes from additional changes to the Soviet foreign policy bureaucracy in 1988. It is suggested below that what made this change in attitude possible was that the Soviets were now prepared to redefine their view of Eastern Europe as part of Soviet vital national security interests. Once this decision was made, there was no need to maintain large numbers of troops in Eastern Europe or the western parts of the Soviet Union itself. If anything can be said to have triggered the end of the Cold War, it must be Gorbachev's speech to the United Nations in December 1988 announcing significant troop withdrawals. It was this above all that signaled to the East Europeans that maybe the tanks were going home to stay.

According to Kramer, Gorbachev's March 1988 visit to Yugoslavia was one of the first indicators of a Soviet change of direction.[42] Although the communiqué issued at the end of the visit was technically limited to Soviet–Yugoslav relations, many East Europeans hoped it had broader applicability. The communiqué pledged "unconditional" respect for "the principles of equality and non-interference" and for the "independence of parties and socialist countries to define, for themselves, the paths of their own development."[43] What was also new was the appearance in Soviet magazines and research institutes of articles critical of Soviet foreign policy in the past.

One of the most influential of these was a paper entitled "A Soviet View of Eastern Europe," which was prepared by the staff at the Institute of Economics of the World Socialist System.[44] This paper was remarkably bold in its criticisms of past Soviet "hegemonic aspirations" in Eastern Europe and its attributing of blame to Soviet policies for the past crises in Soviet–East European relations. The paper also called for radical new Soviet policies toward Eastern Europe. The possibility that these new policies might actually be adopted by official circles was seemingly increased by further changes to the foreign policy bureaucracy.

What these changes essentially amounted to was a reduction of influence for the CPSU in policy making and an increase in influence for the more professionally based Foreign Office, which was now headed by Eduard Shevardnadze. The Department for Liaison with Communist and Workers' Parties in Socialist Countries was specifically abolished and its responsibilities were taken over by an expanded International Department. This decision to treat Eastern Europe the same as any other part of the international system was another early clue that the Soviets no longer considered Eastern Europe as part of their vital national security interests.

Kramer suggests that a number of factors may be used to explain this seeming Soviet change of heart, including Gorbachev's success at consolidating his domestic position; signs of confusion and unrest in Eastern Europe itself; a recognition that political and economic reforms were not as separable as Gorbachev had once assumed; and a significant change in the atmosphere of East-West relations in the aftermath of the signing of the Intermediate Nuclear Forces (INF) Treaty in 1987.[45] Not only was Soviet security now more assured, but also a change in Soviet attitude toward Eastern Europe would open the way for even greater political and especially economic relations with Western Europe.

The linkage between Soviet domestic problems and revised national security definitions is a crucial one.[46] This is not to say, though, that it is necessarily a causal one. While it is certainly possible to argue that the Soviet Union withdrew from Eastern Europe because it could no longer afford to stay there, this was a situation that the Soviets had faced for at least a decade. At minimum, what can be said is that even if the Soviet economy was the primary motivating cause of the end of the Cold War, the Soviets' reclassification of Eastern Europe as not part of their vital national security zone is the most important consequence.

Gorbachev's speech to the United Nations at the end of 1988 was by far the most concrete signal of a fundamental change in Soviet attitude. In this speech, Gorbachev announced that the Soviet Union would make significant unilateral cuts to its forces in Eastern Europe and the western Soviet Union. A total of 500,000 personnel and 10,000 tanks were earmarked for withdrawal. Specifically in relation to Eastern Europe, Gorbachev announced that 50,000 of its 565,000 troops in East Germany, Czechoslovakia, and Hungary would be withdrawn. In addition, six tank divisions were to be removed from the same countries, making a total of 5,000 tanks.[47] It was this announcement and the implications behind it that really sparked all the momentous events of 1989.

Although the December 1988 announcement was not the first time Gorbachev had taken an arms control initiative, it was the first time that such an initiative carried a message for the East Europeans. Prior to this, Soviet arms control policy was concerned primarily with the United States and secondarily with Western Europe. While the December cuts were also sending messages to both these groups, it was the East Europeans who reacted most dramatically.

The substantial reductions of Soviet personnel and armaments in Eastern Europe were highly symbolic. There is no doubt that they were perceived by the East Europeans as meaning or indicating that "Soviet commitment to preserving the 'gains of socialism' . . . was on the wane."[48] However, the reductions also had some practical significance too. Combined with the intrusive verification procedures agreed to at the Stockholm Conference on Disarmament in Europe in 1986, the troop withdrawals meant that it would be virtually impossible for the Soviet Union to intervene in the ways it had in 1956, 1968, and 1980–81. For any invasion or threatened invasion of Eastern Europe to occur now, the tanks would have to gather at some distance from East European borders and all unexpected or suspicious movements could be challenged.

Another and equally important practical significance of the Soviet troop withdrawals was that they left the East European regimes fundamentally reliant on their own legitimacy and on their own troops to maintain order. The hardline regimes of East Germany, Czechoslovakia, Bulgaria, and Romania could no longer rely on Soviet tanks to keep them in power, and the more liberal Poland and Hungary no longer had to be concerned as to just what the limits of Soviet tolerance were. The speed with which all these countries introduced radical reforms provides further evidence of the importance of this realization that the threat of Soviet intervention had been removed.

RAPID REVOLUTION

The details of the East European revolutions are available from various sources.[49] What needs to be emphasized here is the speed with which change was effected once the East Europeans accepted that the Brezhnev Doctrine had been renounced. As might be expected, Poland and Hungary were the first to react in the aftermath of Gorbachev's U.N. speech. In Poland in January 1989, it was announced that Solidarity would be given legal status and that free elections would be held the following June. In the same month in Hungary, legislation was introduced allowing for greater individual freedom, and in May the Hungarians started to dismantle the iron curtain between them and Austria. Both countries, though, continued to play it very cautiously as regards the Warsaw Pact, stressing that it still had an important role to play.

In July 1989, Gorbachev again pushed things along with a speech to the Council of Europe in Strasbourg. In what was, at last, an unambiguous statement, Gorbachev claimed that there could never again be a Soviet invasion of a Hungary or a Czechoslovakia. He declared that "[a]ny interference in internal affairs, any attempt to limit the sovereignty of states—both friends and allies or anybody else—are inadmissible."[50] Taking a cue from this, Hungary instigated one of the boldest moves of 1989 in permitting thousands of East German vacationers to exit into Austria and thereby gain access to West Germany.

This undoubtedly put pressure on the East German regime, which was still finding it difficult to believe that the Soviet Union no longer regarded Eastern Europe, and especially East Germany, as part of its national security zone. Erich Honecker had no choice, however, but to believe, when Gorbachev made it abundantly clear to him during private conversations, that Soviet tanks would not shore up his regime.[51] Within six weeks the communist system in East Germany was essentially dismantled and the Berlin Wall was torn down. Czechoslovakia, Bulgaria, and Romania soon followed suit, so that by the end of the year communism no longer existed as a credible or coherent force in Eastern Europe. Within months other instruments of Soviet control, such as COMECON and even the Warsaw Pact itself, were dismantled.

CONCLUSION

Discovering what ended the Cold War will be no easy task for either the historian or the political scientist. John Lewis Gaddis's recent article in *International Security* poignantly reminds us of the weaknesses and inadequacies of, at least, international relations theories in forecasting the end of the Cold War.[52] Many of the reasons now being offered by analysts for the end of the Cold War, such as economic difficulties in both the Soviet Union and the United States, did not first appear in early 1989. Similarly, in Eastern Europe, problems had existed in the Polish economy for years, as had divisions in the Hungarian Communist party, and throughout the entire bloc dissident groups and general antipathy existed toward the Soviet Union. While it cannot be denied that all these factors were necessary, it is obvious they were not sufficient to cause the East Europeans to remove themselves from the Soviet sphere of influence or to cause the Soviets to let them go.

What this chapter postulates is that at least as far as Europe is concerned, the Cold War ended when the Soviet Union finally conceded that Eastern Europe was not part of its vital national security zone and that therefore there was no need to maintain an oppressive Soviet military presence on East European soil. This concession did not come until the end of 1988, when Gorbachev announced substantial military withdrawals from both Eastern Europe itself and the adjoining districts of the Soviet Union. In short, as soon as the Brezhnev Doctrine was renounced, East European governments and peoples moved to secure their independence from the Soviet Union by, in the main, expunging communism and severing institutional links with the Soviet Union.

Although the Soviet Union at various times saw different roles for Eastern Europe above all—largely resulting from World War II—it saw the countries of Eastern Europe as vital parts of its national security. Maintaining stability and some degree of control over Eastern Europe was always going to be difficult for the Soviet Union, given the traditional hostility that existed toward Russians throughout most of the area. The ultimate instrument for maintaining order in Eastern Europe, and thus enhancing Soviet national security, was the Soviet Red Army. The Soviets developed two complementary justifications for keeping their troops stationed on East European territory: socialist internationalism and the Warsaw Pact. Socialist internationalism gave the Soviet Union an ideological justification for limiting the sovereignty and independence of the countries of Eastern Europe and for making sure that Soviet views were accorded primary importance. The Warsaw Pact gave the Soviets the physical, and to some extent the legal, means to intervene in any country which did not accept socialist internationalism. Although both these justifications existed long before the 1968 invasion of Czechoslovakia, it was this invasion that saw them codified into the Brezhnev Doctrine.

While Gorbachev's assumption of the General Secretaryship of the CPSU in 1985 may have led to some expectations of change, Eastern Europe's role in Soviet national security was one area where Gorbachev initially stressed continuity. Throughout 1985 and into 1986, he continued to refer to socialist internationalism and the "common" interests of bloc members. Some signs of a change in attitude did emerge in speeches, magazine articles, and bureaucratic restructuring between 1986 and 1987. However, these changes were nearly always accompanied by statements that hinted the Brezhnev Doctrine was still in operation. At any rate, even halfway through 1988, no East European government or people could be sure that the Soviets would refrain from ordering in their tanks if they did not like the direction of reform.

Gorbachev's announcement of troop and tank withdrawals from Eastern Europe at the end of 1988 was highly significant. Not only did it symbolize that the Soviet Union had reassessed the position of Eastern Europe in its national security calculations, but the withdrawals also made any intervention or invasion of an East European country physically much more difficult. Confident in the knowledge that they were safe from Soviet tanks, the East Europeans rid themselves of most Soviet connections within the year. It is certainly of far more than symbolic interest that the first action of the new postcommunist Czechoslovakian foreign minister was to declare the 1968 agreement allowing Soviet troops to be stationed on Czechoslovakian soil invalid on the grounds that it had been made under extreme duress.

NOTES

1. S. P. Huntington, "The End of History?" *Quadrant* 33, no. 10 (1989): 28.

2. W. Laqueur, *Europe in Our Time* (Harmondsworth, England: Penguin, 1992) p. 531; J. L. Gaddis, "International Relations Theory and the End of the Cold War," *International Security* 17 (1992–93): 5–58.

3. J. F. Brown, *Surge to Freedom: The End of Communist Rule in Eastern Europe* (Durham, NC: Duke University Press, 1991), pp. 45–46.

4. P. Marer, "The Political Economy of Soviet Relations with Eastern Europe," in *Soviet Foreign Policy in a Changing World,* eds. R. F. Laird and E. P. Hoffmann (New York: Aldine de Gruyter, 1986), p. 571.

5. Ibid., p. 585.

6. Brown, *Surge to Freedom*, p. 46.

7. C. Gati, *The Bloc That Failed* (Bloomington: University of Indiana Press, 1990), p. 140.

8. J. L. Nogee and R. H. Donaldson, *Soviet Foreign Policy since World War II* (Oxford, England: Pergamon, 1988), pp. 326–30.

9. A. Schlesinger, Jr., "Origins of the Cold War," *Foreign Affairs* 46 (1967–68).

10. Z. Mlynar, *Night Frost in Prague,* trans. P. Wilson (London: Hurst and Co., 1980), p. 240.

11. K. Dawisha, *Eastern Europe, Gorbachev, and Reform: The Great Challenge* (New York: Cambridge University Press, 1990), pp. 86–90.

12. Ibid., p. 89.

13. T. H. Rigby, "Stalinism and Mono-Organisational Society," in *Stalinism: Essays in Historical Interpretation*, ed. R. C. Tucker (New York: Norton, 1977), pp. 53–76.

14. R. Kolkowicz, "The Warsaw Pact: Entangling Alliance," *Survey: A Journal of Soviet and East European Studies* 70/71 (1969): 86.

15. W. LaFeber, *America, Russia, and the Cold War, 1945–1992,* 7th ed. (New York: McGraw-Hill, 1993), p. 188.

16. Gati, *The Bloc That Failed*, p. 40.

17. Ibid., p. 41.

18. Ibid.

19. Cited in ibid., p. 43.

20. *Pravda*, September 26, 1968, p. 4; translation from *Current Digest of the Soviet Press* 20, no. 39 (1968): 10–11. For an alternative translation see M. Kramer, "Beyond the Brezhnev Doctrine: A New Era in Soviet–East European Relations," *International Security* 14, no. 3 (1989–90): 25.

21. Kolkowicz, "The Warsaw Pact: Entangling Alliance," p. 89.

22. V. Kusin, "Gorbachev and Eastern Europe," *Problems of Communism* 35 (1986): 42.

23. M. Sheehan, *The Arms Race* (Oxford: Martin Robertson, 1983), p. 157; B. Buzan, *An Introduction to Strategic Studies* (London: Macmillan, 1987), p. 274; and D. M. Hart, "Soviet Approaches to Crisis Management: The Military Dimension," *Survival* 26, no. 5 (1984): 214–23.

24. S. Brown, *New Forces, Old Forces, and the Future of World Politics* (Glenview, IL: Scott, Foresman/Little, 1988), p. 90.

25. Gati, *The Bloc That Failed;* Dawisha, *Eastern Europe, Gorbachev, and Reform;* Brown, *Surge to Freedom;* and Kramer, "Beyond the Brezhnev Doctrine."

26. Cited in Kramer, "Beyond the Brezhnev Doctrine," p. 28.

27. Cited in Kusin, "Gorbachev and Eastern Europe," p. 39.

28. Cited in Dawisha, *Eastern Europe, Gorbachev, and Reform,* p. 203.

29. *Pravda,* June 21, 1985, pp. 3–4; translation taken from Dawisha, *Eastern Europe, Gorbachev, and Reform,* pp. 203–4, and Kramer, "Beyond the Brezhnev Doctrine," pp. 28–29.

30. Cited in Brown, *Surge to Freedom,* p. 65.

31. M. Gorbachev, *Political Report of the CPSU Central Committee to the 27th Party Congress* (Moscow: Novosti Press Agency Publishing House, 1986).

32. Dawisha, *Eastern Europe, Gorbachev, and Reform,* p. 207.

33. Kramer, "Beyond the Brezhnev Doctrine," p. 30.

34. Cited in ibid., p. 32.

35. Cited in *Current Digest of the Soviet Press* 39, no. 15 (1987): 15.

36. Cited in Kramer, "Beyond the Brezhnev Doctrine," p. 34. See also "The Gorbachev Doctrine," *The Times* (London), April 11, 1987.

37. Cited in Dawisha, *Eastern Europe, Gorbachev, and Reform,* p. 87.

38. Cited in ibid., p. 219.

39. The East German regime tried to restrict distribution of *Perestroika,* but its contents were widely covered in West German media outlets.

40. M. Gorbachev, *Perestroika* (London: Fontana, 1988), p. 165.

41. Brown, *Surge to Freedom,* p. 61.

42. Kramer, "Beyond the Brezhnev Doctrine," p. 39.

43. Cited in ibid.

44. This paper is reprinted in full as an appendix in Gati, *The Bloc That Failed,* pp. 205–19.

45. Kramer, "Beyond the Brezhnev Doctrine," pp. 36–38.

46. D. Holloway, "Gorbachev's New Thinking," *Foreign Affairs* 68, no. 1 (1988–89): 66–81; R. Legvold, "Soviet Foreign Policy," *Foreign Affairs* 68, no. 1 (1988–89): 82–98.

47. C. Bremmer and M. Binyon, "Gorbachev Hails 'Era of Peace,'" *The Times* (London), December 8, 1988.

48. Gati, *The Bloc That Failed,* p. 156.

49. M. Kaldor, ed., *Europe from Below* (London: Verso, 1991); P. Brogan, *Eastern Europe, 1939–1989* (London: Bloomsbury, 1990); Gati, *The Bloc That Failed;* Dawisha, *Eastern Europe, Gorbachev, and Reform;* Brown, *Surge to Freedom.*

50. M. Binyon, "West Is Offered Hand of Co-operation," *The Times* (London), July 7, 1989.

51. W. Leonhard, *Das kurze Leben der DDR* (Stuttgart: Deutsche Verlagsanstalt, 1990), p. 212. See also Brown, *Surge to Freedom,* p. 146—citing *The Washington Post,* October 8, 1989.

52. Gaddis, "International Relations Theory and the End of the Cold War."

II

MASS MOVEMENTS
AND "NEW THINKING"

4

Gorbachev, the Peace Movement, and the Death of Lenin

Jennifer Turpin

The Cold War ended as a result of the intersection of complex social forces: the influence of intellectuals, the international peace movement, Soviet mass media, and Gorbachev. These forces converged, allowing Mikhail Gorbachev to subvert both Marxism-Leninism and the Cold War paradigm in favor of "new thinking."

"NEW THINKING"

"New thinking" was not so new. *Perestroika* was rooted in Lenin's New Economic Policy (NEP), which advocated a combined socialist and market economy. It also stemmed from the reforms initiated by Nikita Khrushchev from 1953 to 1964 and from the generation of reformists spawned during Khrushchev's "thaw." These members of the intelligentsia called themselves the "children of the Twentieth Party Congress"—the historical event where Khrushchev revealed Stalin's legacy of crimes. Later they became members of Gorbachev's progressive team.

In addition, "new thinking" should be in part credited to Yuri Andropov. Andropov was known to be a reform-oriented statesman, with ties to younger members of the party.[1] Although his tenure in office was brief, he was responsible for bringing Alexander Yakovlev, the architect of *glasnost*, back from diplomatic exile in Canada, where he was being punished for offending Brezhnev and his conservative allies. Yakovlev was appointed head of the prestigious Institute for World Economy and International Relations (IMEMO), and was later appointed by Gorbachev to head the Department of Propaganda. Gorbachev, who was mentored by Andropov, met Yakovlev on a visit to Canada. Andropov had begun to advocate reforms, but his death in 1983 postponed the process until Gorbachev's ascendence.

Andropov was attracted to Gorbachev's orientation toward reform; Andropov told Georgi Arbatov, "There is a brilliant man working in Stavropol."[2] Gorbachev's ideas arguably go back to his days at Moscow University in the 1950s. In 1978 Gorbachev wrote a confidential memorandum to the Central Committee about the need to reform the agricultural economic system. Once elected general secretary, his thinking may have become more radical due to Soviet conditions, but he proceeded to approach change cautiously, especially in his first year,[3] due to entrenched forces of resistance.

Many in the West have argued that "new thinking" simply meant the Soviet Union was economically driven to its knees, thus forcing political change. However, as April Carter points out in this volume, economic logic alone cannot explain the broad scope of Gorbachev's political agenda, which included cultural freedom and democratization. Clearly, though, the grave state of the economy was important: it produced disillusion with Marxism-Leninism and thus contributed to an ideological shift.[4]

Stephen Cohen argues that a "pre-crisis" existed in the Soviet Union: leaders knew that the economy was in disrepair; alcoholism, corruption, and environmental decay were rampant; and key indicators of health, such as infant mortality and life expectancy, were in decline. At the same time, the population was becoming more educated, more people had exposure to the West, and greater political pluralism was developing within the Communist party. Soviet leaders and key members of the intelligentsia came to believe that Lenin was in fact wrong: socialism would not triumph over capitalism, and the Soviet political-economic system was rife with internal flaws.

A prominent senior member of the Supreme Soviet explained: "We lost the economic and social and the technological edge with capitalism . . . nobody believes [that socialism will spread] in our country now. . . . [The idea is] false that all the world and all countries would follow the same way. . . . Before, we believed we had the best society in the world. Now the young generation believes they live in the worst society in the world."[5]

Gorbachev's writings suggest that the public's realization that the United States could destroy the Soviet Union in a nuclear war also undermined Marxism-Leninism, which argued that communism would win the war against capitalism. This shift in consciousness developed over a number of years, particularly during the 1980s when Cold War rhetoric and weapons production escalated. Television programs shown on Soviet television that were sponsored by International Physicians to Prevent Nuclear War (IPPNW) affected Soviet citizens' thinking about the prospects of "winning" or even surviving a nuclear war.[6] These programs featured prominent scientists who argued that a nuclear war would be so devastating that it would be impossible to care for the population. Nuclear winter studies argued even further that the use of nuclear weapons could mean global suicide. "New thinking" was imperative for survival. Georgi Smirnov, director of the Central Committee's Institute of Marxism-Leninism under Gorbachev, stated: "[I]f the United States and the Soviet Union don't find ways to coexist peacefully as capitalist and socialist systems, we shall all perish. That's why we developed our bold new thinking and overtures to the West."[7] The Chernobyl disaster further magnified the Soviet people's fear of nuclear war and undermined state secrecy in the process. It also showed Soviet officials that nuclear accidents do happen. All of these developments increased the momentum toward renouncing both Cold War military doctrine and Marxist-Leninist opposition to capitalism.

INTELLECTUALS

The Soviet intelligentsia were central to this process: they comprised a constituency for reform and influenced each other's and Gorbachev's thinking. Scholars in diverse areas had been developing reformist ideas for decades. Alexander Yakovlev argues that "the ideas of *perestroika* were nourished in different fields for a long time, sometimes a very long time, even too long. . . . These ideas have been developed over the years by scholars, cultural figures, and people engaged in political activity."[8] These figures kept open certain realms of political discourse and cultural space, and began to speak out in the early 1980s on the arms race and survival, human rights, freedom of expression, and political and economic restructuring.

Among the more influential were policymaker Alexander Yakovlev, dissident scientist Andrei Sakharov (whom Gorbachev released from exile in Gorki), poet Yevgeny Yevtushenko, historians Roy Medvedev and Yuri Afanasyev, sociologist Tatyana Zaslavskaya, philosopher Georgi Smirnov, writer Nikolai Shmelyov, physicist Yevgeny Velikov, political scientist Fyodor Burlatsky, dissident politician Len Karpinsky, filmmaker Elem Klimov, economist Georgi Arbatov, journalists Yegor Yakovlev and Alexander Bovin, and actor Mikhail Ulyanov.[9]

Alexander Yakovlev was the reform leader behind Gorbachev who initiated the radically changed rhetoric about the conflict between East and West. He served as Gorbachev's key adviser, and worked to protect the liberal members of the intelligentsia. He helped other Gorbachev supporters go from being "heretics" to government officials.[10] Even as they preserved and developed their ideas, prior to Gorbachev and Yakovlev, these intellectuals were unable to advance their work far beyond their professional circles. Gorbachev's policy of *glasnost* gave the intelligentsia access to the media, which provided them with a pulpit for promoting their programs. Gorbachev, the intelligentsia, and *glasnost* were mutually reinforcing.

GORBACHEV, THE INTELLIGENTSIA, AND THE MEDIA

Without a revolution in mass media, "new thinking" would have been confined to academic and policy circles. Gorbachev recognized the power of the media (much as Lenin did) and launched his policy of *glasnost*. In the early days of Gorbachev's leadership, the press was baffled by his unprecedented statements. His speeches were edited and published days after they were given. The Soviet press was said to be "unable to stomach the highly controversial issues raised by Gorbachev."[11] As the Soviet specialist Thomas Remington put it: "Under Gorbachev the orchestra has begun performing in a new key."[12] After three or four months Gorbachev consolidated his power over the press. He appointed Alexander Yakovlev to the important post of chief of the CPSU's Central Committee's Department of Propaganda.

Free expression in the Soviet Union blossomed at an unbelievable pace. Michael Urban has shown that Gorbachev's own speech patterns displayed more openness than the traditional Soviet leader's pattern, which he calls "the classic Leninist tale."[13] At times, Gorbachev admitted he did not have all the answers, and he avoided giving authoritative prescriptions for what had to be done in the Soviet Union. Instead, he spoke about the need to deeply analyze the nation's problems and stressed the need to change social relations and practices instead of blaming individuals and the past for current problems.[14]

Gorbachev's language also acknowledged the public's desire to participate in change rather than merely view it as spectators. In these ways, the Soviet leader loosened the constraints imposed by the party's official definition of the world, opening greater social space for communication. This had an important impact on the possibilities for political change. Historically, the Soviet Union exerted tremendous resistance to the Western press. Yet under Gorbachev the press adopted Western styles of news presentation.[15] The mass media traditionally took their direction from party and government propaganda departments. But this relationship weakened as a result of demands for pluralism in the news. The Soviets moved toward the Western view of the media as instruments for advancing "public opinion."[16] New media forms shifted in emphasis from the group to the individual,[17] which was partly reflected in the rapid growth of advertising in Soviet newspapers and magazines.

The Soviet press served as the most significant reflection of political developments in the country. Soviet media played a tremendous role in promoting Gorbachev's policies and even criticized Gorbachev's conservatism late in his presidency. The agency within the Soviet media system that most advanced social change under Gorbachev, Novosti Press Agency (*Agentsvo Pechati Novosti/APN*) was headed by Gorbachev-appointed reformist Valentin Falin. Novosti and *Moscow News* (distributed in forty countries) advocated *perestroika, glasnost,* and an end to the Cold War.[18] The newspaper criticized both Soviet and U.S. nuclear policies and advocated an end to the arms race. *Moscow News* was called "the flagship of *glasnost*" and "Gorbachev's newspaper"; it was run by editor-in-chief Yegor Yakovlev, a longtime dissident journalist.

In August 1985, shortly after Gorbachev became general secretary, Yakovlev was offered the position as *Moscow News* editor-in-chief by Valentin Falin, the head of Novosti Press Agency whom Andropov had appointed while he was general secretary. Falin explained that the newspaper was to be special, publishing what other Soviet newspapers would not publish and reflecting the true spirit of *glasnost.* Yakovlev accepted the job, despite his (and his wife's) fears that he would "end up with his bare ass on the sidewalk again."[19] Yakovlev believed that the U.S.S.R. had to move beyond Leninism, with *glasnost,* public opinion, and democratization. The Soviet Union was, he claimed, ready for these changes.[20]

Mass media played a major role in bringing about internal reform and also conveyed to the rest of the world the changes that Gorbachev was attempting to bring about. The media made public the unorthodox views that were marginalized for decades, and gave an audience to the reformist intellectuals who supported Gorbachev. East European intellectuals and dissidents similarly laid the foundation for their countries to break with the Soviet Union, but it was Gorbachev's policy of noninterference that signaled the opening for those movements to succeed. This renunciation of the Brezhnev Doctrine was legitimized at first through Gorbachev's policy of "peaceful coexistence," which he attributed to Lenin, but which is arguably in direct conflict with Lenin's thinking.[21]

Western intellectuals also played a role in influencing Gorbachev's thinking and the evolution of Soviet policy. "Unseen actors" made important contributions to ending the Cold War, and history must take their efforts into account. Among those American voices that were heard in the Soviet press, for example, are Dr. Bernard Lown, co-president of IPPNW, Sovietologists Marshall Goldman and Stephen Cohen, and businessperson Armand Hammer. They were featured in articles that critiqued former Soviet policies, but they did not simply advocate official U.S. positions.

The Soviet press featured articles by Professor Marshall Goldman on how to salvage the Soviet economy. The executive editor of the *New York Times,* A. M. Rosenthal, wrote condemning Soviet officials for mistreating political prisoners. Robert Scheer of the *Los Angeles Times* wrote on the decline of U.S. conservatism (particularly anti-Sovietism); Sovietologist Stephen Cohen wrote on the rehabilitation of Nikolai Bukharin; John Keegan, the *London Daily Telegraph* defense correspondent, wrote on Soviet military forces in Europe; and Hedrick Smith, journalist and author of *The Russians* and *The New Russians,* declared his support for *perestroika.* Robert Manoff, from the New York–based Center for War, Peace, and the News Media, was interviewed about "enemy images," and Richard Carlson, director of the Voice of America, was interviewed by Vladimir Pozner about freedom of information. In this manner, outsiders had unprecedented access to Soviet audiences. Voices in the peace movement were also heard.

THE INTERNATIONAL PEACE MOVEMENT

The peace movements in the United States, Europe, and Asia and the Pacific Rim influenced the course of events in the Soviet Union and contributed to the end of the Cold War. The peace movement had already had a significant effect on nuclear strategists and policymakers in the United States—before the political changes in Eastern Europe and the Soviet Union. Official U.S. rhetoric on the possibility of winning a nuclear war, for example, changed after 1983, before Gorbachev came to power.[22]

But the peace movement also affected Gorbachev's and leading intellectuals' stance on the arms race. The nuclear freeze movement transformed political discourse, redefining the nuclear arms race in solvable terms which were adopted by Gorbachev, by the official Soviet peace movement, and by the independent Soviet peace movement.

The idea of a nuclear freeze, initiated by Randall Forsberg, was advocated by some U.S. politicians.[23] The proposal became popular internationally and was advocated by Australian Helen Caldicott and others throughout the peace movement. The independent Soviet peace movement, especially the Trust Group,[24] distinguished itself from the official Soviet peace movement by opposing both U.S. and Soviet nuclear weapons, calling for both sides to freeze the arms race.[25]

The nuclear freeze movement also influenced Soviet officials, who submitted a freeze resolution to the United Nations that borrowed much of Randall Forsberg's wording.[26] Gorbachev issued his radical proposal "To Enter the 21st Century Without Nuclear Weapons" on January 15, 1986. The second stage of Gorbachev's proposal, which would start no later than 1990, suggested that he had been influenced by the European peace movement and the Pacific nuclear-free-zone movement. In his plan, all nuclear powers "would pledge to freeze all their nuclear arms and not to have them on the territories of other countries."[27] Gorbachev submitted this proposal to President Ronald Reagan at the Reykjavik summit and declared a renewed Soviet moratorium on nuclear testing as part of the effort toward ending the Cold War. He also released a book of his speeches and proposals called *For a Nuclear-Free World*.[28] In it, Gorbachev stated:

> Time is running out. On behalf of the Soviet people we call on the American people and its government, on the peoples and governments of all countries to work vigorously by practical actions for the ban on nuclear explosions to become a fact, an immutable norm of inter-state relations. Mankind is standing on a line that requires the utmost responsibility. The consequences of the nuclear arms race can become dangerously unpredictable. We must act together. This matter is of concern to everyone.[29]

Perhaps the most significant influence on Gorbachev at this time was Andrei Sakharov, who after only a few months out of exile in Gorki gave an address at the Forum for a Nuclear-Free World and the Survival of Mankind held in Moscow in February 1987. In his speech, Sakharov criticized the Kremlin for linking the Intermediate Nuclear Forces (INF) issue to the Strategic Defense Initiative (SDI). Shortly after that, Gorbachev announced his decision to decouple INF and SDI, and to the astonishment of the Americans, a significant agreement was reached.[30]

The debates about the Cold War escalated, and the Soviet mass media devoted significant attention to criticizing past nuclear weapons policies. Pyotr Gladkov wrote a severe critique of Soviet participation in the arms race:

> Let's see what we've achieved by arming to the teeth. Our friends and allies are economically poor states. The military support we give them costs us a pretty "kopek" which could very well be used for our own needs. . . . Let's imagine for a moment that America decided to invade the USSR. What would it get? A vast country in economic shambles, with a flimsy and morally retrograde technical base and contaminated environment, a population most of which has unlearned how to work, and ethnic conflicts any one of which could lead to civil war.[31]

Writer Ales Adamovich declared, after the signing of the INF treaty, that "everything that has been accumulated in the name of mutual annihilation" was "the most senseless goal in history."[32] Alexei Pankin and Major Mikhail Smagin criticized the viability of deterrence, "the cornerstone of the nuclear world's somber edifice," as a security system and agreed that a nuclear-free future was possible.[33]

Printed debates and round-table discussions served as venues for exploring military problems. British journalist John Keegan and Soviet historian Lev Semenko debated the progress being made on the demilitarization of Europe. Keegan argued that the Soviets must make significant cuts in conventional forces, while Semenko argued that Soviet tanks were obsolete anyway and that NATO must discontinue the modernization of nuclear weapons while calling for conventional cuts.[34] Another debate—between Josef Joffe, the chief of the International News Department at Germany's *Sud Deutsche Zeitung,* and Lev Semenko—examined the concept of "reasonable sufficiency" in defense. Joffe claimed the Soviets should reduce their conventional forces to parity with NATO and orient them defensively rather than offensively to gain the trust of the West.[35] As Johan Galtung argues in this volume, peace research concepts were applied during these discussions.

A series of articles even raised the controversial proposition that the U.S.S.R. should convert to a militia-only defense force. This notion was introduced in a letter to the editor from Lieutenant Colonel Savinkin and further developed by philosopher and lieutenant colonel in the reserves Igor Shatilo. Shatilo argued that militia-only force was in fact Lenin's idea and went on to advocate demilitarization: "Any massive development of the 'man-killing' industry quickly brings civilization closer to military self-destruction or to economic depletion which can, even without a war, bleed our planet white. To prevent this impending disaster, it is necessary to start everywhere limiting and cutting permanent armies, replacing them with a militia defense system."[36]

Georgi Arbatov explained that "old thinking" had become the main threat to security. Bernard Lown presented the case that old thinking's military spending had resulted in a national debt and shameful social consequences in both the United States and the Soviet Union, while Germany and Japan had prospered in the absence of nuclear weapons spending. Lown called for reduced defense spending and the allocation of resources for treating the sick and hungry and for saving the environment.[37] After opening a branch in Leningrad, a Greenpeace representative declared the group's opposition to Soviet nuclear vessels in the Baltic Sea. But the Soviet branch leader of Greenpeace claimed to have learned about the presence of nuclear vessels in the Baltic only the night before the press conference.[38] Peace movement organizations were at the forefront of "new thinking."

It was argued that militarism had not only affected the Soviet economy, environment, and social sphere, but had permeated the national spirit as well. Writer Yuli Krelin went so far as to condemn the shooting down of Korean Airlines Flight 007: "[T]he permanent preoccupation with competition in the military sphere . . . made us swallow the doctrinaire explanation of the need to down a South Korean liner without so much as an apology for the unpremeditated murder of civilians."[39]

Promoting Gorbachev's policies paralleled criticism of Soviet society, since his reforms were designed to reverse the decline of the economy and other aspects of social malaise. The media thus played out their historical role of collective propagandist (promoting desired policies), but *glasnost* brought a new dimension to the news and to Soviet society. In the past, the media's role forbade them from criticizing Soviet leadership and made them rely on misinformation about the state of the economy, the society, and the happiness of Soviet citizens. Under Gorbachev, the mobilization of support for *perestroika* demanded a sober analysis of social conditions.

THE DEATH OF LENIN

Pivotal to promoting Gorbachev's reforms was the notion that he had reinstated Lenin's revolution. Yet at the same time that Gorbachev used Lenin to justify *perestroika*, he was challenging the main tenets of Marxism-Leninism. How much Gorbachev believed in Lenin's ideas has been the subject of considerable debate; publicly he argued that *perestroika* was a continuation of the revolution that Lenin began, but that Stalin perverted.[40]

The objectives of *perestroika*, according to journalist Alla Gracheva, had much in common with Lenin's revolutionary agenda: "to rebuild everything . . . to renew everything so that the mendacious, dirty, dull and ugly life of ours becomes just, clean, joyful, and beautiful."[41] *Perestroika* was not to be mistaken for a turn away from socialism toward capitalism; rather, "*Perestroika* deals with the historical destinies of socialism in its historical competition against capitalism, and in . . . its advantages, its ability to secure a higher than under capitalism labor productivity, and a level of people's well-being that corresponds to it. To do that, socialism must acquire a new quality."[42]

Yegor Yakovlev chimed in that the mass movement for *perestroika* "is being likened more and more often to the legendary times of the October Revolution."[43] Responding to an article by Sovietologist Marshall Goldman, who recommended several market-oriented measures to rescue the Soviet economy, Professor Erik Pletnyov responded that "the aim is to restructure socialism, not restore capitalism."[44] Pletnyov rejected not only the "ideological" nature of Goldman's argument, but also the idea that "there should be voluntary re-establishment of exploitation of hired labor by private capital."[45] Pletnyov claimed that Soviet citizens would never tolerate such a system and were determined to carry out only *perestroika,* or the restructuring of socialism. He was wrong.

Gradually, Lenin would lose his position as the wellspring of all Soviet policies. The first Leninist doctrine to be renounced was that which claimed that struggle was inevitable between capitalism and communism, and would result in a worldwide socialist revolution.[46] In July 1988, Eduard Shevardnadze, then foreign minister, stated in a speech that "[t]he struggle between the two opposing systems is no longer a determining tendency of the present-day era."[47] Gorbachev began to declare that the world was moving toward pluralism, not toward universal socialism—a clear renunciation of Leninism.

Lenin's preoccupation with the class war disappeared from official statements and was replaced with Gorbachev's preoccupation with avoiding nuclear war. In his statements, Gorbachev renounced war and advocated abandoning acceptance of war and armed conflict. As Steven Kull has pointed out, this blatantly contradicts Leninist policy. Lenin wrote:

> Socialists cannot be opposed to all war in general and still be socialists. ... To put "disarmament" on the program is tantamount to making the general declaration: We are opposed to the use of arms. There is as little marxism in this as there would be if we were to say: We are opposed to violence! ... We are living in a class society from which there is no way out. ... [Disarmament] is tantamount to complete abandonment of the class struggle point of view, to renunciation of all thought of revolution.[48]

Some argue that the Cold War ended in 1989 with the revolutions in Eastern Europe. For the Russians, the ultimate death of Lenin occurred in 1991 when Gorbachev claimed on U.S. television that the communist model had failed.[49] Lenin lost his place in Soviet city squares and the Cold War was over.

CONCLUSION

The Cold War would not have ended without Gorbachev, who did more to end it than any other individual. Gorbachev introduced *perestroika,* which included freedom of expression, political reform, and economic change. He renounced the Brezhnev Doctrine, allowing Warsaw Pact countries to become independent (see Joanne Wright's chapter in this volume). He renounced Marxism-Leninism. Most important, he advocated an end to the arms race and the nuclear standoff.

But Gorbachev is not solely responsible for ending the Cold War. The Cold War ended not because of one man, but as a result of the mobilization of efforts from many directions, with Gorbachev as the most notable messenger. He served simultaneously as symptom, catalyst, producer, and product of forces for change.

NOTES

1. Stephen F. Cohen and Katrina vanden Heuvel, *Voices of Glasnost: Interviews with Gorbachev's Reformers* (New York: W. W. Norton, 1989), p. 22.

2. Ibid., p. 312.

3. Ibid., pp. 22–23; see also Robert G. Kaiser, *Why Gorbachev Happened* (New York: Touchstone, 1991), p. 22.

4. Stephen Kull, *Burying Lenin* (Boulder, CO: Westview, 1992); Cohen and vanden Heuvel, *Voices of Glasnost.*

5. Kull, *Burying Lenin,* p. 22.

6. Ibid., p. 18.

7. Cohen and vanden Heuvel, *Voices of Glasnost,* p. 95.

8. Kaiser, *Why Gorbachev Happened,* p. 91.

9. See interviews with many of these in Cohen and vanden Heuvel, *Voices of Glasnost;* see also Kaiser, *Why Gorbachev Happened,* p. 91.

10. Tatyana Zaslavskaya in Cohen and vanden Heuvel, *Voices of Glasnost,* p. 115.

11. Baruch A. Hazan, *From Brezhnev to Gorbachev: Infighting in the Kremlin* (Boulder, CO: Westview, 1987), p. 165.

12. Thomas F. Remington, *The Truth of Authority: Ideology and Communication in the Soviet Union* (Pittsburgh: University of Pittsburgh Press, 1988), p. 28.

13. Michael E. Urban, "Political Language and Political Change in the USSR: Notes on the Gorbachev Leadership," in *The Soviet Union: Party and Society,* ed. Peter Potichnyj (Cambridge: Cambridge University Press, 1988), p. 98.

14. Ibid.

15. James M. Skelly, "Hungarian Television News: Its Role in the Current Transformation and the Implications for Domestic and International Affairs," unpublished research proposal (1989).

16. Ellen Mickiewicz, *Split Signals: Television and Politics in the Soviet Union* (Oxford: Oxford University Press, 1988), p. 49.

17. Ibid., pp. 197–98.

18. Jennifer Turpin, *Reinventing the Soviet Self: Media and Social Change in the Former Soviet Union* (Westport, CT: Praeger, 1995).

19. Cohen and vanden Heuvel, *Voices of Glasnost,* p. 199.

20. Ibid., p. 201.

21. See, for example, Kull, *Burying Lenin.*

22. Paul Joseph, *Peace Politics: The United States Between the Old and New World Orders* (Philadelphia: Temple University Press, 1993), pp. 153–54.

23. Edward M. Kennedy and Mark O. Hatfield, *Freeze: How You Can Prevent Nuclear War* (New York: Bantam Books, 1982).

24. Officially called the Group to Establish Trust Between the USSR and the USA.

25. Humanitas International Human Rights Committee, "The Trials of Moscow's Independent Disarmament Activists," *Humanitas International* 5, no. 4 (1984): 4.

26. P. N. Fedoseyev, *Peace and Disarmament: Academic Studies* (Moscow: Progress Publishers, 1985), p. 395.

27. Mikhail Gorbachev, *To Enter the 21st Century Without Nuclear Weapons* (Moscow: Novosti Press Agency, 1986).

28. Mikhail Gorbachev, *For a Nuclear-Free World* (Moscow: Novosti Press Agency, 1987).

29. Ibid., p. 72.

30. David Cortright, *Peace Works: The Citizen's Role in Ending the Cold War* (Boulder, CO: Westview, 1993), p. 193.

31. Pyotr Gladkov, *Moscow News*, September 10–17, 1989, p. 6.

32. Ales Adamovich, *Moscow News*, January 10–17, 1988, p. 6.

33. Alexei Pankin and Mikhail Smagin, *Moscow News*, May 22–29, 1988, p. 7.

34. John Keegan and Lev Semenko, *Moscow News*, March 27–April 3, 1988, p. 6.

35. Josef Joffe and Lev Semenko, *Moscow News*, January 8–15, 1989, p. 6.

36. Igor Shatilo, *Moscow News*, January 2, 1989, p. 4.

37. Bernard Lown, *Moscow News*, January 22, 1989, p. 7.

38. *Moscow News*, August 13–20, 1989, p. 2.

39. Yuli Krelin, *Moscow News*, July 16–23, 1989, p. 3.

40. Jennifer Turpin, "Glasnost and the End of the Cold War," in *Rethinking Peace,* eds. Robert Elias and Jennifer Turpin (Boulder, CO: Lynne Rienner, 1994).

41. Alla Gracheva, *Moscow News*, January 31–February 7, 1988, p. 13.

42. *Moscow News*, January 10–17, 1988, p. 3.

43. Yegor Yakovlev, *Moscow News*, August 14–21, 1988, p. 3.

44. Erik Pletnyov, *Moscow News*, April 24–May 1, 1988, p. 6.

45. Ibid.

46. Kull, *Burying Lenin,* p. 11.

47. Quoted in ibid., p. 12.

48. Quoted in ibid., pp. 15–16.

49. Ibid., p. 16.

5

The Peace Movement Role
in Ending the Cold War

David Cortright

Conventional wisdom holds that ordinary citizens have no power, that history is made by the privileged few. My perspective is the opposite. I believe that the making of history is a bottom-up process in which social movements can play a central role in bringing about political change. Where conventional history credits the decisions of a few, usually men, in determining world events, my perspective gives voice to the unnamed millions of women and men who participate in the great citizen movements that shape the course of human affairs.

Nowhere is the debate over who makes history more acute than in the controversy over the ending of the Cold War. Two sharply differing interpretations have been offered to explain the dramatic events of the late 1980s. The establishment view, as George Bush once phrased it, is that "America won the Cold War." The signing of the Intermediate Nuclear Forces (INF) Treaty in 1987 and the subsequent easing of East-West tensions resulted from the Reagan administration policies of "peace through strength." In the 1992 presidential election debates, Bush declared, "We never would have got there if we'd gone for the nuclear freeze crowd."[1] By contrast, Randall Forsberg, founder of the Nuclear Weapons Freeze Campaign, declared that the INF Treaty was "a victory for the peace movement."[2] It was not the military build-up, according to Forsberg, but the pressure of citizen activism for peace and human rights that brought an end to the Cold War.

In *Peace Works: The Citizen's Role in Ending the Cold War*, I elaborate and corroborate Forsberg's interpretation, showing that the pressures ending the Cold War were peaceful and democratic in nature, not military. Western peace movements began the process of change in the early 1980s with a massive wave of opposition to nuclear arms and the deployment of new INF weapons. This was followed a few years later by the stunning nonviolent revolution of the East European democracy movement. As Mary Kaldor has written: "The Cold War was ended by a wave of popular movements in both East and West that . . . discredited the Cold War idea. It was the Eastern European democracy movement, not Western governments, that brought about the final collapse of Communism. And it was the Western European peace movements that first challenged the status quo in Europe."[3] The sources of change in the Soviet Union and Eastern Europe were primarily internal, not external. Credit for ending the Cold War belongs to those in both East and West who struggled for peace and freedom, not those who brandished weapons. Peace was achieved in spite of, not because of, the arms build-up.

A central thesis of the peace-through-strength interpretation is that the arms build-up was necessary to bring the Soviets to the bargaining table. In fact, Moscow was ready to begin negotiations with the Reagan administration from the very first days of the administration. It was not Moscow but Washington that rejected serious negotiation. As former secretary of state Alexander Haig reports in his memoirs, "The Soviets were eager to enter into arms talks. . . . [Soviet ambassador Anatoly] Dobrynin raised the subject in his first talk with me and never failed to mention it in subsequent encounters."[4] The White House spurned the Soviet overtures because, in Haig's words, "[t]here was nothing substantive to talk about, nothing to negotiate."[5] It was only when political pressures in the United States and Europe began to build that the White House became serious about negotiations.

The ironic fact is that military pressures from the West reinforced the Soviet system of repression and militarism. As historian and former ambassador George Kennan has observed, "The general effect of Cold War extremism was to delay rather than hasten the great change that overtook the Soviet Union at the end of the 1980s."[6] Whenever Washington resorted to aggressive action, it confirmed the beliefs and strengthened the position of Soviet hardliners. As Mary Kaldor has written, "Far from countering a Soviet military threat to Western Europe, NATO legitimized the Soviet presence in Eastern Europe."[7] In this sense, the military establishments of the two sides were symbiotic, feeding off each other and sustaining a right-wing political climate that reinforced the war system on both sides. In the words of Russian poet Yevgeny Yevtushenko, "Your hardliners help our hardliners, and our hardliners help your hardliners."[8]

It was only when the Reagan administration began to tone down its militaristic rhetoric and policies that East-West relations began to improve and Cold War tensions eased. This change came about through political pressure, through the organized campaigns of peace movements in the United States and Europe. During the first half of the 1980s the peace movement profoundly challenged the Western political establishment. Peace activism in the United States significantly influenced public opinion and created a political climate in Washington for arms control and military restraint.

Throughout the 1980s public opinion surveys consistently found Americans strongly in support of the nuclear weapons freeze—despite vocal Reagan administration opposition to the proposal. According to the most comprehensive survey of public opinion on these matters, conducted by Daniel Yankelovich prior to the 1984 elections, the nuclear freeze was "supported by upwards of 75 percent of the public for several years."[9] One survey by the National Opinion Research Corporation put freeze support at 86 percent.[10] This broadly antinuclear sentiment was frequently translated into direct action and political pressure. On June 12, 1982, nearly one million people thronged to New York's Central Park for the great nuclear freeze rally, the largest political demonstration in U.S. history. That same year nuclear freeze referenda were on the ballot in nine states and dozens of major cities, with eleven million people, 60 percent of those voting, supporting the proposal for a mutual halt to the arms race.[11] The Physicians for Social Responsibility organized symposia in nearly every major U.S. city on the medical effects of nuclear war. The U.S. Catholic bishops and other religious bodies wrote pastoral letters condemning the arms race.[12] In Europe the European disarmament movement generated similar pressure. Millions of people poured into the streets in the fall of 1981 and again in the fall of 1983, demanding a halt to INF deployments.[13] London, Amsterdam, Bonn, Rome, and other European cities witnessed the largest political demonstrations in their histories. The European governments facing this pressure redirected the political heat toward Washington in the form of demands for greater progress at the bargaining table.

What was the result of all this pressure? To determine the impact of citizen activism, we need to assess the specific policy aims of the Reagan administration and how these were altered or redirected by public pressure. Such an exercise will give us a scorecard with which to judge peace movement impact.

Ronald Reagan came into office on a platform highly critical of arms control negotiations and explicitly pledging to achieve "technological and military superiority" over the Soviet Union. Because of the popularity of the freeze movement, however, public opinion became increasingly hostile to this radical philosophy, and a political climate in favor of arms limitation quickly developed. Popular culture became antinuclear, as the freeze movement swept the country. In response the White House toned down the president's often bombastic rhetoric and began to "angle" public statements, as chief speechwriter Aram Bakshian put it, away from the "crazy cowboy" image.[14] The Reagan administration quietly dropped the concept of superiority, abandoned its harshly anti-Soviet rhetoric, and was forced to begin arms control negotiations.

Initially administration officials had asserted that arms talks could not begin until the military build-up was completed, a process Defense Secretary Caspar Weinberger estimated would take eight years.[15] Secretary of State Alexander Haig and senior negotiator Paul Nitze made similar statements, asserting that the White House would not be pressured into early negotiations. Nonetheless, within a year of taking office the administration was forced to the bargaining table. Weinberger admitted in an interview with the author that public pressure influenced the beginning of arms control negotiations.

> *Q.* Did pressures in Congress and in public opinion have anything to do with the timing of the decision to begin the START [Strategic Arms Reduction Talks] talks?
>
> *A.* Well, I suppose something, surely. In a democratic society you've got to respond to what the people want in one way or another.[16]

The Reagan administration also attempted to create a nationwide program of civil defense shelters and the Crisis Relocation Plan, an elaborate evacuation program that would supposedly save 80 percent of the population in the event of a nuclear attack.[17] These ludicrous proposals, part of a conscious nuclear war–fighting strategy,[18] were met with widespread public skepticism and hostility. The Physicians for Social Responsibility overwhelmed the proposal by reminding the public of the medical horrors of nuclear war and the impossibility of surviving a nuclear attack. Officials in dozens of communities rejected federally mandated evacuation plans. In several communities local governments used funds that were to be allocated for this purpose to publish and distribute literature on the prevention of nuclear war. Responding to this pressure, Congress refused to fund the White House's expanded shelter and evacuation programs, slashing 40 percent from the administration's civil defense budget requests.[19]

When the United States and NATO announced the deployment of INF missiles in Western Europe, the European peace movement responded with the largest mobilization of public opposition in the continent's modern history. Millions poured into the streets, and opinion polls showed broad popular opposition to the missile deployments. Even a poll commissioned by the U.S. International Communications Agency found opposition rates ranging as high as 84 percent in Belgium.[20] Despite the vast public campaign against the missiles, military officials succeeded in ramming through the INF deployments, although peace movements managed to delay the process in the Netherlands and Belgium. However, what seemed a political defeat contained the seeds of victory. U.S. and NATO officials had appropriated the peace movement's proposal for a zero solution—no INF missiles East or West—as their official bargaining position in the Geneva negotiations. They did so, despite the opposition of many military officials, as a political maneuver to win acceptance of the missiles. The day the zero-option proposal was announced, State Department official Richard Burt told peace activist Mary Kaldor, "We got the idea from your banners, you know, the ones that say 'no cruise, no Pershing, no SS-20.' "[21] The decision to negotiate on the INF issue was the direct result of political pressure from Europe, as Weinberger notes in his memoirs: "As more and more of the demonstrations were held . . . more and more defense ministers at the NATO meetings urged, either as their views or as the opinions being presented to their governments, that more be done on the 'second track' [i.e., negotiations]."[22] The original assumption had been that the Soviets would reject the zero option, which they did—much to the relief of NATO officials, who believed that new INF weapons were needed regardless of Soviet reaction.[23] When Gorbachev unexpectedly accepted the zero solution in 1987, however, NATO leaders were stuck with their own proposal and had no choice but to remove the missiles they had labored so hard to install. In the end, the peace movement's position prevailed.

Pentagon officials saw the MX missile as the centerpiece of the strategic nuclear build-up. The peace movement made the mobile missile a prime target of political opposition, and a diverse coalition of environmentalists, religious activists, taxpayer groups, trade unions, Native Americans, and farm organizations emerged to battle the MX. A highly successful campaign was waged in the Great Basin area of Nevada and Utah, the most Republican region of the country, to block plans for mobile basing. With prodding and educating from the peace movement, such conservative groups as the Church of Jesus Christ of Latter-day Saints and the Nevada Cattlemen's Association issued statements against MX basing and urged greater efforts to negotiate arms limitation. After the initial success in stopping the basing plan, the anti-MX coalition mounted an intensive multiyear lobbying effort in Washington to halt the missile itself. This campaign, described by a veteran Washington observer as "one of the most effective citizen lobbies ever wrought,"[24] battled the Pentagon and the military-industrial complex through more than twenty major congressional votes, on several occasions actually halting funding for the missile. The anti-MX campaign forced the

administration to create the Scowcroft Commission, which in 1983 recommended that the MX program be cut in half and declared that the "window
of vulnerability," the theory that U.S. missiles were becoming vulnerable to
Soviet attack, did not really exist—a point the peace movement had been
making for years. Trying to preserve the MX became a major dilemma for
the White House. Kenneth Adelman, director of the Arms Control and
Disarmament Agency, called the MX a "dog, the strategic albatross of the
Reagan administration . . . with the President and the Secretaries of State and
Defense doling out staggering political capital each time merely to keep this
dubious project alive."[25] In the end the White House had to settle for a
compromise with MX opponents, when Congress decided in 1985 to cap the
program at fifty missiles, one-quarter the original plan. Another price the
administration had to pay was to accelerate its arms control efforts with the
Soviet Union. Because of the pressure from congressional moderates, led by
Congressman Les Aspin, the White House agreed on two separate occasions
to change the U.S. bargaining position in negotiations with the Soviet
Union.[26] These pressures from Congress were a direct result of peace movement lobbying efforts.[27] The anti-MX campaign significantly impeded the
Reagan administration's vaunted strategic build-up and was a partial victory
for the peace movement.

Another White House priority, an obsession that came to dominate the
second half of the Reagan presidency, was the Strategic Defense Initiative
(SDI), or Star Wars. The proposal for a space shield against nuclear weapons
was in large part a response to the nuclear freeze campaign and the stalemating
of the administration's strategic build-up.[28] The Star Wars proposal was
greeted with widespread skepticism, and intense opposition to SDI developed
within the peace community, among scientists, and within Congress. A
Pledge of Non-Participation, committing signers to refuse government funds
for SDI research, began at the University of Illinois and Cornell University
and circulated among physicists at many other universities. Eventually more
than seven thousand scientists in the United States and twelve thousand
worldwide signed the pledge. Among those signing were nineteen Nobel
laureates in physics and chemistry and 57 percent of the faculty of the top
twenty physics departments in the United States.[29] Opposition within the
scientific community fueled resistance to the president's SDI budget requests
on Capitol Hill, as many of the arms control organizations that had led the
fight against the MX took up the battle against Star Wars. Prodded by
grass-roots activists, Congress voted in 1985 and 1986 to prohibit tests
against antisatellite weapons, a key component of SDI. In 1986 Congress
voted to cut the administration's SDI funding request by 40 percent. The
following year Congress approved the Nunn-Levin amendment, mandating

that SDI testing remain within the limitations of the Anti-Ballistic Missile (ABM) Treaty. This effectively ended the president's dream of a space-based defensive shield, since the ABM Treaty strictly prohibits strategic defense systems in space. While funding for more modest forms of strategic defense continued after 1987, the combination of congressional budget cuts and legislative restrictions on SDI testing defeated the Reagan Star Wars program. Grass-roots peace activists and arms control lobbyists on Capitol Hill played a key role in this important but often overlooked development.

Perhaps no concern was more passionately felt by Reagan and his advisers than the struggle to overthrow the Sandinistas in Central America. Not just in Nicaragua, but in El Salvador as well, the Reagan administration organized and funded proxy wars and threatened direct U.S. intervention. In response a solidarity peace movement based largely in the religious community emerged to contest White House efforts. While the solidarity movement was unable to stop covert war in Central America, it prevented the White House from fully achieving its objectives. The White House was never able to win public support for its policies in Central America, and overt U.S. military intervention was blocked. Nearly every poll taken during the 1980s showed the American people against U.S. policy in Central America—despite elaborate administration attempts to win public support. Disapproval of military aid for the Contras consistently stood above 60 percent.[30] In response to this public sentiment, and with lobbying support from some of the same organizations that fought against the administration's nuclear policies, Congress passed the Boland amendments in 1982 and 1983 blocking military aid for the Contras in Nicaragua. When the White House requested renewed funding in 1984, religious and peace organizations mounted another successful lobbying fight, defeating the president's request in the House of Representatives by a 241-177 vote.[31] The Reagan administration ignored these legislative restrictions, however, and set up the illegal Oliver North Contra supply operation, which led to the Iran-Contra scandal and the administration's worst political crisis. This in turn provided a serendipitous boost to the cause of disarmament. When the Iran-Contra scandal broke in late 1986, the White House was rocked by the sharpest one-month drop in presidential approval ratings ever recorded, according to the CBS/*New York Times* poll.[32] In an attempt to restore the president's image as leader, and to provide a boost for the Republican party going into the presidential elections, the White House turned toward arms control and negotiations with the Soviets. This was just at the time when Gorbachev was preparing to accept the zero-option proposal on INF weapons. Administration officials counseled the president to accept the Soviet offer, despite strong misgivings from military officials, to shore up domestic political support.[33] By raising the political costs of the president's war against Nicaragua, the solidarity movement not only restrained aggression in Central America but inadvertently paved the way for arms control and reduced East-West tensions.

While the peace movement achieved much during the 1980s, it also faced severe limitations. Although citizen pressure influenced some areas of policy, it was unable to alter the larger structures of militarism. Despite the extensive peace campaigns of the decade, the Reagan administration was able to enlarge the military budget, strengthen the CIA, and greatly reinforce the power of military institutions. The continuing legitimacy of military force as an instrument of foreign policy was tragically illustrated by the Bush administration's mobilizing of public support for the Persian Gulf War in 1991. The vicelike grip of militarism on U.S. political institutions is also evident in the Clinton administration's support for Cold War–level military budgets, despite the dissolution of the Soviet Union. The peace movement of the 1980s achieved some success at the margins of policy, but was not able to alter the core structures of the war system.

Nonetheless, it is important to recognize that the peace movement had a real impact on policy. Forcing the Reagan administration to negotiate with the Soviet Union, shaping the zero-option proposal, stalemating the MX missile, rejecting civil defense planning, ending antisatellite weapons testing, imposing limitations on SDI funding and testing, and preventing overt military intervention in Central America—these were all important achievements. They helped to shape the history of the decade.

During the freeze movement, when doubters questioned the worth of these efforts, activists sometimes replied, "Think how much worse things would be if there were no peace movement." The point was well taken. If citizen groups had not campaigned constantly to prevent nuclear war and aggression, the military standoff between East and West might have been much more dangerous. The peace movement played a significant role in restraining the Reagan administration and helped to pull the United States and the world back from the brink of nuclear destruction.

NOTES

1. "The 1992 Campaign: Transcript of First TV Debate Among Bush, Clinton, and Perot," *New York Times*, October 12, 1992, p. A14.

2. Confirmed in communication with David Cortright, March 29, 1993.

3. Mary Kaldor, "Taking the Democratic Way," *The Nation*, April 22, 1991, p. 518.

4. Alexander Haig, *Caveat: Realism, Reagan, and Foreign Policy* (New York: Macmillan, 1984), p. 228.

5. Ibid, p. 105.

6. George Kennan, "The G.O.P. Won the Cold War? Ridiculous," *New York Times*, October 28, 1992, p. 15.

7. Kaldor, "Taking the Democratic Way," p. 516.

8. Quoted in *Moscow News*, October 23–30, 1988.

9. Daniel Yankelovich and John Doble, "The Public Mood: Nuclear Weapons and the USSR," *Foreign Affairs* 63 (fall 1984): 46.

10. Benjamin Page and Robert Shapiro, "Foreign Policy and the Rational Public," *Journal of Conflict Resolution* 32 (1988): 243.

11. David Cortright, *Peace Works: The Citizen's Role in Ending the Cold War* (Boulder, CO: Westview, 1993), pp. 20–22.

12. See Jim Castelli, *The Bishops and the Bomb: Waging Peace in the Nuclear Age* (Garden City, NY: Doubleday, 1983).

13. See Thomas Rochon, *Mobilizing for Peace: The Antinuclear Movements in Western Europe* (Princeton, NJ: Princeton University Press, 1988).

14. Cortright, *Peace Works*, p. 94.

15. Castelli, *Bishops and the Bomb*, p. 83.

16. Interview, Caspar Weinberger with David Cortright, September 23, 1991.

17. See Jennifer Leaning and Langley Keyes, eds., *The Counterfeit Ark: Crisis Relocation for Nuclear War* (Cambridge, MA: Ballinger, 1984).

18. See Robert Scheer, *With Enough Shovels: Reagan, Bush, and Nuclear War* (New York: Vintage Books, 1983).

19. *Congressional Quarterly Weekly Report*, May 1, 1982, p. 983.

20. Connie deBoer, "The Polls: The European Peace Movement and Deployment of Nuclear Missiles," *Public Opinion Quarterly* 49 (spring 1985): 126–27.

21. Mary Kaldor, "We Got the Idea from Your Banners," *New Statesman* 113 (March 18, 1987): 14.

22. Caspar Weinberger, *Fighting for Peace: Seven Critical Years in the Pentagon* (New York: Warner Books, 1990), p. 338.

23. See, for example, John Deutsch, Brent Scowcroft, and R. James Woolsey, "The Danger of Zero Option," *Washington Post*, March 31, 1987, p. 21; and Richard Nixon and Henry Kissinger, "A Real Peace," *National Review* 39 (May 22, 1987): 32.

24. Michael Pertschuk, *Giantkillers* (New York: W. W. Norton, 1986), p. 187.

25. Kenneth Adelman, *The Great Universal Embrace: Arms Summitry—A Skeptic's Account* (New York: Simon and Schuster, 1989), p. 173.

26. See Strobe Talbott, *Deadly Gambits: The Reagan Administration and the Stalemate in Nuclear Arms Control* (New York: Vintage Books, 1985).

27. Interview, Les Aspin with David Cortright, August 1, 1991.

28. See Gregg Herkin, "The Earthly Origins of Star Wars," *Bulletin of Atomic Scientists* 43 (October 1987): 20–28.

29. Lisbeth Gronlund, "Summary and Current Results of the Boycott of Star Wars Research Funds," unpublished report (September 15, 1987).

30. William Leo Grande, *Central America and the Polls: A Study of U.S. Public Opinion Polls on U.S. Foreign Policy Toward El Salvador and Nicaragua under the Reagan Administration* (Washington, DC: Washington Office on Latin America, 1987), p. 27.

31. Cortright, *Peace Works*, p. 288.

32. Richard J. Meislin, "President Invites Inquiry Counsel; Poll Rating Dives," *New York Times*, December 2, 1986, p. 1.

33. See Bruce Russett, "Democracy, Public Opinion and Nuclear Weapons," in *Behavioral Science, Society and Nuclear War*, eds. Philip Tetlock, Jo Husbands et al. (New York: Oxford University Press, 1989), p. 242; also interview, Michael Baroody with David Cortright, July 20, 1990; and interview, Richard Wirthlin with David Cortright, September 5, 1990.

6

Europe 1989: The Role of Peace Research and the Peace Movement

Johan Galtung

What I want to focus on in this chapter is the role of peace research and the peace movement in ending the Cold War. I start by referring to a report by Jonathan Steele[1] concerning some specialists on the peace movement and its role in fomenting dissent. These specialists were not social scientists but were the state security police in the former German Democratic Republic. On a list of what they called "hostile negative forces" there were three elements that had to be watched: a few parsons; their friends; and women for peace. Steele reports that these were the forces that played the main role in bringing down the Berlin Wall. What a compliment.

It was not Chancellor Helmut Kohl nor anyone else in Germany's ruling circles that can take the credit for the social movement leading to German unification. The movement was led by a small group of East German pacifists and parsons who then witnessed the revolution they set in motion stolen from them. The country they wanted to change, while maintaining its own political destiny, has been chaotically annexed. I believe this is a fair judgment about both the causal precipitating factors of what initially happened and what took place later on. This is what I want to explore in some detail.

Let me start by giving the intellectual structure of the argument. The logic of it is simply the following: I start with something called the Cold War System (CWS) and divide it into two components, Stalinism and nuclearism. As I see it, this is the essence of the Cold War; and by the Cold War, I mean

This is an edited and updated version of an address delivered on July 10, 1991, to inaugurate the Peace and Conflict Studies program at the University of Queensland.

the Atlantic theater, for the Cold War is not over in the Pacific theater. There is still a total unnecessary display of brutal nuclearism in the Pacific. There is still a display of Stalinism in its peculiar form in North Korea. What I propose to do is to follow the two syndromes of Stalinism and nuclearism through three processes that took place in the 1980s. These can be referred to as the "triple double P system": people's power; primacy of politics; and peace politics (see Table 1).

Further, the basic thesis is that, given all the contributory causes, the necessary causes for the end of the Cold War were the peace movement, the dissident movement, and Gorbachev. The term *Gorbachev*, however, should not stand for one person; it stands for quite a collection of people whom Gorbachev himself referred to as the "new thinking." These three were sufficient causes together, but each one of them was necessary. You could not explain the end of the Cold War if all three of them had not been there.

Let me complicate my basic thesis by explaining it in terms of the classical Aristotelian format for causal analysis. Aristotle divided causes into four types: *causa efficiens*; *causa finalis*; *causa materialis*; and *causa formalis*. The *causa efficiens* is the pushing force, while the *causa finalis* is the pulling force; that is, there is a goal, a telos—a point not often recognized by modern science. The *causa materialis* can be seen as the matter through which the cause works, and the *causa formalis* is the form through which the cause works. I shall try to give life to these four figures.

Let me say that I find the Aristotelian thinking about causation very important and useful. I now have a couple of jobs to do. First, I have to define Stalinism and nuclearism; then I have to look at what happened in the six cells of Table 1, tracing their interconnectedness. My analysis ends on November 9, 1989, with a command from the leadership of the then German Democratic Republic to open the Berlin Wall. As a matter of fact, what happened was that they sent a man on a motorbike through the wall to the town hall on the other side with a note saying that the wall would be opened at such and such an hour; then came the precise hour and that was the end of it. So the Cold War ended with a bureaucratic message and a man on a motorbike. That itself is quite interesting, and we shall now try to trace the events in chronological order.

Let us start by defining Stalinism and nuclearism. I define Stalinism as a composite of four basic factors (to make it simple I also have four for nuclearism). The four factors for Stalinism are the following: first, a Communist party monopoly not only of power because that one finds in many systems, but a monopoly on truth. Relatively similar to the Christian churches in major periods of European history, there is but one truth and the task is the administration of that truth. The secretary general of the party is the top

Table 1
The Cold War System

		People's Power	Primacy of Politics	Peace Politics
Cold War System	Stalinism			
	Nuclearism			

resident manager of truth. Now this has an interesting implication for intellectuals. One cannot publish any thought that the secretary general has not published. Try to apply that, for example, to Australian politics and see what implications it has. Pick any Australian politician you want and have that as the upper limit to people's publications. The way people handled it in practice was to tell speechwriters to put something into the secretary general's speeches that would prepare the way for the thinking of others.

The second factor is the absence of civil and political rights. The pivotal years in the development of human rights documents—1776, 1787, 1789, 1948—are second in importance to the truth of what was considered Marxism.

The third basic factor is central planning of the economy—not only of production but of distribution and consumption. Four hundred million people were living in the area under Stalinism—290 million in the Soviet Union and the rest in Eastern Europe. They were being planned for by about four hundred persons, that is, about one planner per million people.

I remember landing in Moscow in 1962 and discovering that nearly all the women had green dresses with black polka dots. I asked, "What's on? Is this some kind of special festival?" The answer was that the planning committee had a surplus of that kind of cloth and decided that was the adequate dress for August 1962. When one thinks of the amount of energy women put into not only being dressed differently from other women but also varying their outfits throughout the day, then you could say that this was "planning on top of people's minds"!

The fourth aspect is Russian imperialism—the Red Czar following in the wake of the Black Czar. These four aspects have been pointed out again and again by people on the Right, and they were right to do so. I see nothing particularly wrong; this was exactly the way it was experienced by people in the region. Whether you were on the Right, on the Left, or in the middle, these four factors were weighing on the four hundred million. In addition came the fact that central planning was not able to deliver the goods. There was a scarcity of goods and services. The positive achievements were quickly forgotten, for example, the eradication of a high level of misery in the region. Thus the positive achievements were not acknowledged as a credit whereas the negative aspects of central planning were a yoke on the people. And yet it is quite clear that the system had achieved a balance with the population. People were complaining, but there was, for most people, no outright suffering after the Khrushchev speech in February 1956. There no longer was a fear of a knock on the door at night.

Let us turn to nuclearism in terms of its four syndromes. Its first basic aspect was the readiness of both sides to plan, contemplate, and, if need be, activate massive genocide. The genocide planners, by my counting, were about five hundred. The extermination they were contemplating would easily have come to five hundred million, that is, about one planner per million people. Now it is very important to consider the following. The four hundred planners of people's economic fate in the state planning agencies have lost their jobs; most of the nuclear planners are still working in theirs. The readiness to countenance multiple genocide in several directions at the same time is a feature of the twentieth century, and as such is the basic aspect of nuclearism. The nuclear planners say it did not happen, but of course it could have happened, and the readiness was there! They also made plans for protecting themselves in more or less secret bunkers. In other words, the willingness to sacrifice was to sacrifice others. And yet they would get off scot-free.

Now point two: the authoritarian aspect of the nuclear state—the nuclear state being a security state—is secrecy. Secrecy in most client countries in NATO and in the Warsaw Treaty Organization took the form of concealing basic points from the population. The leaders were more afraid of their population than of the other side, because the other side knew relatively well what was going on since they were planning the same thing. They were experts on the other side so they needed only a tiny bit of information; their population was the one that should be kept ignorant. In most parliaments in the so-called democracies this came to the point where the basic truths were revealed only to handpicked parliamentarians in the nucleus of foreign policy and defense committees and were hidden from the rest. Of course, this is a travesty on any concept of democracy and it fits in well with Winston Churchill's dictum that when we need it most, we abolish it.

The third point was the never-ending arms race. Nuclearism created a justified fear—existential fear—on both sides; it led to an arms race with quantitative and qualitative aspects, one with incessant changes in the quality of weapons, continuous production, and some change in military doctrine. The Russians were better at the quantitative arms race and the Americans better at the qualitative aspect.

The fourth aspect of nuclearism was superpower domination. Whereas on the Stalinist side there was Russian imperialism, there was in the West a hegemonic system exerted by the United States over European countries. Twenty-nine countries (in 1989) were under superpower domination because it also affected the nonaligned and client states and Canada, of course.

These two syndromes, Stalinism and nuclearism, were with us for a period of forty years—from 1949 to 1989. And you can now ask, why did we get it? Well, you have to go back in history, as I think that the Cold War started in 1917. Challenging the Western formulation based on the expansion of capitalism, democracy, human rights, and Christianity, the communists introduced planning instead of market forces; dictatorship and terror instead of democracy and human rights; and scientific atheism instead of God and Christianity.

Those three negations of the West put them on a collision course from the very beginning. You can then argue which one was the most important? Probably the closing of the markets. Thus the Cold War started in 1917 and not with the speech by Churchill on the iron curtain. That means I see Stalinism essentially, like Leninism, as a reaction to Western expansionism. And since Western expansionism continues unabated, there will be other forms of Stalinism coming later. However, now we go to the end of the 1970s after just one remark about the interaction of Stalinism and nuclearism.

This interaction is essential to any understanding of the Cold War. Stalinism encouraged nuclearism and vice versa: it was a positive cybernetic system. Whenever in Eastern Europe the pressure of the four components of Stalinism increased, the planners of nuclearism in the West had what they needed as a rationale. Whenever they stepped up the arms race, the administrators of Stalinism in the East had what they wanted as a rationale. It is this interactive aspect of the system that kept the Cold War in place for such a long time—such a long time that many of us felt it would last forever. So then what happened? I think that the explanation does not lie in the Helsinki conference of 1972–75. That conference stabilized the Cold War System and put some limitations on it, but it did not bring it down. It reassured the Russians that the West was not out to change the borders in Eastern Europe. It reassured Western capitalists that they could establish joint ventures in the East, and it put in place, albeit in slow motion, a human rights process. All of this was important and was a contributory cause, but I think the real explanation lies in what happened in December 1979 and August 1980. In this period two movements sprang up. For the first time the dissident movement became a mass movement in Poland, and the peace movement became a mass movement in the Netherlands and Germany.

Let me give you the four conditions for the peace movement—indeed any mass movement—to be successful. Point one, it has to be sustained over a long time, and its message has to be repeated again and again. Point two, it has to be massive. That does not necessarily mean the 1.4 million that the West German peace movement could mobilize in one day, but it means all kinds of people and many small groups that could network well together. Point three, it has to be against an incontrovertible evil. Point four, it has to present an alternative. Let us look at these points from the Solidarity point of view. Starting in a shipyard in Gdansk with the evils of Stalinism all around them, Solidarity became massive with up to ten million supporters; it went on and on; and it was quite clear that the movement had an alternative. The alternative had one liberal wing and one socialist wing. The liberal wing was human rights–oriented and the socialist wing was oriented toward democratic socialism as expressed in the twenty-one articles from Gdansk in August 1980. Solidarity satisfied, so to speak, the rules of the game. There was a military coup by Wojciech Jaruzelski in December 1981, but that coup did not bring Solidarity to an end. It merely stabilized the confrontation.

Why did Solidarity come into being? It was due to the absurdity of the system. I can remember in the spring of 1980, in Warsaw, actors at the theater dressed up in pink panther suits who had walked into the streets. It was rather astounding to see pink panthers suddenly loose in the streets, but they were part of an absurd theater trying to make it clear to the people and the authorities that their system was absurd. Suddenly the pink panthers queued up at a point; they were all standing queuing and it was quite evident they were queuing for nothing. There was absolutely nothing at the end of the queue. So if you then asked what are these pink panthers queuing up for, the answer was "just the usual thing, for nothing!" The message was very clear and it immediately brings to mind one small point: the relationship between nonviolence and humor. Humor is a fantastic nonviolent weapon. The absurdity had a metaphor and the metaphor was that history was a train. The people were sitting in the waiting room of the Eastern European countries as the train passed by. The people saw the glittering train of history passing by without stopping; they were sidetracked in an ultrastable system.

What brought the peace movement to its gigantic size? It was, of course, the double-track decision[2] of NATO on December 12, 1979, to deploy 108 Pershing II and 464 cruise missiles. But that was just a precipitating event. What brought it into being was a strong sense of absurdity. The system was absurd—its masters had lost control of the system. They did not have the faintest plan as to how to bring the arms race to an end. When they produced something like SALT I and SALT II, these are not arms agreements in the sense of reducing arms. Both agreements were about increasing the level of armaments! And the only intellectual defense advanced was that by having these agreements the increase would be less than it would otherwise be. This did not convince people. There was a feeling of being in a railway station in a waiting room. A train was crossing the tracks marked "nuclear war" and there was a fear that the train might stop, that it could not pass by.

The popular movements of both East and West were movements of reaction to absurdity and of deep distrust with the governments and their elites. That distrust, in both cases, mobilized an enormous amount of intellectual talent. One found it immediately in Eastern Europe in the dissident movement, the reading of human rights speeches and treatises, and in the many proposals of democratic theory. Intellectually armed to the teeth, the peace movement could challenge the thinking of nuclear planners.

I witnessed a discussion between an eighteen-year-old boy and a defense minister. There was not the slightest doubt that the eighteen-year-old was much better informed than the defense minister. This was because the boy had read all the latest pocket books, while all the poor defense minister had read were boring NATO documents. What could one do with bureaucratic gibberish against an eighteen-year-old boy who had read all the pocket books? One found this again and again, and it became clear, as time passed, that the intellectual, political, and moral power had passed into the hands of the people's movements.

At this point, peace research began to play a role. It started in 1981 in West Germany and the Netherlands—the most important countries in terms of the peace movement. The media took the initiative; they felt that when they were organizing debates about the double-track decision of the missiles, people were sick and tired of the old security studies experts. They needed new people. And what happened then was that no debate took place on the missiles without at least one peace researcher on the panel.

After working for more than twenty years we were delighted to be brought into action and to be activated. We certainly found we had an audience—let us say about twenty million on one evening—so it changed the rules of the game. For the usual gang it was no longer the faithful twenty, but twenty million. What happened then was a dialogue, and in that dialogue over time, and out of the peace research movement, there crystallized two ideas. The first can be traced to the U.S. peace researcher Charles Osgood—Graduated and Reciprocated Initiatives in Tension reduction (GRIT). His way of transcending the fake dichotomy between unilateralism and multilateralism was by talking about a sort of unilateral multilateralism or multilateral unilateralism. One party makes more of a downward step than the other, then waits and invites the other to follow. But one party has to take the first step.

The other idea was nonprovocative defense, or defensive defense. This came out of Scandinavian peace research circles inspired by Swiss military doctrine. The Swiss indirectly have played much more of a role than they would want to acknowledge—especially their doctrine of 1973, the idea of having a military that does not provoke because the weapons are defensive and not offensive. Of course one enters the difficult debate of finding a conceptual borderline. There is a grey zone. Nevertheless, there is not the slightest doubt that long-distance missiles or weapons with a large destructive potential are offensive. Nor is there any doubt about a tube that can be built close to the border and is filled with a liquid that can be ignited and exploded so that the terrain above becomes impassable for tanks—it is a defensive weapon. The reason is because the tube does not move. Between those extremes there exist all kinds of weapons systems—the key variable being the logistic capacity to move them. These concepts came out of the peace movement and produced a very lively debate. There were two other things that also came out of peace research and the peace movement: first, very detailed analyses and research on nonviolence; and second, detailed analyses and research on how to build nongovernmental networks and people diplomacy between countries antagonistic to each other.

Thus one finds two people's movements hated by their respective governments. Each of the governments was competing in telling the other how small and insignificant its movement was. The journalists counted the size of the demonstrators hoping they were decreasing as they constantly belittled the phenomenon.

At this stage we come to 1985. If Gorbachev had not gained power, not much more might have happened for some time. It was quite clear that the two systems—Stalinism and nuclearism—had more than enough repressive power to keep a couple of dissidents and "peaceniks" at bay. I remember Stefan Heym, the famous East German dissident, who in a brilliant speech in West Berlin in 1982 compared the two movements and said that when in the West there is a demonstration of less than 200,000 the media do not even like to come; if the numbers reach 200,000, the radio shows up; at 300,000 the TV cameras arrive; and at 400,000 the politicians ask to be on the platform. On the other hand, when we in the East have one person standing on Alexander Platz in East Berlin, the authorities say he or she is crazy; if there are two persons they are arrested; if three, they are put on a train to West Germany; and if four, at least one person on the Politburo has to resign. That shows the relative value of a demonstrator under democracy and under dictatorship being roughly 100,000 to one. Peace demonstrations in a democracy cost little except for the shoes. Any so-called democratic regime knows how to have the demonstrators circle the parliament fifteen times and then send them back home, and of course receive 100,000 or 1,000,000 signatures, putting them down in the basement and burning them the day after. The cynicism of the democratic establishment is incredible. It has also been said that in a democracy everybody talks, hence nobody listens; and in a dictatorship everybody listens, hence nobody talks. These were two very different systems for articulating power.

However, how did Gorbachev come to power? In 1986 a key adviser to Soviet politicians, Georgi Arbatov, made a speech at a symposium in Washington where he told what had happened. He said the peace movement represented an expression of a change in consciousness that the West German population had been undergoing. This was a factor in our decision to elect Gorbachev, who was a spokesman for that thought as secretary general. To understand the implications of that observation, let us look at how the Soviets were viewing the world. They had one major problem; the problem was not the United States—the problem was Germany. Germany had killed twenty-six million Soviets, and 95 percent of the German military deaths in World War II were on the eastern front. The Soviet Union was the country that had defeated Nazi Germany. The United States was the country that defeated Japan. The Soviet Union took the brunt of the war in Europe and were the ones that won it. The Russians were conscious of that and they knew something perfectly well from history—if you beat somebody who has traumatized you, then that somebody also has a trauma and might like to come back and do something in return. For that reason, from May 8, 1945, on, the Russians had one question: is Germany revanchist or not? This was not a paranoid problem; it was perfectly reasonable, and a sizeable amount of their intellectuals were working full-time on exactly that question.

I have witnessed some of the discussions on the German question the twenty-five times I was in the Soviet Union between 1953 and 1989. The discussions were a little overdrawn and focused on morbid and harsh conservative statements, but they were understandable. However, what made the Soviets change their minds? There were two factors. One was Willy Brandt's *Ostpolitik,* the opening to the East in 1970; and the other was, as I have mentioned, the peace movement. I remember myself having a discussion with a Soviet Politburo member in 1983 who said that "what impresses us most about the peace movement is that we did not organize it." Of course, the Soviets had a very heavy share in organizing the movement in the 1950s and 1960s, but that share was, practically speaking, nil in the 1970s and early 1980s, except for small groups attached to the World Peace Council. What happened, according to Arbatov's reasoning, was the following: the peace movement reflects a change of heart in the population, especially for the young generation. It now looked as if the country is no longer dangerous, and as a consequence we can elect Mikhail Gorbachev as secretary general. As far as I understood, he was elected by a majority of one. The significance of the narrow margin is that if he had been elected unanimously, one could have argued that Arbatov's argument was not so important. When it was just one vote which made the difference in electing Gorbachev, it is quite evident that Arbatov's argument had been extremely significant. Gorbachev's victory was not trivial.

In the above manner the world got Gorbachev, so then what viewpoint did he represent? Very simply told, he represented the intelligentsia. Some Russians say he did not represent "new thinking"—he simply represented *thinking*. That was a new perspective, totally novel. This situation arose from the fact that the Soviet Union had the highest number of intelligentsia in the world, thirty-five million—fifteen million who had university degrees and twenty million who in the United States would be community-college graduates. In some statistical reports, this is supposed to account for some 25 percent of the intelligentsia in the world. Significantly, that intelligentsia had 2 percent of the quotes in official Communist party documents, the remaining 98 percent coming from Marx, Engels, Lenin, Stalin, the current secretary general, and a couple of others. One could say that the intelligentsia felt itself highly underquoted. Then in comes Gorbachev with two degrees—one in law and one in agriculture—and his wife, Raisa, with one degree in philosophy of sociology—a Ph.D.

What had clearly happened was that Gorbachev's accession to power opened doors for a number of people. About these people much can be said; they had been sitting and reading throughout the 1970s and early 1980s. Let me illustrate the significance of this by one personal story. We at the international Peace Research Institute, Oslo (PRIO) sent all our products to the Institute for World Economic and World Affairs in Moscow, and it was as if you sent something into a black hole—you heard absolutely nothing, no echo, not a thing. In 1982, I gave some lectures at that institute and up to me came a librarian who said, "Are you Galtung? Come!" So I followed her down some corridors and into a room where on a shelf sat everything we had sent from Oslo; the black hole had been located! But what was significant was that all the documents had been read, as was evident from crease marks. When you find that there were people in Gorbachev's brain trust who had been reading all those things and were putting many of the ideas to work, one feels gratified. I had naively assumed that the things I had been doing would have an effect on some Western establishment—not at all. They would rather read anything from one hundred U.S. think tank documents than anything from PRIO. Yet Moscow was the place where a group of young people were digesting our work, as we noted when a deputy foreign minister later, in 1991, expressed his gratitude during a visit to Oslo.

Gorbachev wanted to get away from the Geneva process of balanced disarmament by launching some policy initiatives. To get the process started he did two things: "asymmetric disarmament," exactly according to the

Osgood recipe; and "defensive defense" as an alternative military doctrine. The defensive defense was called "sufficient defense" and it is possible to see immediately the two functions that the doctrine has: one was not to provoke the other side; and the other not to provoke one's own military by saying we are sending you all home, disarming you, and retiring you all tomorrow. It is nonprovocative in both directions. Gorbachev did this and the whole West said something new has happened. The INF Treaty was concluded for intermediate nuclear forces, and the signatories started destroying their missiles. By June 2, 1989, the *International Herald Tribune* could report that the Soviet Union had destroyed 945 missiles and the United States 324—a ratio of 3 to 1. I asked one of the Politburo members, "Why did you do this?" and the answer was, "We did it for two reasons: first of all, somebody has to take the first step to get the ball rolling; second, we thought it would have a good impact on world public opinion." Everyone can remember the public opinion polls of this period, when Gorbachev's rating kept on rising, leading Jimmy Carter to say that if there were an election just then for a world president, it would be won by Gorbachev.

Yet the INF agreement was not the end of the Cold War. We have to move further along in time to a doctrine announced by Gorbachev in January 1986 which nobody paid much attention to. He simply said that the Eastern European countries were now on their own and could decide their own policies. Of course, you did not believe that if you lived in an East European country, but for those of us who had been listening to the signals we felt that this was indicative of something very new.

We now move on to 1989, and at this point the movements take over and the demonstrations start in Eastern Europe. Let me try to characterize the demonstrations. In East Germany we are talking about 500,000 people who participated in them. A fairly good estimate of those who migrated to the West after Hungary and Czechoslovakia opened their borders is also 500,000. Migration is a very old and venerable method of nonviolence. It is not the most courageous one—the most courageous is to stand face to face with the state security police in the streets, looking them in the eyes and engaging them in dialogue. If at the precise moment in Leipzig on October 9, 1989, somebody had thrown a bomb under a state security police car, the whole game would have been lost. The government would have had exactly the argument they needed. And they desperately needed arguments. The East Germans had invented a very powerful symbolism—*wir sind das Volk* (we are the people). For the Communist party, which said that "we are the representation of the essence of the people," such symbolism had a tremendous significance.

Let us momentarily switch back four years and imagine that in 1985 it was not the peace movement that was on the streets in West Germany but the revanchist movement—the people who had been driven out of the eastern parts of the old Germany—and that they had been shouting in favor of an attack. Or imagine that there was nobody in the streets at all. Gorbachev would never have been elected. We are at the edge of history where one little cause in one direction or the other has great historic significance.

We return to 1989; the Estonians were singing themselves to freedom. They organized groups of up to 200,000 singing—singing in shifts for forty-eight hours. I met a Russian party secretary in Estonia who told me, "Believe me, it is very demoralizing to see so many people singing." In my country (Norway) you may perhaps find 500 to 1,000 singing in any political demonstration, but 200,000 is what Hegel calls a transition from quantity to quality. It is a new phenomenon. The Baltics chained their arms together in a chain from Tallin to Vilnius of human beings, a chain of solidarity for independence from Russian imperialism. Where did they learn this technique? Singing in great masses is an old Estonian tradition. They picked up the human chain technique from the West German peace movement, because that is what they did in an act of solidarity in 1983, from one end of West Germany to the other. This was broadcast by East German television in order to show the population how much conflict there was in West Germany.

One can now go to the candlelight vigils outside churches. The Christians found their idiom, the non-Christians found theirs. What impressed me most in this massive display of nonviolent imagination is that this was not the old European tradition. The old European tradition when fighting for freedom is to take furniture out of the house, build barricades, overturn buses, and then burn cars and tires. Now the inner relationship between burning cars and democracy is not clear to me, and how burning tires can bring one closer to freedom, I simply fail to understand.

If one goes back to the May 1968 demonstrations by French students, it was not nonviolence. The game they were playing was to uproot all the cobblestones from the streets for use in their demonstrations. It is very easy to remove cobblestones after you have removed the first one, because you can then easily remove the others. The trick is to get the first one. For that they had constructed a special fork with four prongs which could be used to get the first cobblestone and could then be passed on to the next guy who runs over to the next street to do the same. What they did then was to build barricades—a kind of ritualistic termite behavior—and then you play a game that has some fascination. It is to roll a cobblestone so it ends ten centimeters before the feet of the police on the other side. The point is to come as close as possible without hitting them. Again, the intrinsic relationship between this form of behavior and democracy is unclear.

What had happened to change the European tradition of demonstrating was that the political culture of Europe had changed toward nonviolence. Why? Gandhi, Martin Luther King? Not that these people had read Gandhi. Many of us who had visited Eastern Europe had given many talks on such subjects, but there were few people who listened to these. No, it was more than the political culture that had changed.

The capitulation that ultimately came about was through the courage of the few who made use of nonviolence and through the networking of people's diplomacy. In all of these demonstrations one saw that more than 50 percent participating were women. Let me mention the Nordic women in 1981–83 who had organized the march to Paris, the march to Moscow, and the march to Washington for disarmament, peace, and human rights. When they arrived in Paris they were received by cynical French comments over their attractiveness and nonattractiveness as women. When they arrived in the Soviet Union they stimulated debates with Soviet groups from the very beginning and this resulted in a Soviet peace committee changing its slogan from "down with atomic weapons in the capitalist/imperialist West" to "nuclear disarmament East and West." When the Nordic women arrived in the United States, people threw stones at their cars, they were spat at, there were shouts for them to go back to the Soviet Union where they presumably belonged, and they were, practically speaking, denied any place to stay, apart from some Quakers' homes and some hospitable houses along the road. Now these were the expressions of three different political cultures. It is not so difficult to guess which of the three changed first.

Let me now draw my analysis to a close. The *causa efficiens*, when one examines the final process, was the sense of the absurdity of Stalinism and nuclearism. It took time for that sense to grow and find its intellectual formulation. You have to remember that Stalinism had as its rationale that it takes time to build a successful socioeconomic system, that a generation or two or three have to be sacrificed, and many people believed that. Perhaps what they feared most in the United States was that it could be true—the communist system might succeed. By 1980, at least the Poles did not believe it; some years later, the others did not believe it either. It was not only because there was a lack of goods on the shelves—to say that would be an insult to the Eastern European population. It is tantamount to saying that they only reacted with their stomachs. I can here mention one factor that was at least as important, the denial of freedom to travel. Deny somebody the right to travel abroad and he or she will think of nothing else. There was no limit to the tricks and gimmicks East Europeans invented so as to travel abroad.

If that was the *causa efficiens*, the *causa materialis* was the two movements and an enlightened leadership in Moscow. Gorbachev himself was not a "peacenik" but was rather a disguised "dissidentnik." He was moved by the inner absurdities of his own system, and he wanted some kind of re-creation of a socialist Soviet Union. The *causa formalis* can be summarized in one word—"revolution" by the people. The *causa materialis* and *causa formalis* found each other in these two movements. The two movements had problematic relationships. The dissidents talked about the peace movement as only being concerned with nuclear war and not giving a damn about the plight of Eastern Europe, and the peace movement often said of the dissident movement that they were only thinking of their own human rights, even at the cost of a possible nuclear war. There was some truth in the two arguments, and in 1983 the two movements came to a solution after a debate in Perugia, Italy: let both of us accept the agenda of the other and agree that one agenda does not exclude the other. That strengthened both movements, although you could still see dissidents in the East kowtowing to the more reactionary parts of the Washington establishment by speaking of the naivete of the peace movement.

What now of the *causa finalis*—what is the pulling force? Here I am ending on a pessimistic note. What I have asserted up to now was that what happened on November 9, 1989, was the triumph of people's movements, nonviolence, and enlightened political leadership, above all in the Soviet Union. Through the peace movement and the dissident movement one sees the women's movement as a leading force. But what is the *causa finalis*? For that I am afraid one has to look in some other direction: European cosmology—deep European ideology. What I mean by that is another force that had also been building up all the time—that is, the European Community (EC) on its way from being a community to a superpower.

The EC is about reconstructing a Western Europe that once again can dominate Eastern Europe and Russia and perhaps do the same for the rest of the world. If this had not been the case, the Eastern European countries would now be in the hands of those who caused the downfall of the Berlin Wall. One can object that Lech Walesa is the president in Poland. But even here one can find a basic schism between Walesa and the major forces of Solidarity; and in East Germany the sixteen million who did not participate in the revolt have been supported by those forces from Western Europe. Thus one sees a *causa finalis*, and it is a Western European expansionism. The two people's movements in a sense did the job that the military did not do, that is, removing the obstacles that stood in the way. All of this culminated with much anguish from the East German dissident movement when the election results were in for the first free elections in the German Democratic Republic, and Helmut Kohl and the Christian Democratic Union had won.

One can thus say that the events in Eastern Europe did not end the way they started. And yet it was a brilliant victory. It was victory for the peace movement, the women's movement, and nonviolence; and it showed the significance of mobilization, tenacity, and having a vision. It was a victory for the dissident movement for exactly the same reason. I can also add that it was a victory for peace research. Basic ideas from peace research played a role: GRIT, defensive defense, and so on. And you could ask yourself where do you learn singing for 200,000? Which military academy teaches that? Which strategic think tank tells you how to chain your hands together? Where do you learn about candlelight vigils? Where do you learn the courage required in nonviolent protest?

So what did the leaders in the West say? Throughout the months of November and December they all said the same thing: "Nobody could have predicted this." And why did they say that? Because *they* could not have predicted it, because it all happened away from their horizon. Did the East European statesmen say that? No, they did not say, "Nobody could have predicted it," because they knew perfectly well how shaky their regimes were. The Cold War ended not because of the balance of power, not because of nuclear strength. It ended because the people's movements were able to bring down the two syndromes. What happened afterward is another chapter and is calling for new people's movements. Let us resolve to continue; don't let one victory stand in the way of the other.

NOTES

1. *Guardian Weekly,* October 7, 1990 (published in England).

2. The double-track decision was the West's strategy to arm in order to disarm. It was thought that deployment of cruise and Pershing missiles would force the Soviets to the negotiating table where they would trade off their S-20 missiles for the withdrawal of the new NATO weapons. This acceleration of the nuclear arms race is what sparked the revival of the peace movement in the 1980s.

7

The Erosion of Regime Legitimacy in Eastern European Satellite States: The Case of the German Democratic Republic

Ulf Sundhaussen

INTRODUCTION

The collapse of communism in the former Soviet Union and its European satellites is now widely attributed to two "interrelated causes: the failure of centrally planned command economies, and rising citizen demands for greater freedom."[1] This "politically correct" interpretation is difficult to refute. Yet it tells us nothing about the reasons for the sudden collapse of communism at a point in time when reforms were under way, nor does it identify the forces which were at work—or failed to play their designated parts—in this most momentous political process of the second half of the twentieth century.

Many attempts have already been made, and will continue to be made, to pinpoint precisely the cause(s) for the collapse of communism; but the issue is far too complex to expect that observers will be able to agree on a single cause or even a clear rank-ordering of a variety of causes. What seems to be required at this stage of the debate is to prevent oversimplistic, plainly inadequate, if not inaccurate, explanations from gaining greater currency than they deserve, and new and questionable orthodoxies from emerging.[2]

This chapter explores the collapse of communism in the German Democratic Republic (GDR), geographically the premier front-line state along the East/West divide, militarily the launching pad for the potential drive of Warsaw Pact troops across the Central European plains to the Atlantic Ocean, and economically—due to its comparatively advanced stage of industrialization—the jewel of the Soviet empire. But this chapter is not a blow-by-blow

I wish to acknowledge the assistance of Sheridan Kearnan in the preparation of this chapter.

account or overall analysis of the fall of the SED (Socialist Unity Party) regime in the GDR: this is provided elsewhere.[3] Rather, it focuses on three central aspects of the demise of the regime in East Berlin which have become blurred due to the myths that have been spun since they occurred. To begin with, the nature of political dissent in the GDR is analyzed in an attempt to clear up misconceptions in regard to who did what, for what purpose, and with what result. Second, the puzzle of the ineffective reaction of a highly authoritarian regime to popular dissent has to be investigated; obviously, in view of the formidable coercive forces at the disposal of the government, the unfolding political abstinence of the Soviet occupation army cannot be the only point of reference. Finally, by critically investigating the state of the East German economy, it ought to become evident that no alternatives were available to the policies as they were pursued in 1989–90.

THE NATURE OF DISSENT IN THE GDR

According to the *Guardian Weekly*, the East German state security police (Stasi) had identified "three elements that had to be watched: a few parsons; their friends; and women for peace. . . . [t]hese were the forces that played the main role in bringing down the Berlin Wall."[4] The obvious question here, and one that is tackled in the next section of this chapter, is, Why didn't they watch closely enough? A handful of parsons, women, and friends should have been no match for a security agency with a full-time staff of eighty-five thousand agents and a quarter of a million regular informers.

This piece of information—or, rather, disinformation—serves as the introduction to Johan Galtung's contribution to this collection. He cites it with obvious approval because it serves his purpose, which is "to focus on . . . the role of peace research and the peace movement in ending the Cold War." He then goes on, and it is worth quoting him at some length:

It was not Chancellor Helmut Kohl nor anyone else in Germany's ruling circles that can take the credit for the social movement leading to German unification. The movement was led by a small group of East German pacifists and parsons who then witnessed the revolution they set in motion stolen from them. The country they wanted to change, while maintaining its own political destiny, has been chaotically annexed. I believe this is a fair judgment about both the causal precipitating factors of what initially happened and what took place later on.[5]

This, in my view, is a rather partisan and, more important, highly elitist attempt at myth building which contemptuously dismisses the role and wishes of the dissident East German masses. Recording dissent in the German Democratic Republic would have to start with the notion that its population never increased. This has less to do with a diminished inclination of East Germans to procreate than with the fact that between 1949, the year the GDR was founded, and 1989, the year in which it—for all practical purposes—collapsed, some five million out of less than seventeen million people left the German workers' and peasants' state. Roughly one-quarter of these were allowed to emigrate to the Federal Republic of Germany (FRG) because as pensioners they were of no economic value to the state; and three-quarters of the emigrants, half of them under the age of twenty-five, left East Germany "illegally."[6] These figures are all the more remarkable because the building of the "Anti-Fascist Protection Wall" in 1961 between East and West Germany, the most heavily fortified boundary in the history of the human race, effectively stopped mass emigration until the opening of the border between Hungary and Austria in mid-1989 allowed East German vacationers an escape route to the West. By contrast, only some sixty thousand people left the West to live in East Germany. But they included cultural heavyweights such as the writers Bertolt Brecht and Stefan Heym and the philosopher Ernst Bloch who were of enormous propagandistic value to the regime.

But those who did not leave the GDR were not necessarily in support of the regime. This became most obvious when, in June 1953, the industrial proletariat—the very people the regime claimed to represent—rose in protest against harsh working conditions, an uprising contemptuously dismissed by Stefan Heym as an antisocialist plot hatched in Washington and Bonn.[7] With the police unable to cope with the uprising and no East German military at the disposal of the regime at this time,[8] the protest movement had to be crushed by the tanks of the Soviet occupation army. The intervention of the Soviet tanks taught the East Germans the lesson which Hungarians and Czechs had to learn in years to come, namely, that popular dissent in any form and shape in any corner of the Soviet empire was unacceptable to the rulers in the Kremlin.

Those East Germans who, for a variety of reasons, neither left East Germany nor supported the regime had to come to terms with their situation. They normally found their own niches in the system, retreating from public life as far as possible and learning to exploit the existing conditions to their greatest advantage. Every evening they—in the words of Konrad Weiss, a prominent figure in the dissident movement to come—"mentally emigrated"[9] by switching on West German television and dreaming of a better life.

While a variety of informal civil rights, peace, and environmental groups had formed during the 1980s, often protected by the Protestant Church against the ever vigilant inquisitiveness of the Stasi, they only challenged the regime openly in mid-1989. The Western media had informed them of the dissident politics in Poland, Hungary, and the Soviet Union itself, and the more than measured response of the new man in the Kremlin. Internally, the normal, passive cynicism about the regime had given way to outrage when it became evident that the communists had, as usual, falsified the results of communal elections in May 1989. But the most important factor propelling both activists and normally passive people into action was the accelerating flight of young East Germans across the Hungarian-Austrian border, and the many thousands who had come to occupy the West German embassies in Prague and Warsaw demanding free passage to the West.

The citizen initiative groups, of which the New Forum of painter Baerbel Bohley and writer-cum-biologist Jens Reich became the most prominent, recruited primarily among intellectuals and Protestant ministers and, at least initially, found little support among the working class, the students, and what was left of the middle classes. In a bold move these groups jointly called on October 4, 1989, for free and democratic elections, to be supervised by the United Nations. But their real agenda was the creation of a purified form of socialism, a "socialism with a human face." They abhorred capitalism, and for many of those connected with the church, capitalists were no better than the money lenders Jesus Christ evicted from the House of God. It is instructive to quote Friedrich Schorlemer, the most eloquent and charismatic among the Protestant parsons, who drew conviction not only from prototype communist literature but from *Soviet* (my emphasis) political writing which he considered "liberating": "My conclusion is: either socialism from Peking to Berlin is capable of reforming itself, or it will disappear. . . . I hope this will not be the case. . . . If I look at the capitalist campaign to destroy nature, and its exploitative expansion vis-à-vis the Third World, I can only conclude that it would not only be regrettable if socialism were to vanish, but it would endanger the survival of the human race!"[10]

During October and November antigovernment demonstrations spread to all corners of the GDR. Leipzig, the second-largest city in the republic, soon emerged as the main center of the dissident movement, with regular demonstrations every Monday attracting up to a quarter of a million participants. Under the guidance of the intellectuals of the New Forum and associated groups, the initial demands for the right to emigrate gradually changed to a defiant vow to stay and change the living conditions for the better, culminating in the popular slogan of "We are the people!"—not the nomenklatura which claim the right to make all the decisions in the name of the people.

But the more that hitherto passive people came out of their niches and partook in the demonstrations, the more it became obvious that the interests of the masses and those of the prosocialist idealists among the intellectuals were irreconcilable. At the Leipzig Monday demonstration of October 30, "massive calls for the reunification"[11] of Germany were heard, a demand diametrically opposed to the intellectuals' intention of rebuilding socialism in an independent East German state. But lacking eloquent speakers of their own, the masses had to wait until the Monday demonstration of November 20, when an unknown toolmaker, encouraged by the spontaneous applause of the masses, argued that East Germans had suffered enough under forty years of socialism and were not prepared to experiment with other varieties of essentially the same. The route to take was to reunite with West Germany and partake in a system which had brought both prosperity and freedom to its citizens. Only a week later the intellectuals, who had been instrumental in organizing the protest movement, were publicly jeered. The direction of dissent had irrevocably changed from "We are the people!" to "We are one people!"[12] Probably the clearest manifestation of how far the mass of the demonstrators and the intellectuals had grown apart came when the authorities in a last bid to regain control over the rapidly unfolding events decided, on November 9, to open the Berlin Wall. While tens, if not hundreds, of thousands of East Germans crossed the border within hours of the announcement to a tumultuous welcome in the West, Baerbel Bohley, at the first national conference of the New Forum, patronizingly condemned this exposure of Western affluence and form of political democracy to an admiring and disbelieving East German crowd as "hasty and ill-considered."[13]

When the East Germans went to the polls in 1990—casting their votes four times during one year—the intellectuals' design for a separate East German state based on a new brand of socialism was overwhelmingly rejected by the electorate. The Christian Democrats, who had never enjoyed much electoral support in this part of Germany, emerged as the winners because they stood for the fastest track toward reunification with the West. The citizen initiative groups which had done so much to start up the protest movement, ensuring that it remained strictly nonviolent, and which of late had exercised enormous influence in the "Round Tables," a kind of basic democratic, semianarchistic system of Soviets supervising and auditing government activities, fared very poorly. Campaigning jointly under the name of Buendnis 90, in the elections for a new national parliament in March, they polled a meager 2.9 percent, declining even further in communal elections in May. Their performance in the October elections for the refounded states is difficult to measure because they contested these elections in a variety of combinations, and their vote may have further declined when in the December elections for the all-German Bundestag, their combined vote with the Green Party amounted to just 6 percent.[14]

The intellectuals were less than graceful in their electoral defeat to create a "third way" between the capitalism of the West and the "real existing socialism." Blaming West German interference in the internal affairs of the GDR and Western promises of a better life, Jens Reich explained this defeat by deploring that "[w]e could not develop our own form of democracy: the Bonn hippopotamus trampled that fragile flower to death."[15] Even more scathing was Friedrich Schorlemer, who denounced the East Germans "as obliging anyone who stuffs their mouths in a pleasant manner. They are nothing more than what they have always been: a private rabble" (*Privatpeobel*).[16]

INTERNAL SECURITY

In one of this volume's chapters it is asserted that it was Gorbachev's renouncement of the Brezhnev Doctrine which "really sparked all the momentous events in 1989 . . . [and] left the East European regimes fundamentally reliant on their own legitimacy and on their own troops to maintain order."[17] There can, indeed, be no doubt that Gorbachev's virtual undertaking not to intervene in the internal politics of East European states had enormous ramifications for many, but by no means all, of the revolutions in this region. It may, in fact, be more correct to argue that the new Soviet political abstinence did not so much trigger these revolutions as it provided the opportunity for radical politics to occur. This may be seen as a rather insubstantial difference, yet it is important when investigating causal relationships.

This leaves us to explore how East European regimes fared in their newly found self-reliance. While the crumbling of regime legitimacy is always well documented, the role of the regimes' security forces is normally neglected. In the case of the GDR, Erich Honecker had at his disposal the tightly woven network of the Stasi, with one full-time agent for less than every two hundred inhabitants; a huge People's Police; a Mobile Police Force; a crack Border Defense Force; and a workplace-based Workers Militia (*Betriebskampfgruppen*). Most important, unlike in 1953, the regime had at its disposal a supposedly politically loyal National People's Army (NVA)[18] of 173,000 men with more tanks than could possibly be required to end any number of demonstrations in any part of the country.

It may well be that, given the existence of such a formidable monopoly over the means of violence, Honecker was not particularly worried about the emergence of the New Forum and similar groups, even despite Gorbachev's warning, while he was attending the fortieth anniversary of the GDR on October 7, 1989, that communist leaders must take into account the wishes of ordinary people, or "otherwise life will punish us!"[19] Alternatively, Honecker may have genuinely been convinced that his regime was safe: the GDR was clearly the most prosperous country in the Eastern bloc, and communist rule had softened considerably since 1953. Popular support for him and his state appeared to be all too evident with jubilant columns of people marching through the streets of East Berlin, celebrating four decades of communist rule, waving banners, and shouting approval for socialist achievements.

But as it was soon to turn out, Honecker's confidence in his personal strength and security was misplaced: on October 18, the Party replaced him as its secretary general with Egon Krenz, his designated "crown prince." Presumably, the Politburo was frightened at the prospects of having to live without the protective umbrella of Soviet tanks, and it tried to appease the increasingly vocal dissidents by sacrificing its leader. Honecker was later to deny explicitly that it was the antigovernment demonstrations which brought him down; rather, he hinted darkly, his downfall was due to the machinations of Soviet foreign minister Eduard Shevardnadze, who had conspired against him behind his back.[20] There is probably no point in trying to assess which of the above explanations is the correct one; it is much more likely that all three factors, and perhaps others like the fragile state of Honecker's health, contributed to his sacking.

The security forces apparently played no role in the replacement of Honecker except that doubts in their resolve to handle the political crisis may have weighed heavily on the minds of the members of the Politburo. Indeed, the writing had been on the Berlin Wall for some time. Since the founding of the GDR, soldiers, especially from the Border Defense Force, consisting of people considered to be particularly loyal to the party, had crossed the Wall to the West[21]; according to some estimates enough soldiers had defected to West Germany to form a whole army division. More ominously, while the police, particularly on October 7 and 8, 1989, moved resolutely against peaceful demonstrators in East Berlin and Dresden, respectively, and arrested large numbers of people, the brutality with which dissidents were treated in the streets and especially once in custody was so extraordinary that police officers were horrified, and enlisted men refused to participate in further actions.[22] With the front line of the regime's defense—the police—crumbling fast, party functionaries took to dialogue and negotiations with dissidents, striking deals without waiting for the Politburo to work out a strategy for coping with the protest movement.

But what about the military? As has been mentioned, practically the whole officer corps were party members, and the regime ought to have been able to rely on them. Despite the fact that the officers regarded themselves as military professionals, or "experts" in external defense, and like their counterparts in any part of the world loathed to be drafted into "doing police work," they also were supposed to be "Red," and therefore ready to confront the enemies of the party within the state.

However, disenchantment with the conservative SED leaders had set in during the 1980s, along with doubts whether necessary change could be brought about as long as regime inflexibility remained. According to a ranking staff officer, whole party organizations within the NVA had by 1988 begun to criticize regime policies without, however, questioning the socialist state as such.[23] Reportedly, the majority of officers disapproved of the military involvement in crushing the protest movement in 1989 in Beijing despite East Berlin's wholehearted approval. When demonstrations occurred in the GDR, the irritations with the regime's inability to find sensible solutions strengthened the sentiment that the National People's Army was, indeed, an army of the people and not of the party and that therefore "action of the NVA against the people for the purpose of defending the failed policies of the SED, was out of the question."[24] According to Admiral Theodor Hoffmann, the last communist minister of defense in the GDR, this principle of the NVA being responsible to the people rather than the party was to be enshrined in a reform program[25] and presumably in the constitution, but before these reforms could be drafted the collapse of the GDR made the issue irrelevant. By the end of 1989, the NVA was in a state of acute decay, with desertions on the increase and demonstrations, strikes, and mutinies spreading.[26] Military officers, just like party members throughout society, returned their party membership cards.[27] The NVA was simply not willing to prevent the collapse of the socialist order in East Germany and its subsequent incorporation into the Federal Republic of Germany.

THE ECONOMICS OF THE GDR

The GDR's economy was centrally planned and, through COMECON, firmly locked into trading mainly with Eastern Europe, and particularly with the Soviet Union. It was the most successful economy in the Eastern bloc, and according to the *1980 World Bank Atlas*, it surpassed in 1978–79 the per capita income of Britain. Publications, which ignored the World Bank's warning that its statistics for Eastern Europe were "tentative,"[28] spread the good news that East Germany had overtaken the United Kingdom,[29] a truly grotesque distortion of the truth. But many people, particularly in the ranks of the citizen initiative groups, were only too willing to believe in the recuperative strength of the East German economy, which was to serve as the basis of a new socialist order.

But the realities did not bear out such optimism. While economic development had been hampered by such factors as extraordinarily heavy war reparation payments to the Soviet patron state and the drain on manpower by the flight of particularly young and skilled workers to the West, the state had embarked on an investment policy which centered on the greatest possible economic autarky, a principal decision which for a country of the size of the GDR (less than seventeen million people) was bound to be disastrous. The normal features of centrally planned command economies, such as the lack of incentives for greater efforts at the workplace, the inflexibility toward consumer wishes, and the enshrined "right to work" (or, rather, to be on a payroll), enhanced economic problems. By 1988 overstaffing in the agricultural sector had made the prices for cereals 75 percent higher than in high-labor-cost West Germany, and the price for livestock even 160 percent higher. Overstaffing and a declining rate of investment had made industry uncompetitive on the world market; the country's energy supply had become unreliable; and the polluting effects of its mining and chemical industry sectors required nothing less than closing down these industries altogether.[30] Financially, the government had run up substantial budget deficits which were due mainly to the fact that almost 20 percent of the annual budget was spent on subsidizing basic foodstuffs, public transport, and housing.[31] The status of the foreign debt situation was a state secret, known only to three people in the Politburo of which only one, Guenther Mittag, the regime's chief economic planner, comprehended its magnitude and significance. Greater openness in the debate about financial matters occurred only after the whole government including the SED Politburo had resigned, and Hans Modrow, the party secretary of the district of Dresden, had on November 13 been elected as the new prime minister.

Due to the new economic openness of the Modrow administration, the true state of the economy was publicly disclosed. According to Modrow, growth rates and productivity had been falling for years, and goals set in the Five-Year Plans had not been met since the middle of the 1970s. Moreover, the high level of foreign debts was creating problems.[32] This should have come as no surprise to anyone who was willing to look at reality without ideological blinkers. The earlier solemn prediction by the regime that the GDR would overtake West Germany before the turn of the century in terms of prosperity had become a joke which elicited no smiles. According to Mittag, the "collapse of the economy had become a probability in 1981, and was apparent by 1983."[33]

It rapidly became obvious that the existing economic structure would have to undergo radical change. But for people who had never been exposed to the notion of economic efficiency, it was difficult to devise different economic structures. What, for instance, is to be made of a professor of (socialist) economics whose advice for economic reforms includes profound insights such as "a dress only becomes a dress through the act of being worn"?[34] Modrow himself was more pragmatic, asking the West German chancellor, Helmut Kohl, for a grant of DM 15 billion, which he considered justified on the grounds that it was primarily the GDR which had to shoulder the burden of compensating the Soviet Union for war damages.[35] Kohl, indeed, made available substantial amounts of money[36] but linked further aid to fundamental changes in the economy. But Modrow's new economics minister, Christa Luft, formerly the director of the highly prestigious Socialist Institute of Economics, appeared to be either reluctant or incapable of opening up the East German economy to market forces. In early February 1990 she entered the election campaign for a new national parliament with the admission that "our present economic system has turned out to be too inefficient and cannot somehow be improved."[37] The GDR's economic situation was further hampered by the fact that its traditional market, other socialist countries, also experienced economic collapse and, for all practical purposes, had ceased to import East German products.

Despite these facts the SED, renamed the Party of Democratic Socialism (PDS), insisted that although some loose form of unification with West Germany had become inevitable, the GDR brought substantial assets into the marriage[38] and, in any case, economic merger should come about slowly and gradually. The citizen initiative groups which had formed an alliance to contest the elections were even firmer in their rejection of an early economic and political merger, entertaining hopes that the East German economy could somehow be resurrected.[39] They envisaged West German capitalists swamping East Germany, snapping up valuable state enterprises for a song, and robbing East Germans of the opportunity to rebuild their economic future. At the very least, if reunification could not be prevented, they demanded that the right to work, enshrined in the East German constitution, ought to become law in a unified Germany as well, apparently unaware that this right had been a major cause for the decline of the East German economy and was incompatible with a market economy.

When Modrow asked that the elections planned for May 1990 be brought forward to March because he had lost the political as well as the economic capacity to govern, he set the country on a course of rapid unification. When after reunification the East German economy broke down almost completely despite an annual transfer of approximately DM 150 billion from West to East, and unemployment reached horrendous levels, the forces of the Left could argue that rapid economic integration had been an obvious failure. They could say, "We told you so!" and they found plenty of listeners.

CONCLUSION

The East German revolution of 1989 is closely linked to attitudes in the Kremlin, and particularly to Gorbachev's unwillingness to use his formidable garrison to protect the Honecker regime. This is not to say that unrest and protest would have to be categorically ruled out had Moscow exhibited a tougher stance on dissidents in its empire, but the course, and probably the nature, of such protests would almost certainly have produced a different outcome.

The trigger effect of this revolution is usually attributed to the brave decision of a few tiny dissident groups, taken independently of each other, to come out in the open and make public demands. The fact that initially only a handful of people were involved leaves one wondering why the Stasi failed to pick them up and either lock them away or sell them to West Germany. Apparently, the regime and its secret police may have misjudged the potential threat emanating from these groups: after all, the people involved and their political views, which were known to the Stasi, had so far not harmed the regime in any perceptible way. A factor which undoubtedly had an impact was the dissidents' clever timing, just before the fortieth anniversary of the GDR: surely, it would be embarrassing to engage in a political witch hunt while at the very time jubilant columns marched past the regime leaders and their international guests celebrating the achievements of socialism.

In a way, the regime's assessment of the limited importance of these groups was not incorrect provided they were denied mass support. But the regime, unaccustomed to gauging popular sentiment, failed particularly badly on this account. Clearly, the recent mass defection of young and skilled people had affected substantial sections of society, either at home or at the workplace, and the party grossly misjudged popular sentiment when it denounced the refugees as social misfits and congratulated itself on the riddance of such people. That caused fury and provided the dissidents with mass attendance at their protest rallies.

But attendance at demonstrations does not equal total political support. The intellectuals leading the protest movement were soon perceived to have come to praise socialism, not to bury it. Galtung's "fair judgment" that the revolution was somehow "stolen" from them is simply not borne out by facts. For the masses socialism in any form or shape, no matter how purified, had become anathema. In the end, they articulated their own agenda long before West German politicians began formulating a policy; and it was the demands of the masses which the regime had to respond to. Moreover, it was the will of the masses which, in the end, counted at the ballot box.

In regard to marshaling forces to crush the dissident movement, the fixation on the availability or otherwise of Soviet tanks has to be extended to include an investigation into the coercive forces at the disposal of national governments. In the case of the GDR, the inept handling of the masses by regime politicians unaccustomed to wooing the populace clearly affected the security forces which, it is worth remembering, were created to protect not only the state, but also the regime and the party. The Stasi, despite all its ineffectiveness in a time of crisis, stayed loyal to the regime: their interests were inextricably linked to the survival of the political order. The same applies to sections of the People's Police. But those police formations staffed by draftees, as well as the NVA, including its officers, became appalled by the brutality with which the few initial counteractions against demonstrators had been carried out, and were disillusioned with the regime's inability to find acceptable political solutions to the problems at hand. While the sacking of Honecker as well as his successor, Egon Krenz, the resignation of the whole Politburo, the appointment of the "moderate" Hans Modrow as prime minister, and the election of a young, charismatic, and reformist lawyer, Gregor Gysi, as secretary general of a revamped Party of Democratic Socialism were all steps in the right direction, they came too late to arrest the disenchantment of the former dissidents and many of the party faithful alike.

To give Modrow his due, the regime was beyond salvation. The economy was not just in decline; it was in ruins. He was therefore deprived of the means to buy electoral support, and in his efforts to shore up support for a new start had to depend solely on nonmaterial appeals at a moment when socialist ideology had lost all credibility. The result of this impasse was not, as Galtung asserts, chaotic annexation, but annexation—if this really is the correct word—as the only way out of existing chaos.

In the final analysis, the notion at the beginning of this chapter—that communism collapsed because of the failure of its economic system and the increased demands for political freedom—is borne out. But the details of the collapse in the case of East Germany also suggest that once the system was challenged by large numbers of dissidents, there was no way to reform its antiquated structures and policies radically and swiftly enough to save it from destruction. What for a long time had been regarded as a rather monolithic power structure had revealed itself to be a fragile house of cards, with its stewards helplessly incapable of crisis management.

NOTES

1. See, for instance, Kyung-won Kim, "Marx, Schumpeter, and the East Asian Experience," *Journal of Democracy* 3, no. 3 (July 1992): 18.

2. See R. Summy, "Challenging the Emergent Orthodoxy," the introduction to this volume.

3. See U. Sundhaussen, "The Disappearance of the East German State: The Interaction Between Structures, Political Culture, and Policy," *European Studies Journal* (forthcoming).

4. *Guardian Weekly,* October 7, 1990; cited in Johan Galtung, "Europe 1989: The Role of Peace Research and the Peace Movement," Chapter 6, p. 91 in this volume.

5. Ibid.

6. See H. Wendt, "Die deutsch-deutschen Wanderungen—Bilanz einer 40 jaehrigen Geschichte von Flucht und Ausreise," *Deutschland Archiv* 24, no. 4 (1991): 387–89.

7. For an evaluation of Heym and his novel *5 Tage im Juni,* see J. P. Wallmann, "Persoenliches von Stefan Heym," *Deutschland Archiv* 23, no. 10 (October 1990): 1633.

8. The National People's Army (Nationale Volksarmee, or NVA) was created only in 1956.

9. Quoted in G. Rein, *Die Opposition in der DDR* (West Berlin: Wichern, 1989), p. 72.

10. F. Schorlemer, *Traeume und Alptraeume* (Berlin: Verlag der Nation, 1990), pp. 101, 107.

11. See S. Ailisch, "Die Gebetswand in der Leipziger Thomaskirche," in *Leipzig im Oktober,* eds. W. J. Grabner et al. (West Berlin: Wichern, 1990), p. 142.

12. See H. Bahrmann and C. Links, *Wir sind das Volk* (East Berlin and Weimar: Aufbau, 1990), pp. 124, 125, 146; also T. G. Ash, *Ein Jahrhundert wird abgewaehlt* (Munich: Hanser, 1990), 394–95.

13. See *The Times* (London daily), November 14, 1989.

14. In the October elections the Greens had gained 4.09 percent on their own. For a detailed analysis of all four elections, see U. Sundhaussen, "Voting for Reunification: East Germany's Four Elections in 1990," *Australian Journal of Politics and History* 37, no. 2 (1991).

15. See *Der Spiegel* (Hamburg weekly news magazine), March 19, 1990. Normally, Reich is a more reflective political commentator. See, for instance, his *Rueckkehr nach Europa* (Munich: Hanser, 1991).

16. See *Freitag* (East Berlin weekly), August 9, 1991.

17. See chapter by Joanne Wright in this volume, "The End of the Cold War: The Brezhnev Doctrine," pp. 60, 61.

18. Ninety-eight percent of the NVA officer corps were members (or candidates for membership) of the SED. See W. Markus, "Das Offizierskorps der NVA: ein soziales Portraet," in *Die Nationale Volksarmee,* ed. D. Bald (Baden-Baden: Nomos, 1992), p. 55.

19. *New York Times,* October 19 and November 10, 1989; see also M. Wimmer et al., *Wir sind das Volk!* (Munich: Heyne, 1990), p. 62.

20. Interview, televised on ARD TV, October 10, 1991.

21. See K. Held, "Soldat des Volkes? Ueber das politische Selbstverstaendnis des Soldaten der Nationalen Volksarmee," in *Die Nationale Volksarmee,* ed. D. Bald (Baden-Baden: Nomos, 1992), p. 72.

22. See *Der Spiegel,* February 12, 1990. The Mobile Police Force was largely staffed by draftees who were not trained in handling demonstrators, nor were they particularly well indoctrinated for this kind of task.

23. See Held, "Soldat des Volkes?" p. 70.

24. See Markus, "Das Offizierskorps der NVA: ein soziales Portraet," pp. 52, 56; Held, "Soldat des Volkes?" p. 71.

25. See T. Hoffmann, "Zur nicht-vollendenten Militaerreform der DDR," in *Die National-ale Volksarmee*, ed. D. Bald (Baden-Baden: Nomos, 1992), p. 110.

26. Ibid., pp. 108–9; also *Le Monde* appearing in *Guardian Weekly*, December 24, 1989, and *Berliner Zeitung* (East Berlin daily), March 22, 1990.

27. By December 1989 half a million members had resigned from the SED.

28. See D. Childs, *The GDR: Moscow's German Ally,* 2nd ed. (London: Unwin Hyman, 1988), p. 147.

29. For instance, R. Hague and M. Harrop, *Comparative Government and Politics*, 2nd ed. (London: Macmillan, 1987), p. 57.

30. See L. Hoffmann, "Integrating the East German States into the German Economy: Opportunities, Burdens and Options," in *Economic Aspects of German Unification*, ed. J. J. Welfens (Berlin and Heidelberg: Springer, 1992), pp. 60–62.

31. Interview with E. Hoefner, minister of finance, in *Neues Deutschland* (central socialist daily), November 8, 1989.

32. See *Freie Erde* (Neubrandenburg socialist daily), December 11, 1989.

33. *Der Spiegel*, September 9, 1991.

34. *Berliner Zeitung*, November 16, 1989.

35. Modrow claimed that the GDR had paid DM 99.1 billion, while the richer FRG had paid only DM 2.1 billion. See H. Modrow, *Aufbruch und Ende* (Hamburg: Konkret, 1991), p. 98.

36. For the rather complicated details of the aid package, see P. J. Bryson and M. Melzer, *The End of the East German Economy* (New York: St. Martin's Press, 1991), pp. 135–37.

37. *Neues Deutschland*, February 3/4, 1990.

38. Modrow mentions a figure of DM 980 billion of state property alone. See Modrow, *Aufbruch und Ende*, p. 135.

39. See, for instance, J. Becher, "Das Ringen um die Wirtschaftsreform in der DDR," *Deutschland Archiv* 23 (May 5, 1990).

III

ECONOMIC
DETERMINANTS

8

"Upper Volta with Rockets": Internal Versus External Factors in the Decline of the Soviet Union

Dennis Phillips

It is an exaggeration to claim that America's military spending in the 1980s prompted the Soviet counter-measures and economic dislocations that forced the evil empire to surrender.[1]

Gorbachev's desire for a more relaxed Soviet-American relationship seems to have arisen much more from domestic needs than international pressure.[2]

Perestroika emerged from the perception that the greatest threat to the Soviet Union's security was of its own making.[3]

[T]he foreign policy of any government is determined first of all by internal demands.[4]

The end of the Cold War marks the most significant historical divide in the latter half of the twentieth century. Experts agree that the debate over why and how the Cold War ended is of more than mere academic interest. At stake, for the United States at least, is the vindication not only of the nation's entire postwar foreign policy orientation, but also the legitimization of a worldview that defined superpower rivalry as a contest between good and evil.[5]

From at least 1947, when the Truman Doctrine and the Marshall Plan institutionalized "containment," U.S. foreign policy was based on the notion that the world was divided into two halves, one slave and one free. Endemic Soviet aggression could be contained only "by the adroit and vigilant application of counterforce at a series of constantly shifting geographical and political points."[6] The foreign policy orientation of the United States remained remarkably consistent throughout the Cold War. More than thirty years after the Cold War began, former president Richard Nixon wrote that World War III had begun before World War II ended. He defined World War III as "the first truly total war," the long-term struggle between the United States and the Soviet Union for global supremacy—"a struggle of titans, the like of which the world has never seen." Six years after his resignation in the wake of the Watergate scandal, Nixon, now rehabilitated as the "elder statesman" of U.S. foreign policy, wrote:

> It may seem melodramatic to treat the twin poles of human experience represented by the United States and the Soviet Union as the equivalent of Good and Evil, Light and Darkness, God and the Devil; yet if we allow ourselves to think of them that way, even hypothetically, it can clarify our perspective on the world struggle. . . . The United States represents hope, freedom, security, and peace. The Soviet Union stands for fear, tyranny, aggression, and war. If these are not poles of good and evil in human affairs, then the concepts of good and evil have no meaning.[7]

Richard Nixon was neither the first nor the last U.S. president to argue that the United States had to gird its loins for history's most decisive struggle, firm in the belief that "we are on God's side, that our cause is right, that we act for all mankind."[8] The rhetoric of all Cold War U.S. presidents, Republican or Democrat, resounded with the same call to arms. A policy of deterrence, given rhetorical justification by the phrase "peace through strength," linked each administration to the next. It was assumed as self-evident that peace could be protected only if the United States were more heavily armed than the Soviet Union. As Ronald Reagan put it in 1980, "The Soviet Union underlies all the unrest that is going on. If they weren't engaged in this game of dominoes, there wouldn't be any hot spots in the world."[9]

Given the heady mixture of self-righteousness and power that marked U.S. foreign policy during the Cold War, it is not surprising that some people now celebrate the end of superpower rivalry as a vindication of a hardline approach. In particular, they congratulate President Reagan for exorcising the ghost of Vietnam and replacing it "with a new posture of American assertiveness."[10] As members of this "Reagan victory school" see it, their hero was able to restore American pride and win the Cold War through his costly rearmament program, his commitment to the notion of "peace through strength," his eagerness to support counterrevolutionary (Contra) forces, and his determination to consign the "evil empire" to "the ash heap of history." By upping the ante in the Cold War, President Reagan pushed the Soviet Union over the brink and won for the United States and the Free World one of history's sweetest victories. As soon as the Soviet Union collapsed in the early 1990s, the "Reagan victory school" (also known as "triumphalism") sought—what Ralph Summy describes in the introduction to this book—"the status of unassailable orthodoxy" as an explanation for the end of the Cold War.[11]

A moment's reflection, however, reveals numerous problems with triumphalism. In the first instance, the end of the Cold War caught almost everyone, particularly the hardliners, by surprise. In 1986 Zbigniew Brzezinski predicted that U.S.-Soviet rivalry "will long endure."[12] Conservative commentators continued their incessant warnings that the West was not doing enough to counter communism. Hardliners repeatedly predicted a Soviet victory in the Cold War unless the United States spent even more on defense and adopted a more interventionist foreign policy. A year into his first term, Ronald Reagan was astonished to find prominent conservatives openly critical of him for "going soft" on the Soviet Union. In the early 1980s, Reagan's policies on trade with the Soviets, his failure to forcefully support Solidarity, and his reluctance to oppose a natural gas pipeline linking the Soviet Union with Western Europe all incited conservative criticism. In 1982 columnist George Will complained that "a crisis of American conservatism is at hand. This administration evidently loves commerce more than it loathes Communism." Reagan complained that "columnists that I respect . . . are kicking my brains out as if, well, here we are backing away."[13]

Western hardliners were caught by surprise at the end of the Cold War because the collapse of communism and the demise of the Soviet Union had less to do with a U.S. policy of containment than with developments within the Soviet Union itself. As Daniel Deudney and G. John Ikenberry have written, the "Reagan victory school" represents "a remarkably simplistic and self-serving conventional wisdom." While containment forced the Soviet Union to spend on defense a much larger percentage of a much smaller gross national product, "it cannot explain either the end of the Cold War or the direction of Soviet policy responses."[14] Ultimately, it was not military strength and ideological warfare that moved the Cold War toward a rapid conclusion, for these factors had been characteristic of the superpower confrontation for more than forty years. Far more important was the emergence of a new generation of Soviet leaders determined to do something about their nation's deteriorating productivity and economic position. If we were to measure the significance of domestic as opposed to international factors as an explanation for the collapse of Soviet communism, the former are by far the more important. To the extent that international factors played a role, containment was only one—and by no means the most significant—of the forces at work.[15]

The beginning of the end of the Cold War can be identified not in the collapse of the Berlin Wall, or the Eastern European revolutions of 1989, or in any aspect of U.S. foreign policy under Reagan or Bush. Long before these events took place, the Soviet Union had begun to suffer from economic failure and political and social paralysis. In his popular 1987 book on *The Rise and Fall of the Great Powers*, Yale historian Paul Kennedy reminds us that throughout history, imperial power has grown from a firm economic base. In the modern world, the prerequisite for hegemonic success is a balance between commitments and resources. Without a domestic economic base characterized by productivity and technological dynamism, no nation can long sustain great-power status. Writing shortly after Gorbachev came to power, Paul Kennedy noted the decline in the Soviet Union's relative economic standing and the urgent need to address "contradictions" in the Soviet system.[16]

PERESTROIKA

It did not require a British-born, Yale historian to inform the Soviet leadership that their economy was in trouble. Soviet economists and politicians had been concerned for years with the economic, social, and moral stagnation of their country—the "gathering sense of loss of control and direction" that bedeviled the Soviet system.[17]

It is important here to emphasize the deep roots of the reform impulse. The failure of the Soviet economic system, and hence the beginning of the end of the Cold War, was not a product of the 1980s. It can be traced at least to the death of Stalin in 1953. As Ed Hewett, senior fellow at the Brookings Institution, has noted in *Reforming the Soviet Economy*, from the death of Stalin onward "Soviet leaders have never been even close to fully satisfied with the performance of the economic system."[18] The condition of the Soviet economy made the U.S.S.R. look increasingly like "Upper Volta with rockets," as one wag put it.[19] In the twenty years prior to Gorbachev's accession to power, Soviet national income (with the exception of alcohol production) did not increase in real terms at all. The Stalinist model of the economy, whatever purposes it may have served in the past, simply was not appropriate as a strategy for economic growth in a late twentieth-century global marketplace—one that demanded efficiency, productivity, declining relative costs of production, conservation of raw materials, improved quality control, and a build-up of the infrastructure. U.S. foreign policy had very little to do with these economic realities. Soviet economists were more concerned with the fact that over half of the vegetables and fruits produced in the Soviet Union did not reach the consumer due to deficiencies in transport, storage, and administration.[20]

After the death of Stalin, a whole series of attempts were made to address the problems plaguing the Soviet economy (Khrushchev's 1957 *sovnarkhoz* reforms; the Brezhnev-Kosygin 1965 reforms; industrial reorganization in 1973, the 1979 Decree, etc.). By the 1980s the Soviet leadership faced not only a failing economy but a record of reform failure as well. All previous reform efforts shared common faults: an excessively cautious, inflexible, and bureaucratic approach, a commitment to centrally controlled microeconomic reform, misguided definitions of incentive, inadequate attention to efficiency and quality control, and an ideologically determined antipathy to any consideration of the role of market forces.[21]

The situation demanded urgent and radical action. As the economy faltered, so too did the legitimacy of the state. After the death of Stalin an unspoken social contract had emerged between the Soviet people and the Communist party whereby the masses accepted continued authoritarian rule and a one-party state in return for the promise of rising living standards. Soviet specialist David Christian has noted that "declining growth rates and declining legitimacy posed severe threats to the Soviet government." In order to overcome those threats, more sophisticated methods of rule had to be found, along with bold new attempts to reinvigorate the economy.[22]

To initiate such a reform policy, the Soviet Union required a new generation of leaders, better educated and less paranoid than their predecessors. The significance of this "generation shift" in Soviet politics should not be underestimated. Not only did the "Gorbachev generation" mature at a relatively secure time in Soviet history (despite U.S. nuclear weapons, containment, and the Cold War), but the most influential political event in the formative years of this generation was de-Stalinization. University-educated and lacking "the rough peasant style of a Khrushchev or a Brezhnev," the Gorbachev generation were far less paranoid and far more inclined toward radical reform than their aging predecessors.[23]

When Mikhail Gorbachev introduced *ekonomicheskaia perestroika* in 1987, he did not intend to dump socialism or imitate capitalism. *Perestroika* began as an attempt to correct the obvious failure of Stalinist economic planning. This failure was seen as "a correctable defect arising out of the distortions of 'true socialism' imposed during the period of the 'cult of personality.' "[24] As Gorbachev himself explained it in the opening pages of *Perestroika*, the idea was to *renew* the Soviet economic system by breathing new life into socialism.[25] Rather than imitate capitalism, Gorbachev argued that *perestroika* was aimed at creating a "third way," one that would preserve the values of socialism and yet reform the Soviet system so that it was more efficient, more productive, and well placed to benefit from the dynamism of a global market economy. The problem was that it is virtually impossible to restore a structure riddled with rot. Even though radical transformation was the goal, the process of change was further accelerated by the very forces that change unleashed. Furthermore, the links between domestic and international factors in Gorbachev's reforms were complex. As R. Craig Nation wrote in *Black Earth, Red Star*, time had simply run out on the Soviet experiment:

> Ultimately, *perestroika* sought to eliminate the terms of the Soviet security dilemma altogether by bringing the country in from the cold, voiding its claim to embody the future, and facing up to the realities of international society as it is. The terrible burden of representing a cause imbued with revolutionary messianism, either sincerely or as a callous justification for the exercise of power, had defined much of the Soviet experience and cost the Soviet peoples dearly. By the 1980s the pretense to stand for such a cause had become a pathetic farce that strained the state's resources beyond measure and undermined popular morale by encouraging a pervasive cynicism.[26]

"NEW THINKING"

In order to achieve the domestic economic breakthroughs he required, Gorbachev needed a new and more benign global political environment. He realized that neither the Soviet Union nor the United States could afford the costs of the Cold War. His appeal for "new thinking" in international affairs was not a retreat imposed upon him by Reagan's rearmament program. Rather, it was designed to provide the intellectual framework in which both a domestic and a foreign reform agenda could succeed. The phrase "new thinking" originated not with Gorbachev, but with Bertrand Russell and Albert Einstein, who used it when launching the Pugwash peace movement in 1954. Further evidence of the pre-Gorbachev roots of radical reform in the U.S.S.R. can be found in the fact that the term was also used by foreign policy specialists Anatoli Gromyko and Vladimir Lomeiko in 1984 "at a low point of the 'new Cold War.' "[27]

As the words suggest, Gorbachev called for a profound shift in the conceptual basis of how nations interact with each other. He argued that the familiar confrontational model of world politics that had existed for centuries—the zero-sum approach that had characterized the policies of *both* superpowers throughout the Cold War—had to be replaced by a radical new concept of interdependence based on mutual efforts to solve global political, economic, social, and environmental problems. Because the very essence of international politics had changed, cooperative effort and genuinely *mutual* security had become prerequisites for survival. Gorbachev first articulated these revolutionary ideas to the French parliament on October 3, 1985, during his initial trip abroad. Since he had only come to power a few months earlier, it cannot be argued credibly that he was using the occasion of his first trip outside the Soviet Union to end the Cold War by "surrendering" to Reagan and the West.[28]

If taken seriously, Gorbachev's proposal represented a quantum leap in the way most people (East or West) perceive international relations. For the Soviet people it meant transcending the Marxist-Leninist doctrine of class conflict and capitalist perfidy in favor of the urgent need for cooperative effort and common goals. For the West, it constituted an appeal to abandon the Cold War mentality and the "inherent bad faith" model whereby every conciliatory gesture on the part of the Soviet Union was interpreted as an exercise in deception. Western conservatives dismissed the Gorbachev appeal as a rhetorical flourish, a "charm offensive," while liberals reeled in astonishment that the Cold War might end, not in a nuclear holocaust, but in a more tranquil and less dangerous world. So stunning was the proposal that neither Reagan nor Bush knew quite what to do about Gorbachev. Indeed, during the late 1980s, it was not uncommon for the Bush administration to be praised for having the wisdom to do *nothing*.[29]

THE SOVIET EMPIRE IN EASTERN EUROPE

Perestroika and "new thinking" within the U.S.S.R. paved the way for dramatic change in the Soviet Union's external empire. As part of his reorientation of Soviet foreign policy, Gorbachev signaled that he intended to abandon the use of the Red Army to shore up corrupt communist regimes in Eastern Europe. According to one observer, Gorbachev replaced the Brezhnev Doctrine with a "Sinatra Doctrine" (I did it my way) that left already unpopular satellite governments to their own devices. In 1989 those governments collapsed in quick succession. Following years of protest by Solidarity, elections in Poland led to the appointment of a noncommunist prime minister. In October 1989 antigovernment demonstrations broke out in East Berlin and the East German leader, Erich Honecker, resigned. On the night of November 9–10, wildly enthusiastic demonstrators began to dismantle the Berlin Wall. Communist governments fell in Czechoslovakia, Bulgaria, and Romania. By January 1990 every pro-Soviet regime in Eastern Europe had disappeared.[30]

Conservative commentators in the West were quick to argue that the Soviet Union abandoned its Eastern European satellite states because it had "lost" the Cold War. Their thesis was that Gorbachev was forced to forsake the Soviet empire in Europe because the costs of maintaining it were too great. Containment had triumphed. Just as George F. Kennan had predicted in 1947, the adroit and vigilant application of counterforce had turned the Soviet empire in on itself and produced the revolutions of 1989.

The basic problem with this view is that it puts primary responsibility for the dramatic events of 1989 in the wrong place. As R. Craig Nation, Valerie Bunce, and others have pointed out, far from being surprised by what happened in Eastern Europe in 1989, Moscow "actively encouraged" change. In reformulating Soviet policy toward Europe, Gorbachev was not primarily concerned about containment, Ronald Reagan, or pressure from the West. Nor did he back away from the Brezhnev Doctrine because he felt economically squeezed by the United States. Gorbachev's motives were not reactive but proactive and there were three main reasons for this. First, a territorial buffer against the West obviously meant less to the Soviet Union in the 1980s than it had in the 1940s. Second, "Gorbachev's domestic program . . . was becoming incompatible with the continued existence of dependent satellite regimes embodying the very system that the Soviet Union was seeking to discard." Third, the existence of a Cold War "bloc system" was seen as an impediment to Soviet cooperation with a new and more unified Europe. Furthermore, Gorbachev was fully aware that the demise of a Soviet empire in Eastern Europe would provide not only an opportunity for enhanced Soviet access to the economic vitality of a new, unified Europe, but also an inevitably reduced role for the United States in that important part of the world.[31] With these facts in mind, Daniel Deudney and G. John Ikenberry argue that the Cold War ended "despite the assertiveness of Western hardliners, rather than because of it."[32]

ARMS CONTROL

Proponents of the "Reagan victory school" have seized upon Gorbachev's arms control initiatives in an attempt to prove that the Soviets were forced, by virtue of Reagan's rearmament program, to scale down their military expenditures in order to save their domestic economy. Conservative analysts—who never had much time for arms control in any event—interpreted Soviet willingness to negotiate substantive military reductions as unmistakable evidence of the success of containment. At the height of the Cold War, writers like Colin Gray viewed arms control as either "an irrelevance" or a process potentially damaging to U.S. security.[33] When the Soviets began making substantial concessions in order to move from "managerial" to "visionary" arms control, what the conservative commentators had called an irrelevance was now cited as a victory for the West.

With arms control, as in all the other areas we are discussing here, the truth is considerably more complex. Ironically, the simplistic "Reagan victory school" undervalues both Reagan and Gorbachev. Despite his administration's massive arms expenditure and his reputation for hardline rhetoric, Reagan was deeply ambivalent about nuclear weapons. Like his predecessors in the Oval Office, he realized that, short of global suicide, nuclear weapons were militarily useless. He longed to get rid of them without making America, and himself, appear weak. The Strategic Defense Initiative (SDI), his Star Wars dream for rendering nuclear weapons "obsolete," was a naive attempt to conjure up a way of delegitimizing nuclear weapons from a position of strength.[34]

Taken at another level, Reagan's tenure as president is marked by what appears to be a baffling change of policy toward the Soviet Union and arms control. In 1983 Reagan called the U.S.S.R. the "evil empire." Some years earlier he had proclaimed that the main achievement of detente had been the right to sell Pepsi in Siberia. In the early 1980s Reagan oscillated wildly between predictions of Soviet decline and declarations of U.S. nuclear inferiority. He certainly used anti-Soviet rhetoric as a way of neutralizing domestic opponents of accommodation. But by the beginning of Reagan's second term, writers like A. L. Horelick and E. L. Warner III were able to identify an administration divided between hardliners or "squeezers" (Weinberger, Perle, etc.), and accommodationists, or "dealers" (such as Secretary of State George Schultz, who had gone from "nuclear neophyte" to one prepared to "engage in hand-to-hand combat" on relations with the Soviet Union). With the departure in 1987 of the assistant secretary for international security affairs, Richard Perle, the "dealers" gained the upper hand.[35]

Reagan's hardline approach was far from being responsible for a major breakthrough in arms control; rather, the president's rhetoric had come in for increasing criticism at home. His off-the-cuff gaffes, such as the one about beginning the bombing of the Soviet Union in five minutes, sent a chill through the public. Throughout the early 1980s the peace movement grew rapidly, partly in response to Reagan's bellicose rhetoric and partly out of a conviction that better ways than the Cold War had to be found to conduct great-power relations. The peace movement represented more than the hopes of an idealistic minority. By the late 1980s John Gaddis described a U.S. Congress which had become "curiously impervious to the logic of trying to exhaust the Russians by tripling our own national debt."[36] Far from Reagan forcing the Soviets to the disarmament bargaining table, there was ample personal and domestic pressure put on him to moderate his line on the U.S.S.R. and get serious about arms control.

The decisive initiative came not from Reagan but from Gorbachev. At the Reykjavik summit in October 1986 Reagan and the Soviet premier came close to agreeing on a plan for global denuclearization. Even though SDI proved a stumbling block at Reykjavik, Gorbachev came away from the summit convinced that further bold arms control initiatives on his part would be reciprocated rather than exploited. This paved the way for the successful conclusion of the INF Treaty in 1987 and, eventually, the U.S.-Soviet Treaty on the Reduction and Limitation of Strategic Offensive Arms (START I) signed in July 1991. As Walter Stutzle noted in 1988, Gorbachev more than anyone else deserves the credit for turning "the originally anti-Soviet and anti-arms control policy of President Reagan and the US-Soviet arms control impasse into a productive co-operative arms control approach."[37]

Even when Gorbachev himself was overtaken by the momentum of events he initiated, Boris Yeltsin and others accelerated the pace of arms control negotiations. If fully implemented, the START treaties and all the other arms control initiatives undertaken in the last four years will constitute a reduction in the bilateral balance of terror never dreamed of when Ronald Reagan came to power in 1981.

In his summary comments on the symposium that produced this book, Michael Salla notes that no event as complex and significant as the end of the Cold War is achieved through the efforts of one person or a single set of policies. Indeed, Salla suggests seven interpretive frameworks that may be offered for explaining the end of the Cold War.[38] It is historically inaccurate, therefore, to argue that Ronald Reagan or the American policy of containment was solely responsible for bringing the Cold War to an end. If China was not America's to "lose" in 1949, the Soviet Union was not America's to "win" in 1989. In their contributions to this volume, Kevin Clements, Keith Suter, and others discuss some of the many factors which contributed to the end of the Cold War. Writing in the *Washington Quarterly* in 1992, Robert E. Hunter summarized it this way:

> The fall of the Berlin Wall symbolized the coming together of several trends in historical development: the playing out, at long last, of the end-game in Europe from World War II; the amelioration of irrational fears of one another on the part of the two superpowers, plus their mutual recognition that neither had anything to gain from continued conflict; the widespread perception of the success of Western market systems in comparison with centrally planned economies; the penetration of closed societies by modern means of communication; and the

human rights.

propagation and popularity of ideas fundamental to human dignity and self-realization.[39]

THE UNITED STATES AND RUSSIA'S FUTURE

An essay on the end of the Cold War should not itself end without some comment on U.S. policy and Russia's future. The breakup of the Soviet Union and the widespread belief that the United States and the West "won" the Cold War have contributed to a popular image of contemporary U.S.-Russian relations which is based on a number of questionable assumptions. According to Stephen F. Cohen, director of Russian studies at Princeton University, those assumptions include the following:

- that the events of 1991 constituted a "new Russian Revolution" that destroyed most of the obstacles to fundamental reform

- that fundamental reform in Russia necessarily means the creation of a democratic and capitalist system based on the U.S. model

- that success in this reform effort depends largely on Boris Yeltsin supported by Western financial aid

- that by teaching the Russians how to do it right, the United States will transform the postcommunist Commonwealth of Independent States (CIS) into a friend and a partner so that a "new world order" under U.S./U.N. leadership will be possible[40]

Cohen contends that, as a by-product of the Reagan victory interpretation of the end of the Cold War, this popular image of contemporary U.S.-Russian relations is simplistic, inadequate, and potentially dangerous. Policies based on such an image reflect American conceit more than Russian reality. Cohen argues that recent change in Russia should not blind us to what remains the same: "Crucial aspects of the Soviet system still exist today, particularly those responsible for people's essential needs—housing, employment, basic supplies, health care, welfare and public order." Furthermore, the United States lacks "the right, wisdom and power to convert Russia to America's way of life."[41]

Cohen goes on to note that if the study of twentieth-century U.S. foreign policy teaches us anything at all, it teaches us that intrusive, missionary-minded U.S. policies are often self-defeating: "Excessive intervention by US agencies will always be counterproductive, inspiring more resentment against America, undermining domestic and foreign policies we favor and further strengthening enemies of those policies." The United States has a role to play in Russia's immediate future, and Russia will certainly borrow from the West, but Russia will devise its own economic and political future "within its own historical experiences" and in the midst of complex domestic circumstances which are still only dimly understood in the West.[42]

Cohen outlines some of the more significant aspects of the bilateral relationship that demand prompt and effective attention from the U.S. government and the West. The first involves generous and well-directed aid. The sum of $3 to $6 billion annually for direct aid to Russia would constitute barely 1 to 2 percent of current U.S. defense spending and it would be "the cheapest investment America could make in real national security."[43] Other items on Cohen's list include the following:

- prompt ratification of SALT II by all parties

- U.S. acceptance of the Russian offer for a permanent ban on nuclear testing

- concerted efforts to locate all ex-Soviet tactical nuclear weapons and negotiation of major reductions in both CIS and U.S. arsenals of these weapons

- proper funding for modernizing and safeguarding Soviet-built nuclear reactors

- massive humanitarian support, especially in the form of food and medicines to those Russians imperiled by economic change, that is, the very young, old, and sick

- prompt restructuring of Russia's $84 billion foreign debt, perhaps even to the point of forgiving interest payment and a large portion of the principal

- creation of an effective program to convert military plants in excess of Russia's need to civilian production

- start-up loans to small private enterprises in Russia

- a program to subsidize unemployment benefits for Russians left jobless by economic restructuring

- the administration of programs such as those just mentioned "by Russian agencies staffed by Russians using rubles, not by Americans using dollars"

- increased, well-conceived U.S. private investment in Russia supported, where Russian law is inadequate, by U.S. government guarantees

- encouragement for U.S. private industry to put its money where its mouth has been throughout the Cold War, and financial support given by private foundations "to the universities and other education centers that were the crucible of Soviet Russia's middle classes and now are nearly destitute."[44]

For seventy years the United States demanded that the Soviet Union give up its "evil" system. America and the West spent trillions of dollars during the Cold War to "defend" themselves against a Soviet "threat" that was said to be global and pervasive. Conservative commentators constantly complained that the West was losing the Cold War due to inadequate defense spending and a failure of nerve.

Now that the Soviet Union no longer exists, the question presents itself whether the West has the wisdom to manage peace as enthusiastically as it managed the Cold War. Soviet experts like Stephen Cohen remind us that Russia will eventually emerge from its present time of troubles. It may reappear governed by some form of parliamentary democracy, or it could descend into chaos or return to its old, totalitarian traditions.[45] At this critical point, will history show that the West generously assisted Russia to make that gigantic leap into a new era of stability, prosperity, and cooperative effort, or will it show that policies guided by selfishness and neglect doomed our children to live through another period of global hostility and great-power confrontation?

NOTES

1. J. Garry Clifford, "History and the End of the Cold War: A Whole New Ball Game?" *Organization of American Historians: Magazine of History* 7, no. 2 (Fall 1992): 26.

2. Phil Williams, "US-Soviet Relations: Beyond the Cold War?" *International Affairs* 65 (spring 1989): 279.

3. R. Craig Nation, *Black Earth, Red Star: A History of Soviet Security Policy, 1917–1991* (Ithaca, NY: Cornell University Press, 1992), p. 321.

4. Mikhail Gorbachev, *Perestroika: New Thinking for Our Country and the World* (London: Collins, 1987).

5. Daniel Deudney and G. John Ikenberry, "Who Won the Cold War?" *Foreign Policy* 87 (summer 1992): 123.

6. George F. Kennan, "The Sources of Soviet Conduct," *Foreign Affairs* 25 (July 1947): 566–82. See also Walter LaFeber, *America, Russia and the Cold War, 1945–1992,* 7th ed. (New York: McGraw-Hill, 1993), especially Chapters 3 and 4.

7. Richard Nixon, *The Real War* (New York: Warner, 1980), pp. 314–15.

8. Ibid., p. 314.

9. Quoted in Robert Dallek, *Ronald Reagan: The Politics of Symbolism* (Cambridge, MA: Harvard University Press, 1984), p. 141. In view of the many "hot spots" which have emerged

around the world since the collapse of the Soviet Union, this must stand, even by Reagan standards, as one of the most ill-informed presidential comments of recent times.

10. Daniel Yankelovich and Larry Kaagan, "Assertive America," *Foreign Affairs: America and the World 1980* 59, no. 3 (1981): 696.

11. See Ralph Summy, "Challenging the Emergent Orthodoxy," the introduction to this volume, pp. 4–6. Summy identifies former president George Bush, former secretary of state Zbigniew Brzezinski, ex-Pentagon officials Caspar Weinberger and Richard Perle, columnist George Will, Republican senator Richard Lugar, and neoconservative intellectual Irving Kristol as leading proponents of triumphalism. See also George P. Shultz, *Turmoil and Triumph: My Years as Secretary of State* (New York: Charles Scribner's Sons, 1993), pp. 1130–38. Colin S. Gray warns against euphoria over "the apparent Western victory in the Cold War," but he goes on to quote approvingly D. W. Brogan's 1944 description of the American way in war: "For Americans . . . the battle is *always* the pay-off. . . . Victory is the aim, and the elegance of the means is a European irrelevance. . . . To Americans, war is not the sport of kings but the most serious national and personal concern which they like to fight in their own way and which, when they do fight it in their own way, they win." See Colin S. Gray, *War, Peace, and Victory: Strategy and Statecraft for the Next Century* (New York: Simon and Schuster, 1990), pp. 9, 356.

12. Quoted in Deudney and Ikenberry, "Who Won the Cold War?" p. 124.

13. Quoted in Laurence I. Barrett, *Gambling with History: Ronald Reagan in the White House* (New York: Penguin, 1984), p. 299. On the eve of Soviet collapse, Edward Luttwak wrote, "The West has become comfortably habituated to defeat. Victory is viewed with great suspicion, if not outright hostility." Luttwak feared, above all, "the counsel of impotence" that would leave the West with two possible policy choices, "appeasement or outright retreat." Edward Luttwak, *On the Meaning of Victory: Essays on Strategy* (New York: Simon and Schuster, 1986), pp. 289, 293.

14. Deudney and Ikenberry, "Who Won the Cold War?" p. 131.

15. Ibid., pp. 123, 131, 137–38. See also Richard E. Ericson, "Soviet Economic Reforms: The Motivation and Content of *Perestroika*," *Journal of International Affairs* 42 (spring 1989): 330.

16. Paul Kennedy, *The Rise and Fall of the Great Powers: Economic Change and Military Conflict from 1500 to 2000* (New York: Random House, 1987), pp. 430–31, 488–98.

17. Ericson, "Soviet Economic Reforms," p. 318.

18. Ed A. Hewett, *Reforming the Soviet Economy: Equality Versus Efficiency* (Washington, DC: Brookings Institution, 1988), p. 221.

19. Quoted in Clifford, "History and the End of the Cold War," p. 26.

20. Seweryn Bialer, "Domestic and International Factors in the Formation of Gorbachev's Reforms," *Journal of International Affairs* 42 (spring 1989): 285–86.

21. Ibid. See also Hewett, *Reforming the Soviet Economy*, Chapter 5, especially pp. 255–56.

22. David Christian, " 'Perestroika' and the End of the Soviet Experiment, 1982–1991," *Teaching History* 27, no. 1 (March 1993): 4. I would like to thank Dr. David Christian for his helpful advice during the preparation of this article.

23. David Christian, "Mikhail Gorbachev and the End of the Stalin Generation," *Teaching History* 20, no. 2 (July 1986): 3–11.

24. Ericson, "Soviet Economic Reforms," p. 317.

25. Gorbachev, *Perestroika*, pp. 17–59.

26. Nation, *Black Earth, Red Star*, p. 326. See also Bialer, "Domestic and International Factors in the Formation of Gorbachev's Reforms," pp. 283–91.

27. Nation, *Black Earth, Red Star*, p. 288.

28. Bruce Parrott, "Soviet National Security under Gorbachev," *Problems of Communism* 6 (November-December 1988): 1–36.

29. Michael Mandelbaum, "The Bush Foreign Policy," *Foreign Affairs* 70, no. 1 (1991): 5–22.

30. Christian, " 'Perestrioka' and the End of the Soviet Experiment, 1982–1991," p. 15.

31. Nation, *Black Earth, Red Star*, pp. 306–10. See also Valerie Bunce, "The Empire Strikes Back: The Evolution of the Eastern Bloc from a Soviet Asset to a Soviet Liability," *International Organization* 39 (winter 1985): 1–46.

32. Deudney and Ikenberry, "Who Won the Cold War?" p. 132. See also Joanne Wright's chapter on the Brezhnev Doctrine in this book.

33. Gray, *War, Peace, and Victory*, p. 230.

34. Deudney and Ikenberry, "Who Won the Cold War?" pp. 126–27, 130.

35. A. L. Horelick and E. L. Warner III, "US-Soviet Nuclear Arms Control: The Next Phase," in *US-Soviet Relations: The Next Phase*, ed. A. L. Horelick (Ithaca, NY: Cornell University Press, 1986), pp. 225–56; Barrett, *Gambling with History*, pp. 321–22, 369. See also William G. Hyland, *The Cold War Is Over* (New York: Random House, 1990). Summy discusses aspects of Hyland's thesis in the introduction to this volume, p. 4.

36. Quoted in Phil Williams, "US-Soviet Relations: Beyond the Cold War?" pp. 278–79.

37. Walter Stutzle, "1987—The Turning-Point?" in *SIPRI Yearbook 1988: World Armaments and Disarmament* (Oxford: Oxford University Press, 1988), pp. 3–6.

38. See Michael Salla's conclusion to this volume, especially his table of interpretive frameworks, p. 257.

39. Robert E. Hunter, "Starting at Zero: U.S. Foreign Policy for the 1990s," *Washington Quarterly* 15, no. 1 (winter 1992): 42.

40. Stephen F. Cohen, "American Policy and Russia's Future," *The Nation* 256, no. 14 (April 12, 1993): 476–85.

41. Ibid., pp. 478, 481.

42. Ibid.

43. Ibid.

44. Ibid., pp. 482–85.

45. The emergence of Russian ultranationalist leader Vladimir Zhirinovsky indicates both the wisdom in Stephen F. Cohen's warnings and the worrisome prospect that the West's "window of opportunity" for constructive assistance to the CIS may be closing.

9

Marxism, Capitalism, and Democracy: Some Post-Soviet Dilemmas

Geoff Dow

This chapter presumes that the end of the Cold War and the disintegration of the Soviet economy are two aspects of the same phenomenon. It is this phenomenon that has been underwritten by a complicit intellectual failure which itself helped to define both the Cold War and its subsequent dissipation: the absence of a systematic differentiation between the economic problems of development and the economic problems of socialism. In the former Soviet system, many apparent problems derived from low levels of material development; only part of these ought to be attributed to the attempt to create a distinctively socialist route to affluence.

The Cold War came into being because an experiment in "socialism before capitalism" was attempted. Its most alarming manifestation, the possibility of real war, concluded because that experiment has been abandoned. But another of its manifestations, intellectual impoverishment, lingers. Perhaps controversially, this chapter suggests that Western intellectuals with a commitment, however vague and nondoctrinaire, to socialist or antiliberal principles are culpable insofar as less analytical energy has been devoted to the task of anticipating and specifying the difficulties of a nonmarket and nonrepressive mode of economic development than has been marshaled in the cause of undermining it. Just as the Cold War smothered Keynesian and social democratic attempts to impose political criteria on economic development in the West, thus keeping levels of economic development lower than they might have been in capitalist economies, so too has it ensured political and economic failure in the East. The politics of the Left has not been well served by its theorists or politicians.

The core concern of this chapter, then, is that an antiliberal or postliberal political economy has been insufficiently developed.[1] This key part of the Cold War phenomenon has been too little specified, analyzed, or explained— though there was a putative recognition during and just after World War II of humans' potential to produce ignoble, squalid, misanthropic, dishearten- ing, and unprincipled responses to problems. In the absence of an ongoing investigation of those aspects of the Cold War milieu which resulted in the suppression of living standards in both East and West, are we really entitled to declare that it is over?

What the Cold War involved was a sustained abrogation of the possibilities of politics. The gap between potential and actual living standards has been larger than it needed to be, not just because of the diversion of productive activity to military deployments, but because the entire world has not developed political or institutional mechanisms capable of utilizing all its resources. Generally high standards of living or security cannot even be guaranteed in the rich capitalist countries. The economies of the West have been poorer and more inegalitarian than they should have been ever since 1945, partly as a result of hysterical political objections, and partly because an intellectual task has remained largely uncommenced.

The Cold War ended because of the economic burden its continuation had imposed on the Soviet economy. The Gorbachev era signaled, more than anything else, an overdue realization that the burden was unsustainable. The subsequent commitment by the regime to dismantle the distortions implied by its long-term involvement in the arms race led inexorably to the events of 1989 and to the breakup of the Soviet Union. The Soviet experiment probably should not have been attempted; but neither should we forget that the Western response to the experiment was more tawdry and unnecessary than the experiment itself. Until the West recognizes that contemporary liberal politics has been just as debilitating as the arms race, we will continue to live with the legacy of the Cold War.[2]

Underlying the structural incapacity of the Soviet economy to "keep up" with other economies' unproductive expenditures has been a serious, scarcely specified, intellectual failing. This is constituted by (1) the historical unwill- ingness of Marxism to provide a conceptual model of a noncapitalist, nonmarket, but developed, economy; (2) an underdeveloped understanding of the nature (and capacities) of the Soviet economy; (3) the persistence of "planning without theory"; and (4) a reluctance in Marxist social science (especially since the late 1940s) to acknowledge the interrelatedness of capital accumulation and nation building, even in the West. In turn, these concep- tual weaknesses or abrogations have bequeathed to us some distinctively new problems: first, the specificity of Marxism has been diluted, and its analyses and pretensions discredited, even though it has much to say, potentially, about the possibilities of politics in capitalist economies; and second, the post-Soviet responses to systemic breakdown, within Russia, owe too much to outside organizations' conceptions of the value of "shock therapy" and austerity, and too little to auditing the actual infrastructural needs (which implies the need for a clearer appreciation of the extent of Russia's infrastructural inheritance).

The ongoing "infantile disorder" in capitalist polities—an underdevelopment of contemporary politics—remains. The intellectual dimensions of political abrogation continue to cause major damage to social, political, and economic development—in the countries that have retained the liberal route to development as well as in those that attempted to bypass it.

MARXISM AS POLITICAL ECONOMY

Marxian political economy, like its classical precursor, was conceived as a coherent discipline committed to understanding the dynamic development of *capitalist* economies. Not even tangentially can Marx's mature work be a guide to the construction or operation of a socialist economy. The principles of historical materialism suggest, remarkably strongly, that any attempt to create socialism voluntaristically before the forces of production "have matured within the framework of the old society"—that is, before there is a level of general affluence sufficient to sustain the distributive pretensions and citizenship entitlements of socialism—would most likely result in precisely the repression that in fact occurred.[3]

There are four aspects of Marx's concept of capital that framed the whole of *Capital* and that remain pertinent. First, Marx provided a "critique of political economy" whose purpose was to extend the contributions of Smith and Ricardo to understanding the progressive nature of capitalist economic activity. The socialist element in Marxian political economy derives from the insistence that however productive and progressive capitalism has been, it cannot last forever. Second, Marx argued that the defining features of a capitalist economy (the "social relations" of capitalist production[4]—which needed to be imposed on societies unwilling to accept them) would *initially facilitate but later impede* the development of the forces of production (societal wealth and productive potential). This is what gives rise to tension between market modes of economic regulation and more explicitly political controls, with an expected transition from the former to the latter. Though this tension is anticipated in the political economy of Marx, it has been less apparent and its implications almost wholly undeveloped in later Marxian political economy. That there is a possibility of "socialist" politics (in liberal capitalist contexts) emerges from this circumstance. Third, political dimensions of notionally depoliticized market activity resurface as a result of recurrent crises in capitalist economic development. Politics is implicated in attempts either to preserve or to transcend the defining social relations, as tendencies toward crisis are either allowed to run their course or countered by explicit retaliatory maneuvers. That the crisis tendencies need not play themselves out to fruition was explicitly acknowledged by Marx, but subsequent generations of Marxists have been reluctant to expend energy delineating progressive from reactionary countertendencies. Fourth, as successive crises are countered, by capital directly or by the state acting on its behalf, or by the state acting at the instigation of socialist movements—through policies and institutions with a market-displacing charter—"an epoch of social revolution" might begin.

The elements of crisis which Marx highlighted do not contribute to a theory of apocalyptic transformation from capitalism to some succeeding mode of production. Transformation is a result of recurrent interventions to usurp market mechanisms, in the interests of renewed accumulation; for this reason, socialist politics can claim not only a strategic opportunity but legitimacy and success. Marx, of course, offered no prescription for how, or how quickly, these political and economic changes would transpire. There is no theory of postliberal politics in Marx; but the logic of the argument indicates that such tensions would be ongoing, intensifying as capitalist economies matured, presumably defining much of the political and economic turmoil that he expected to continue.[5]

The important point to emerge from these rehearsals of Marxian political economy is that there is no reasonable conception of socialism that does not depict it as the (contingent) outgrowth of capitalist success. Socialist politics within capitalism consists of the attempt to politicize the accumulation process to ensure that it continues. Only after capitalist development has created the infrastructure on the basis of which antiliberal (or postliberal) distributive principles can be enunciated and effected does it make sense to contemplate the erosion of markets and the development of those citizenship entitlements that it has been the "historic mission" of labor, through the state, to assert. As a mode of production, socialism is not something that can be constructed through will, from a low base of prior development, before capitalism has done the dirty work.

In Marx's work, the essential outcome of capitalist development and crisis is transformation, after centuries rather than decades, of the essentially capitalist nature of the system into one reasonably classifiable as "postcapital-ist."[6] It is a revolutionary transformation in the sense that tendencies generated from within the market dynamic produce something antithetical to market capitalism. But the transition can be expected to occur only insofar as the political and institutional structure facilitates progressive responses to systemic decay. It is always possible that political responses reaffirm or reinforce conditions that give rise to crisis in the first place. This is what has characterized much of the neoliberal response to recession, in the advanced capitalist countries, in the past twenty years. Politics can be a force for the consolidation or the transcendence of past practices: a facilitator of or impediment to social improvement. New institutional structures of economic management are necessary, and they are a part of the socialist project; but their purpose is to compensate for the recurrent failure of market capitalism to maintain high levels of activity, not to engineer those high levels of activity and affluence from scratch.

Leninist attempts to create socialism differently were doomed to proceed only by dint of long-term, large-scale, repressive efforts to replicate capitalist accumulation. There is no easy or painless route to capital accumulation or to the development of the forces of production because exploitation is ineradicable. Whatever the Soviet system's accomplishments in terms of the decommodification of labor, health, education, and housing, the distortions, failures, sufferings, and problems of "actually existing socialism" were probably inevitable—producing, as the critics have long insisted, grotesque caricatures of the original intentions.[7]

MARXISM AS POLITICS

None of this constitutes a new or unfamiliar conclusion, having been prefigured in Bolshevik-Menshevik debates and the (unresolved) Bernstein-Kautsky debates and elsewhere over revolutionary socialism and the revolutionary theory of Marx. Nonetheless, many contemporary contributors to the general discussion of what went wrong (with the Soviet experiment, or with socialism, or with Marxism) have produced such weird and nihilistic conclusions that some systematic reconsideration is now necessary. Göran Therborn, for example, has recently objected to the view that "the epochal turn of 1989" was "the final extinction of a non-viable social species."[8] Conceding that successful industrialization cannot justify the attendant brutality, his argument is that the communist era cannot be depicted in terms of repression alone. Therborn sees the collapse as "conjunctural" rather than "structural," contingent upon the appearance of new problems, "beyond the scope of industrial modernity."[9] On the other hand, it has been suggested that "the prevailing crisis of confidence in the possibility of socialism is . . . due to the absence of any convincing theoretical model of how a socialist society, and in particular a socialist economy, might be organized."[10]

While noting the Marxian proposition that "genuine socialism could be built only on the basis already laid by capitalism," Robin Blackburn has been even more defensive, ascribing the failure to *Marx's* reticence in not sketching out "exactly how the socialist economy would function"![11] He resuscitates the socialist idea by arguing that leftist sentiment underwrote "the fruits of 1945, in the form of more democratic rights and more generous social provision."[12] He notes: "We should not forget that the Cold War policies of the West . . . were successfully designed to cut the Soviet Union off from Western technology and also forced Soviet planners to waste huge resources on military expenditures."[13] Blackburn acknowledges Maurice Dobb's claim that one of the virtues of a nonmarket economy was its ability to "command" the production of large-scale projects which would not be sanctioned under market modes of regulation.[14] This reflects the preoccupation of the 1940s with discussion of the relative merits of socialist and capitalist calculation *tout court*. However, the actual issues at stake then concerned the economic underdevelopment of socialism alongside a well-developed capitalism. The debate that was needed then, and it still is, concerns the appropriate stage (of development or of crisis) at which to shift the balance from market forms of calculation to political, commanded or negotiated, forms of calculation.

Blackburn argues plausibly that "socialism postulates the necessity of developing forms of social life that will allow for conscious human control of economic processes, with the aim of banishing want, furnishing every individual with the material means for self realization, preventing class divisions and ensuring a sustainable relationship with the natural environment. What is implied is not a single mind but institutions that will encourage a meeting of minds."[15] He errs, though, in not recognizing that this is an unreasonable demand until societies' productive capacities are sufficiently well developed to allow it. Maurice Dobb was courageous enough to admit that a real trade-off between authoritarian planning and consumer preferences was inevitable during the process of socialist development (as it is in capitalist development); a commensurate trade-off exists still between security and freedom. Blackburn is among those who even now want to believe that choosing authoritarian planning and security represented a mistake by the socialists.

Marxism has always seen capitalist societies as *inherently* undemocratic because they give voice to possessors of money and property rather than to people as citizens in making economic decisions. Their existence also removes from the public realm discussion and debate over the general course and specifics of social and economic development, which are then determined unintentionally as the outcome of a myriad of privatized calculations by economic actors who have vastly unequal access to economic resources and who are motivated by incentives that may affect macrolevel outcomes detrimentally.

Much of the Cold War's legitimacy derived from the West's ability to represent the absence of political democracy as the absence of democracy per se. Marxism and the Soviet experiment are still frequently portrayed as the antitheses of democracy. But of course the critics of liberal democracy always argued that the integrity of political democracy was somewhat compromised by the ubiquitous economic inequality which accompanied it. To the advocates of meaningful democracy (social, industrial, and economic conditions as the basis of citizenship entitlement rather than capacity to pay for things), the bypassing of electoral democracy always seemed minor. Though this judgment was probably wrong, the theme recurs from pre-Marxist critics of the French revolution to C. B. Macpherson and beyond. While it is no longer reasonable to argue that the elements of social and economic democracy that existed in the Soviet Union compensated for the absence of democratic elections, it should be mentioned more often that much of the West's insistence is hypocritical. And the transition to a market economy will exacerbate rather than relieve the undemocratic nature of these societies, by definition, because many of the entitlements that have been forged—regarding employment, housing, education, health, and security—are now being lost. The dominant liberal anti-interventionism that lubricated Cold War ideology in the West prevented these social democratic ideas and possibilities from receiving the airing they deserved, and hence contributed to the harsh terms in which the Soviet experiment is now evaluated.

Those who decry the experiment presumably accept that this critique of liberalism is unimportant; and they may be right. But they ought to put the point explicitly. Is social and economic democracy irrelevant, or just premature? Certainly markets and political democracy together are compatible with the exclusion of large segments of living standards from democratic determination.

POST-SOVIET DILEMMAS

The economic crisis in Russia since 1990 is in many respects an outgrowth of the situation that had developed in the Soviet Union prior to 1985. Nonetheless, the post-1990 problems are in some respects *sui generis*. They are well known and do not need to be elaborated. The Australian Department of Foreign Affairs and Trade (DFAT) recently presented what is doubtless close to conventional wisdom concerning the current situation in Russia: "the future of capitalism seems assured . . . [though] in the short term things will remain confused in just about every way as the capitalist revolution sorts itself out."[16] The relief stemmed of course from the presumption that "structural distortion, technological backwardness, low efficiency of resource utilization and massive non-economic burdens on the state budget" had been endemic features of the pre-Yeltsin regime and that the emergency measures and policy changes since 1991 would begin to reverse all that.

The problems that exist now in the post-Soviet Russian economy can be gleaned from a variety of documents (see Table 2). Most important, economic decline has accelerated since 1991 with successive falls in production in 1991, 1992, and 1993. But there is an infrastructure of some significance in Russia. Although the country was poor prior to 1990, its education, health, and, to some extent, housing[17] were impressive compared with many other countries. Its citizenship rights in respect of employment were also well developed. The country still has enormous agricultural and energy resources which contributed 21 percent of gross domestic procuct (GDP) in 1990. Even managerial quality at the highest levels is good.[18] In addition, scientific, industrial, and cultural capacities, while below those of the best of the Organization for Economic Cooperation and Development (OECD) countries, are far above the standards of Third World and semideveloped countries. In any reconstruction program, this threshold ought not to be disregarded.

Table 2
Summary of Structural Problems in Post-Soviet Economy

Structural problems in agriculture:
>   poorly maintained equipment, poor storage facilities, inefficient distribution, low state-administered prices; farms withholding produce from state shops

Vertical integration in industry (still powerful conglomerates):
>   "gigantomania," dedicated technology, single suppliers, single customers; conversion to civilian production almost impossible; credits to allow inefficient producers continue as necessary to prevent "cascade of failures" up and down the chain; restructuring and retooling impeded; rising inventories in state enterprises; supplies not reaching retail outlets

High inflation (1,000% per year) and falling production (except energy):
>   unavailability of working capital for new enterprises; unintended incentives for routinization of speculative and criminal activity; reduction of living conditions for honest, well-qualified workers; urban transport services reduced because of insufficient fuel; hard-currency shortages; inability to service foreign debt (but a trade surplus); countertrade and barter arrangements

Regional "mercantilism"

Systematic production of defective products

Uncertain property rights

Since 1991 there has begun another experiment. In commenting on the advice offered to Russians, Adam Przeworski has referred to "the greatest ideologically inspired experiment" since Stalin. *The Economist* called it the "second biggest economic experiment in history."[19] The Yeltsin-Gaidar proposals, presumably now reinstated, are a development of the Yavlinsky program of 1991, itself a successor to the Shatalin "500-day plan" proposed in 1990 before Gorbachev departed. It is instructive to examine these proposals because they are mainly timetables without institutional mechanisms for the implementation of substantive policy goals. The Yavlinsky program expected institutional agreements (a new union, uniform monetary policy, legalization of illegal private economic activity, privatization of small enterprises, land reform, cuts in government spending, and help from the West) in the first year. In the second year, it proposed stabilization of market reforms (a new constitution, election, cuts in military spending, exchange rate and banking reform, trade liberalization, and marketization of agriculture); the third year would require consolidation and privatization (structural reform and conversion of military industry, privatization of large enterprises, elimination of monopolies, the creation of financial markets, improvements to infrastructure—especially telecommunications, and foreign investment). A fourth stage envisaged reconstruction of the service sector, creation of new private corporations, private housing, taxation reform, deregulation of the labor market, integration into the world market, and gradual reductions in Western assistance. The program is, then, a "wish list" drawn up to appeal to the West by Western-trained economists without regard for the existing peculiarities of Russian industry or of the time and difficulty involved in generating industrial activity. There is an extraordinary presumption, to be found in economic policy proposals outside Russia too, that the "right conditions" will result in spontaneous development at an appropriate level and content of economic activity, as if no explicit decisions need to be made concerning priorities, mechanisms, location, timing, purposes, and linkages.

"Shock therapy" in Russia is as sadistic as austerity responses to economic recession in the West. Everybody has known that something dramatic had to happen; but the response by Yeltsin, Gaidar, and the International Monetary Fund (IMF) may well build in a permanent weakness from which there will be no recovery at all. Perhaps Yeltsin has made the same mistake as Gorbachev in that he has done what was easiest: liberalization does not regenerate production, or if it does there is no way of ensuring that it is in the correct sectors. The experience of industry policy in the successful capitalist countries suggests that a high degree of institutional development is necessary to determine appropriate patterns of investment, access to finance, workforce training, and so on. It can be done with private enterprise, but it cannot be done under private decision-making auspices. Genuine opposition to the "reforms" is coming from the industrial managers, but they are not troglodytes:

> When they express opposition to the policies by which the transformation is being attempted . . . we should not be too quick to dismiss their criticisms. . . . It may be that they sometimes understand the immediate economic consequences of certain policies better than we newcomers do. A Russian manager with an engineering degree and some schooling in Marxist economics, let us say, will not express himself in the terms we use. But he may still understand perfectly well that pell-mell privatization may wreak havoc with vertically integrated industries.[20]

In large measure the argument that the transition must be achieved quickly comes from outsiders skeptical of the ability of the system to reform itself[21] and is resisted by insiders.[22] Suggestions that essential changes to correct serious systemic malfunction will violate the expectations of Marx and the Marxist tradition are not new,[23] but they are not unimpeachable suggestions. The part of the Marxist tradition that is faithful to Marx's purpose could hardly expect that capital accumulation before capitalist accumulation, under noncapitalist social relations, would lead unproblematically to socialism. And it is the problem of development and the difficulties of accumulation, wholly anticipatable, that are now being faced. The material impost of the Cold War made these problems worse than they might have been, but they stem from 1917, not from 1945. The intellectual legacy of the Cold War continues to frustrate our attempts to correctly specify these problems.

The structure of Soviet industry may well be such that market reform is an impossible as well as an inappropriate strategy for economic reconstruction.[24] Many of the problems are unique. Something akin to the Marshall Plan reconstruction from 1947 to 1950 may be more appropriate. That was distorted by the Cold War, too, insofar as the U.S. Congress was initially reluctant to approve assistance to the Soviet Union and the prohibition on use of the funds for rearmament was relaxed. In recent times, much of the Western assistance pledged to Russian reconstruction has been on inappropriate terms or withheld for inappropriate reasons. In addition, "there have been almost no aid flows during 1992 and 1993, especially in comparison with Russia's needs, and in comparison with the levels of assistance advertized by the Western governments and the IMF."[25] What is needed now in Russia is fewer carpetbaggers and more industrial production, less speculation and more modernization, fewer advertising joint ventures and more construction joint ventures such as the Finns and the Germans had negotiated in the 1980s.

To put the case bluntly, Marxism would recommend more capital and skill formation, and liberalism would not.

CONCLUSION

Marxism, especially Marxian political economy, is less scathed than are Marxists by the collapse of the Soviet economy because specification of the nature or dynamics of a noncapitalist economy was always outside its self-proclaimed sphere of competence. Marxian social science had little to say about how to construct a socialist society, and still less about the possibility of a socialism unaided by a prior *capitalist* development of national forces of production. Mature Marxism provided no guide beyond a few cryptic aphorisms of Lenin.

Yet the knowledge and direction that Marxism did not provide are still needed. More than anything else, Russia is today in need of knowledge it does not have: how to reconstruct a deteriorated productive capacity and how to avoid the exacerbation of social and economic sufferings already being intensified by policy advice wrought from different contexts. This is why, in the debate about the downfall of "actually existing communism," I am forced, *contra* Therborn, to take the position that the problem has been structural rather than conjunctural. Post-Soviet politics will continue to be plagued by the unavailability of a decent, pragmatic model of what is to be done, of what can be done, or how. There is also reason to believe that the continuing underdevelopment of Russia implies consequences at least as debilitating for the West as those posed by the Cold War from which none of us has quite yet escaped.

This chapter has argued three points. First, the Cold War ended insofar as the Soviet economy could no longer sustain the diversion of resources to the military (about 40 percent of research and development and about 15 to 18 percent of GDP). The weakness in the economy devolved from an ideological reliance on Marxism, which provided no help. Intellectuals in the West had devoted little time or energy to the definition or analysis of a socialist economy in terms that would have helped. Second, intellectuals in the West have difficulty understanding capitalism, too. Insofar as attempts have been made to implement interventionist policies or to develop interventionist institutions, Cold War–derived political impediments have been mobilized quickly and effectively. The Cold War and its associated climate of hysterical anti-communism have greatly damaged the wealth and productive capacities of the liberal economies (the less liberal regimes of Japan, Sweden, and Germany have fared better). In this respect the Cold War distortions remain and are still afflicting us. Third, insofar as apparently inappropriate economic "reme-

dies" are now being imposed upon the former Soviet Union, damage continues to be done. There remains insufficient intellectual attention to specific
problems, and too much readiness to pass on solutions derived from ideological preferences developed in other contexts, even when they have a proven
record of failure there. There is reason to believe that we would all be better
off if all countries developed to the maximum extent of their resource
availability. But this requires quite different political commitments from
those that have prevailed for the past fifty years. It seems that, as Keynes
complained in 1930, for some time yet "we must pretend to ourselves and to
everyone that foul is fair and fair is foul; for foul is useful and fair is not."[26]

NOTES

1. My concern is with the drying up of sympathetic contributions to the political economy
of socialism by the 1960s. I exclude, therefore, the impressive efforts of an earlier generation
of political economists such as Maurice Dobb, Michal Kalecki, and perhaps Alec Nove, Oskar
Lange, Karl Polanyi, and the historian E. H. Carr. See, for example, Maurice Dobb, "The
Question of 'Investment Priority for Heavy Industry,'" *Papers on Capitalism, Development
and Planning* (New York: International Publishers, 1967), pp. 107–23; Tadeusz Kowalik,
"Oskar Lange," in *The New Palgrave: Problems of the Planned Economy*, eds. John Eatwell,
Murray Milgate, and Peter Newman (London: Macmillan, 1990) pp. 133–46; Alec Nove,
"The Defense Burden: Some General Observations," in *Studies in Economics and Russia*
(London: Macmillan, 1990), pp. 325–39; Alec Nove, "Socialism," in *The New Palgrave*, pp.
227–49.

2. It may be that the Soviet economy would have collapsed anyway, even without the
military burden. The evidence does not seem to support such a proposition, but in any case,
the issues raised in this chapter, concerning our incomplete knowledge of the possibilities of
postliberal economic activity, would still be pertinent.

3. This ought not preclude, of course, the development of socialist political strategies
oriented to the politicization of economic decision making within capitalism in order to
promote either efficiency or democracy or rationalization according to nonmarket principles.

4. They are (1) market allocation of resources, (2) the use of profitability as the key
criterion for investment, (3) commodity production, including the treatment of labor as if
it were a commodity, and (4) hierarchical (managerial or ownership) control of the labor
(production) process.

5. This is not to deny, of course, the equally prevalent possibility that political opportunities and legitimacy might be squandered.

6. It is retrieval or reconstruction of conceptually strong and defensible Marxian themes
that leads to the development of a postliberal view of *contemporary* change. What is important
in the writings of Marx is not each utterance, for there are inconsistencies and great variation
in purpose, but the logic of the argument.

7. Leszek Kolakowski, "Introduction" and "The Myth of Human Self-Identity: Unity of
Civil and Political Society in Socialist Thought," in *The Socialist Idea: A Reappraisal*, eds.
Leszek Kolakowski and Stuart Hampshire (London: Weidenfeld & Nicolson, 1974), pp.
1–17, 18–44.

8. Göran Therborn, "Reply to Mouzelis," *New Left Review* 200 (July-August 1993): 186.

9. Ibid., p. 184. He had been replying to Nicos Mouzelis's insistence that "the Soviet experiment was from beginning to end an unmitigated disaster . . . a colossal failure," not mitigated either by "the enduring contempt . . . most left-wing intellectuals and activists have for social democratic 'revisionism,' gradualism and reformism."

10. Fikret Adaman and Pat Devine, "Socialist Renewal: Lessons from the 'Calculation' Debate," *Studies in Political Economy: A Socialist Review* 43 (spring 1994): 63.

11. Robin Blackburn, "Fin de Siècle: Socialism after the Crash," in *After the Fall: The Failure of Communism and the Future of Socialism*, ed. Robin Blackburn (London: Verso, 1991), p. 182; see also Warren J. Samuels, "The Status of Marx after the Disintegration of the USSR," *Challenge: The Magazine of Economic Affairs* 36, no. 4 (July-August 1993): 45–49; Pekka Sutela, *Economic Thought and Economic Reform in the Soviet Union* (Cambridge: Cambridge University Press, 1991), pp. 6–8.

12. Blackburn, "Fin de Siècle," p. 192.

13. Ibid., p. 198.

14. See Adaman and Devine, "Socialist Renewal," pp. 67–75.

15. Blackburn, "Fin de Siècle," p. 208.

16. Department of Foreign Affairs and Trade, *Country Economic Brief: Russia* (Canberra: DFAT, 1992), p. 4. A 1993 update is denoted "Commercial in confidence—not for attribution."

17. Quality is low but rents are extremely low; International Monetary Fund et al., *The Economy of the USSR: Summary and Recommendations* (Washington, DC: World Bank, 1990).

18. Ibid., p. 22.

19. "Talking to Gaidar: From the Hot Seat," *The Economist*, April 25, 1992, p. 17.

20. Axel Leijonhufvud, "The Nature of the Depression in the Former Soviet Union," *New Left Review* 199 (May-June 1993): 126.

21. Anders Åslund, *Gorbachev's Struggle for Economic Reform: The Soviet Reform Process, 1985–1988* (London: Pinter, 1989), Chapters 2 and 7.

22. See Anders Åslund, ed., *The Post-Soviet Economy: Soviet and Western Perspectives* (London: Pinter, 1992), pp. 167–68.

23. See Alec Nove, "Marxism and Really Existing Socialism," in *Studies in Economics and Russia* (London: Macmillan, 1990), p. 218.

24. See Thomas Weisskopf, "Russia in Transition: Perils of the Fast Track to Capitalism," *Challenge: The Magazine of Economic Affairs* 35, no. 6 (November-December 1992): 28–37; Amitai Etzioni, "How Is Russia Bearing Up?" *Challenge: The Magazine of Economic Affairs* 35, no. 3 (May-June 1992): 40–43.

25. Jeffrey Sachs, "Toward Glasnost in the IMF," *Challenge: The Magazine of Economic Affairs* 37, no. 3 (May-June 1994): 5.

26. John Maynard Keynes, *Essays in Persuasion* (New York: W. W. Norton, 1931, 1963), p. 372.

10

Whose Cold War?

Rick Kuhn

DEFINITIONS AND PREHISTORY

If we are to understand the end of the "cold war" it seems useful to first consider what it was, as conceptions of the nature of the "cold war" are likely to shape the position commentators take on its demise. The following argument begins with a discussion of the "cold war" as the conflation of the class conflict between capital and labor (cold war) with conflicts between two imperialist powers, the U.S.S.R. and the United States (Cold War). The demise of the Soviet workers' state during the 1920s is considered in this context. The achievements of the Russian state capitalist model of economic development are then examined. The subsequent sections deal with structural elements in, and then factors associated with, *perestroika* which immediately precipitated the collapse of the Soviet Union. The final section very briefly assesses the implications of the Cold War's end.

The conflict that underlay the Cold War predated not only post–World War II superpower rivalry but also the 1917 Russian revolution. It is the conflict between capital and labor, or international civil war.[1] This cold war saw its own arms race and hot conflicts. Thus, for example, popular unrest in England during the French revolution, struggles of trade unions against masters, and the Chartist movement against the oligarchic English state

I am grateful to Jim Craven of Clark University for his observations on the end of the Cold War, which inspired the broad concept of the "cold war" used in this chapter, although his own analysis is a distinct one. John Passant's and Mary Gorman's thoughtful comments on drafts were the basis for substantial improvements in content and presentation.

during the 1830s and 1840s saw an early, though one-sided, arms race. The ruling class built up its resources for violent repression of the domestic population. The military proved inadequate, because of their limited reper-toire of responses, to deal with civil unrest. The Peterloo massacre had successfully dispersed peacefully protesting workers. But in the process the murderous use of army and militia units generated a massive public outcry. After five previous parliamentary committees from 1770 on had rejected proposals to establish police forces, the Metropolitan Police was set up in 1829. The immediate context was the rise of organized labor and a strike movement. Police forces were established across the country to help deal with the Chartist movement, the first mass expression of working-class politics in history. "The new police had little to do with crime prevention and everything to do with what the ruling class saw as public order."[2] Farrell has also demonstrated close parallels between levels of strike activity and growth in police numbers between 1888 and 1913.[3]

The conflict between capital and labor also took international forms. Marx wrote that "[a] specter is haunting Europe, the specter of communism"—not in 1948, but in 1848. The hottest international conflict between capital and labor during the nineteenth century was the suppression of the Paris Com-mune in 1871, executed by the rabid Versailles government with the aid of the new German Reich and applauded by ruling-class opinion and the press of Europe. Anticommunist witch hunts followed the suppression of both the 1848 revolutions and the Paris Commune. Even in the United States, far from the Parisian uprising, the red menace was a preoccupation of the press from the spring of 1871: "Anticommunism was being developed as a weapon to isolate labor organizations and control the untamed urban masses."[4]

The immediate antecedents of the Cold War go back to the period immediately after November 1917, when the Entente powers sought to get Russia back into the war and to deny Russian assets to Germany by over-throwing the Soviet regime. After the war's end the latter means were subordinated to a related goal. The new workers' government in Russia,[5] first of all, damaged the immediate interests of capital under the protection of the imperialist powers, through expropriation, workers' control, and disruption of trade; and second, constituted a threat to the world capitalist political order. As U.S. Secretary of State Bainbridge Colby put it: "The existing regime in Russia is based upon the negation of every principle of honor and good faith, and every usage and convention, underlying the whole structure of international law; the negation, in short, of every principle upon which it is possible to base harmonious and trustful relations, whether of nations or of individuals."[6] Indeed, the struggle between capital and labor now had a heightened international aspect.

From the side of the imperialist powers the first phase of hostilities primarily took a hot form, through military support for the opponents of the Soviet government and outright intervention by units of their armies or volunteer and mercenary groups under their officers.[7] An economic blockade and anti-Bolshevik hysteria accompanied this initial stage. The former was dropped in the interests of profits in 1921; the latter continued as a means both of isolating the workers' state and of persecuting militant labor movements around the world. Even when competition between other capitalist states and enterprises led to a reopening of trade, these continued to wage war on workers at home.[8] Heale explains how the cold war between capital and labor started to be transformed into the Cold War with the Soviet Union, in the consciousness of the U.S. ruling class: "In the aftermath of the Russian Revolution . . . American perceptions of the communist threat gradually changed. Communism had ceased to be a free-floating European 'ism' that might excite the 'dangerous classes' and had become identified with the implacable regime in Russia, whence revolutions directed at capitalist states could henceforth be plotted. The class war was being replaced by a global struggle."[9] By regarding domestic class conflicts as an aspect of international rivalry with the Soviet state, this conception inverted the real relationship, so long as vestiges of workers' power continued to exist in the Soviet Union. After the revolution had been totally destroyed, it oversimplified the connections between Soviet foreign policy and militant labor movements around the world.

The Soviet state's belligerence toward the West initially indicated that it was a product and aspect of the struggle between the international working and capitalist classes. It embodied a commitment to world revolution. Lenin explained on the third anniversary of the October revolution that "[w]e knew at that time that our victory would be a lasting one only when our cause had triumphed the world over, and so when we began working for our cause we counted exclusively on the world revolution."[10] In practical terms, this meant support for and dialogue with the radical wings of labor movements wherever contact could be established. The assistance provided to organizations inside and outside the Communist International (Comintern) was overwhelmingly moral in form. The Bolshevik/communist leadership of the Russian revolution and discussions in the Comintern helped clarify analyses of the nature of capitalist state power, as well as revolutionary strategy and tactics which crystallized a world communist movement, with varying levels of popular support in different countries.[11] During and after 1917 the leaders of the Russian workers' state (including Stalin) conceived its future as inextricably tied to the spread of revolution, particularly to Germany. The end of the revolutionary wave that had produced the Russian revolution, brief soviet regimes in Hungary and Bavaria, factory occupations in Italy, and mass strikes in Glasgow, Seattle, and Winnipeg was signaled by the stabilization of the German economic and political crisis of 1923 in terms favorable to capital.

While the process of degeneration of the Russian revolution began early—with the decimation of the working class during the civil war and the period of imperialist intervention—it took a decade to complete. The depoliticization and numerical decline of the working class and the failure of the revolution to spread to more industrially advanced countries with powerful labor movements emptied the soviets of their democratic content. The bureaucratic apparatus, increasingly populated by opportunists attracted by the exercise of power and the prospects of privilege, displaced militant workers as the defining element in the party and state. "The implementation of Stalin's program," as Reiman points out, "required the existence of a ruling stratum, separated from the people and hostilely disposed to it. . . . [S]talinism appears as a regime with a strongly expressed social character based on inequality and privilege."[12] With Stalin as their figurehead and master, the interest of the ruling stratum in preserving their prerogatives was embodied in the slogan of "socialism in one country." The Russian state and party bureaucracy announced its independent existence as a class in the late 1920s.[13] In the face of domestic economic problems, the end of the New Economic Policy, collectivization and rapid industrialization consolidated the power of this class against the other main domestic classes—workers,[14] peasants, and small capitalists—as well as its foreign competitors. This shift in policy also indicated the nature of the new order—all social activity was ruthlessly subordinated to rapid capital accumulation.

The Bolshevization of the member parties of the Communist International during the period after 1924 extended the effects of the degeneration of the revolution to militant sections of the international working class. The new bureaucratic capitalist class's project of rapid capital accumulation meant that the regime's early commitment to working-class internationalism, with its subordination of Russian developments to a broader project of world revolution, had to be turned into its opposite, a rhetoric that justified the subordination of the Comintern to the interests of the Russian state and its rulers.[15]

The nature of the "cold war" between Russia and the imperialist powers changed. From a class conflict at a global level, it became a conflict among rival states, to one of which a section of the world's labor movement had subordinated itself: the Cold War.[16] The cold war between capital and labor continued. But the orientation of one of the key actors had changed decisively. Transformed in a creeping counterrevolution, the Russian state stood on the side of reaction, against the interests of labor both at home and overseas.[17] The rivalries of the imperialist powers, now including Russia, and the congealing of an ideological residue, called Marxism-Leninism, from the cinders of the analyses which had made the Russian revolution possible confused the issue. In the West, the campaign against "Bolshevism," which meant both revolutionary Russia and local working-class militancy, provided policymakers both with a framework of understanding and an established repertoire of vilification to use against the Stalinist state. It also suited the Stalinist regime to clothe itself in a religion that amounted to little more than out-of-context quotations from the works of Marx, Lenin, and a few others in order to justify current policy ex post facto. The idea "that the emancipation of the working classes must be conquered by the working classes themselves"[18] or, in Hal Draper's words, "socialism from below,"[19] which had animated the political activity and theory of Marx and Lenin, was thus eliminated from the state dogma that bore their names. This conflation of Stalinism with working-class interests, of Stalinist ideology with Marxism, was particularly important in maintaining the support of working-class militants outside Russia. Yet the identification of workers' interests with the Russian state, which had been valid so long as that state retained at least an element of the content of the revolution, no longer had any basis. The equation "Soviet Union equals working-class militancy" (often presented as the work of a few communist agitators) had become a conflation. It survived because it served the interests of the ruling classes in both East and West—to the detriment of workers on both sides.

The arms race of the 1930s, unlike that of the post–World War II period, was not bipolar but multipolar. The private capitalist powers had built up their military strength in mutual rivalry. But Russian participation in the scramble for arms was both a premonition of the central fracture of the post–World War II Cold War and an aspect of its "state capitalist character." Russian production was oriented toward rapid economic growth, the fastest possible build-up of industry as the explicit basis for economic independence, and from 1933, a massive arms program.[20] As Stalin put it: "The tempo must not be reduced! On the contrary, we must increase it. . . . We are fifty or a hundred years behind the advanced countries. We must make good this distance in ten years. Either we do so, or we shall go under."[21] The consequences for Soviet peasants and most workers were disastrous.[22]

In Marxist terms the logic of the Russian economy and state was underpinned by capitalist accumulation: production to make profits in order to invest on an expanded scale. This was driven by a military competition with other capitalist states and based on the extraction of a surplus from the peasantry and, increasingly as the process advanced, on the exploitation of wage labor.

There were, of course, distinctive features to the restored capitalism of Russia. The means of production were juridically in the hands of the people through "their" state. But in practical terms, ownership, the right to deploy and dispose of resources, was the monopoly of a tiny proportion of the population, as in private capitalism. This group exercised control collectively, however, like the managers of a giant corporation with J. D. Stalin as managing director, chairman of the board, and auditor, rather than as separate owners of distinct lumps of capital as in the West. There was, consequently, on the domestic level an absence of the kind of market competition characteristic of private capitalism, though not of the rivalry and competition among departments, subsidiaries, and individual managers apparent in large public and private corporations and bureaucracies in the West. Competition at a higher level, between Russia as a bloc of capital and rival imperialist blocs, mediated through an arms race rather than product markets, was fundamental to the economic dynamic of this peculiar new society.

This foray into the prehistory of the Cold War after World War II has been a step in understanding its logic, because it challenges the argument, convenient for both the most virulent advocates of the free market and social democratic apologists for capitalism, that the end of the Cold War was precipitated by the death of socialism and/or Marxism. The Russian socialist state had already died six decades before the dissolution of the Soviet Union.

FAILURE OF A SUCCESSFUL STRATEGY

Once it is established that the U.S.S.R. was a capitalist superpower, the question still has to be asked, why did it collapse?; for the process of collapse itself and Gorbachev's efforts to prevent it signaled the end of the Cold War. Chris Harman, on whose work the following argument draws, has provided a persuasive answer.[23] The seeds of the Soviet Union's decline are to be found in the very success of Stalin's strategy for competing with the West. This relied on the extreme centralization of meager national resources in order to build up priority heavy industry. In economics, centralization took the form of the arbitrary but imperative decision making which went under the double-speak label of "planning." Its political form was the concentration of power in Stalin's hands.

Stalinist industrialization was, in Stalinist terms, miraculous. Industrial output grew at a cracking pace. "The basic tools of industrialization, and of arms production, were, by 1937, made in the Soviet Union."[24] Table 3 shows the rapidity of growth of key indicators during the 1930s.

Table 3
Indices of Soviet Economic Growth

Handwritten note: Yet halted after. Could not keep up with new times. Little invest-ment.

Year	1927–28	1932	1937	1940
Steel (million tons)	4	6	18	18
Electricity (billion kilowatt hours)	5	13	36	48
Industrial employment (millions)		8	10	
Total employment (millions)	11	23	27	

Source: A. Nove, *An Economic History of the USSR 1917–1991* (Harmondsworth, England: Penguin, 1992), pp.194, 228, 278.

Impressive showpiece projects like the Moscow Metro and the Dniepr Dam were completed. Mass starvation in the countryside, low incomes, unsanitary housing and unsafe workplaces in the cities, and everywhere repression by a vicious police state were simply means to the end of maximizing accumulation. The waste consequent on bottlenecks and the arbitrariness of planning from above were both encouraged and disguised by a mendacious system of statistics and accounting which was a necessity for the physical survival of individual managers.[25]

This pattern of state capitalist accumulation achieved the results its architects sought during the 1930s and again in the post–World War II period. Russia was able to build up an industrial base and hence military power that prevented conquest by the (recently allied) Nazi regime. This build-up also enabled the Soviet Union to hold its own in the interimperialist rivalry with the United States which took the form of the Cold War arms race from the late 1940s on, despite the larger size of the U.S. economy and its freedom from wartime damage.

The Western powers, too, adopted a partial state capitalist road to the mobilization of resources for industrialization as a temporary expedient during World War I and then more systematically during World War II. In the form of "import substitution industrialization," the enforced autarky of state capitalism became an optional model for development in the Third World, both under regimes which adopted the label communist (China, Vietnam, and Cuba) and those that did not (Burma, Algeria, Tanzania, India, Iraq, Syria, Egypt, Brazil, and Argentina).

The large and powerful institutions of state capitalist management and accumulation were most developed, integrated, and dominant in Russia and its satellites. The thoroughness and success, first in the U.S.S.R. and then elsewhere in Eastern Europe, of the implantation of the strategy meant the elimination of almost all other organized political and economic forces. There were exceptions, notably the Catholic Church and the peasantry in Poland

and the Evangelical Church and the bloc parties in East Germany. But throughout Eastern Europe the political and social institutions and the economic structures (social relations and relations of production) were closely meshed and very rigid.

Outside the Eastern bloc, however, capitalist competition during the postwar period generated new techniques of production and the skills that they entailed (the forces of production). These gave rise to new ways of organizing the production process (relations of production). The integration of the world economy accelerated, with transnational corporations emerging as a form of economic organization which particularly exploited and advanced these developments. Private capitalist production could therefore, either through transnationals or arms-length trade, combine resources and components from all over the planet to manufacture goods that competed more effectively with those of rivals on the basis of lower cost or innovative design. Cars, computers, and even salads have become global products.

The geopolitical situation and the rigidity of economic and political institutions in the Eastern bloc militated against the emergence of the more dynamic relations of production—trans-state capitalism—which became increasingly characteristic in the West during the post–World War II period.[26] Already in the early 1960s, Russian economists like Abel Aganbegyan, later senior adviser to Gorbachev, were pointing to the stagnation of growth rates.[27] The problem was exacerbated by two other factors. The first was a relative exhaustion of the scope for easy gains through extensive growth, bringing un- or underutilized labor and raw material resources into production by means of existing technology. Intensive growth was, in the postwar period, increasingly predicated on technologies associated with international economies of scale greater than those available in the large, but on average poor, Eastern bloc and its outriders in the Third World, and on access to global sources of inputs. Second, the strategy of concentrating on the production of capital goods increased output in the short term. But its corollary in poor housing, clothing, and food also limited both the quality of labor and the incentives to work. As Andrzej Gwiazda pointed out for Poland, a reliable workforce does not come cheap:

> I have been working in industry for thirty years, and the workers still surprise me by their imagination. Their norms are increased, and despite that they manage to maintain their wages at the same level. I am a worker with a number of skills. I have worked as a lathe-operator, a welder, and now I am a painter. So, I can judge how much time is necessary to make a given product. The norms are such that it seems totally impossible to

do the work in the assigned time, but they manage it. Simply, they do not respect the technological process. From the outside, the product seems to meet specifications. It even has, if necessary, the indicated dimensions, but this product maintains its use value ten times less than it should, because it is produced by eliminating 80 percent of the specified technical operations. All the workers' inventiveness is directed toward finding means for eliminating them.[28]

Marx theorized the process which undermined the Soviet Union's once successful economic strategy: "At a certain stage of development, the material productive forces of society come into conflict with the existing relations of production or—this merely expresses the same thing in legal terms—with the property relations within the framework of which they have operated hitherto. From forms of development of the productive forces these relations turn into their fetters."[29] This is characteristic of changes between and within modes of production.

The impasse reached by state capitalist organization is paralleled by problems faced by individual private capitalist enterprises in their struggle to innovate and compete. Corporations such as General Motors and IBM are not immune to such difficulties: "Five years ago IBM was one of the world's most profitable companies, and reputedly one of the best-managed. Today it is one of the biggest loss makers in corporate history. It needs a new strategy and, many think, a new boss."[30]

ECONOMIC CRISIS

A further factor contributed to the weakness of the Eastern bloc and especially the Soviet Union: the end of the postwar boom and the onset of a period of low and declining profit rates which also had detrimental effects on the West. The boom had been sustained by the arms race. The mechanism involved was not a Keynesian one of effective demand stimulated by government expenditure powering growth. It was more profound, rooted in the production process itself.

The rate of profit is a decisive determinant of the health of an economy. It measures the ratio of new value created and appropriated by capital or profits, to the outlay on resources necessary to produce it. Given that labor is the source of new value, investment which improves the productivity of labor and cheapens the final product also tends to lower the rate of profit. That is, increased productivity means that less value-creating labor is employed compared with the total investment. The impulse to new investment is, however, unavoidable. Capitals gain an initial competitive advantage by

using new technology and modern equipment and by being able to produce
cheaper goods. Rivals are forced to invest if they want to stay afloat. This
applies to both market and military competition. At the end of a round of
investment, other things being held equal, the average rate of profit in an
industry will be lower.[31]

The arms race slowed down this process by siphoning off a significant
proportion of funds available for investment in the world's largest economy,
the United States, and in several others, the U.S.S.R., France, and Britain.
But while these countries stabilized world profit rates, others whose arms
spending was lower, notably Japan and Germany, could devote a much higher
proportion of their resources in productive investment as opposed to the
accumulation of the (unproductive) means of destruction. Their faster reno-
vation of capital stock and innovation gave them a competitive advantage.
Their economies grew more rapidly than those of the major arms producers.
Eventually, as the weight of the latter in the world economy declined, the
mechanism of the "permanent arms economy," after sustaining a boom for
about twenty years from 1951, declined in effectiveness. The U.S.S.R. and
the United States were doubly disadvantaged. They were affected by the
global crisis that meant relatively stagnant growth from the mid-1970s. In
additon, since they were the largest arms spenders, their competitiveness
compared to that of their rivals also declined. The consequences were more
devastating for the U.S.S.R. for two reasons. The arms race compelled the
Soviet Union to attempt to match the military build-up of the United States.
Its economy was much smaller and therefore the proportion of new value
devoted to the arms industry was commensurately greater. Second, for the
reasons outlined above, the Soviet economy was, by the 1970s, much less
efficient than that of the United States. It got less rockets for its rubles than
the United States got bangs for its bucks. Russian statistics, whose reliability
has, in some respects, improved since *perestroika*, suggest that the Soviet
economy was not half the size of that of the United States, as indicated by
both the CIA and pre-*perestroika* numbers, but only an eighth to a quarter.[32]
On the other hand, according to Nove, defense expenditure was up to four
times higher than the earlier official figures showed.[33] Rutland argues that
Soviet living standards were also drastically below those of the developed
West, and points out that in 1988 infant mortality in the Soviet Union ranked
fiftieth in the word, behind Barbados. Basic consumer items were still in short
supply, and in 1990, food ration books were issued in the Ukraine.[34]

John Gaddis, a U.S. historian of the Cold War and Reagan supporter, has
even, ironically and ex post facto, identified the Soviet Union's weakness in
Marxist terms: "The means [*sic*; the term should be "forces"] of production
themselves had shifted—very much as Marx had described them as doing a

century before the Cold War began—and it was this, as much as anything else, that brought the Cold War to an end."[35]

So far the discussion has concentrated on seemingly impersonal and long-term developments. The factors which precipitated the end of the Cold War were of more recent vintage. They fall into two categories: calculations at the top and ferment below.

THE GAMBLE OF *PERESTROIKA*

forcing Soviet economic collapse

The Reagan administration seemed to have accelerated the arms race in the "new Cold War" in the expectation that this would exhaust the Soviet Union. The need to match higher U.S. outlays during the early 1980s did undoubtedly exacerbate the burden of arms production on the weaker Russian economy. Aslund argues that already in 1984, Gorbachev recognized "that the USSR was losing out in the arms race with the USA because of insufficient economic strength."[36] While quickly propelling the United States out of the 1982 recession, through a short-term military Keynesian stimulus, massive new arms spending weakened the U.S. economy compared to the economies of its Western competitors. Reagan's strategy underpinned the now chronic budget and trade deficits of the United States.[37]

double edged sword

Gorbachev's program, after a final voluntarist fling with an anti-alcohol campaign, was an attempt, summed up as *perestroika*, to modernize and restructure the Soviet economy. *Glasnost*, political openness, was a necessary preliminary. It was designed to build a wider constituency among intellectuals and middle levels of the apparatus for reform, against the large ostrich sectors of the ruling class.[38] Gorbachev zigzagged pragmatically, to avoid alienating conservative members of the nomenklatura on the one hand and his hoped-for popular base on the other. Detente, in this strategy, was desirable as a means of reducing the weight of arms spending, gaining greater access to Western technology and goods, and building his domestic popularity. As Eyal puts it, "Gorbachev's first priority was the establishment of his own power base and the revitalization of his country and party. Eastern Europe—rather like the Soviet Union's ethnic and territorial problems—was an issue which he did not propose to tackle as a matter of urgency."[39]

The withdrawal from Afghanistan, completed in February 1989, was an important and successful element of detente, as were arms limitations treaties with the United States. Both helped wind back the burden of military spending. Soviet enthusiasm for detente and good relations with the United States, however, opened the way for the Eastern European revolutions.

Although initial developments looked favorable, *perestroika* was quickly associated with a rapidly deteriorating economic situation in the Soviet

Union.[40] By late 1988, a recession on the same scale as the cyclical downturn at the beginning of the decade was apparent. The economic contraction accelerated. The process of reform from above had disrupted the old means of economic coordination and control. At the same time increasing discontent below, culminating in the Eastern European revolutions of 1989, made economic management more difficult. By the second half of 1990, according to Khanin, the situation was better characterized as one of economic catastrophe rather than crisis.[41] Russia is currently experiencing an economic collapse on a similar scale to that in countries worst hit by the Depression of the 1930s.

Gorbachev had not counted on the volatility of Russian society outside the charmed circle of the nomenklatura and the elitist intelligentsia. The experience of workers' opposition to Stalinist regimes since World War II had been considerable: Germany in 1953; Hungary in 1956; Poland in 1956, 1970–71, and 1980–81; even the U.S.S.R., notably in Novocherkask in 1962.[42] There were elements of cross-class alliances against Stalinist regimes and the Soviet Union in events in Eastern Europe, particularly the Prague Spring of 1968 and the early stages of the 1956 Hungarian revolution. The self-confidence of the Soviet ruling class was crucial in the suppression of these uprisings.

Unlike their hostile brothers across the Chinese border, the U.S.S.R.'s rulers did not have a recent object lesson like the Cultural Revolution of the dangers that arose when one side in a dispute within the nomenklatura appealed to wider social layers for support. Gorbachev's liberalization not only provided an opening for popular involvement in politics, but it also shook the assurance and cohesion of the ruling class. When workers moved to resist further austerity measures in Poland in 1988 and in the coal mining districts of the U.S.S.R. in 1989 and 1991, the rulers were incapable of responding decisively. One of the most important products of successful industrialization in Eastern Europe—a working class which was now the largest section of the population—also started to constitute a major threat to the state capitalist regimes.[43]

Sections of the communist parties in Russia's inner and outer empires dressed themselves in nationalist colors to save their skins. Many managers have made a transition from bureaucratic official to private capitalist entrepreneur, often at the head of the same enterprise. Nevertheless, the revolutions of 1989–90 saw mass mobilizations in East Germany, Czechoslovakia, Bulgaria, Romania, and Albania sweep away the most vicious machinery of the police states and the most compromised and dogmatic Stalinist leaders. The impact of these events accelerated the more gradual liberalizations in Poland, Hungary, and the U.S.S.R. which had helped precipitate them. The disintegration of the inner Soviet empire followed successful resistance to the heavy-handed attempted coup of August 1991 by a section of a divided, incoherent, and incompetent ruling class.

The state capitalist regimes of Eastern Europe did not, therefore, just collapse. They were destroyed by the actions of ordinary people in factories and particularly on the streets. The Western ruling classes, however, have been more concerned with stability than with stopping oppression in the "communist" world. Western banks and governments, including Reagan's, were relieved when General Wojciech Jaruzelski suppressed Solidarity in December 1981. The national debt was guaranteed and Poland received new loans and credits. Similarly, President Bush was prepared to overtly support Gorbachev in 1989, "prompted by fears that an economic crisis and bitter winter could threaten Mr. Gorbachev's hold on power and throw his nation into political crisis as Eastern Europe experiences major change."[44] The fear was as much that Gorbachev would be toppled by the actions of the mass of the Soviet population as by reactionaries in the Communist Party of the Soviet Union.

A PYRRHIC VICTORY

The end of the Cold War should give little comfort to those who claim to be the victors. The factors which resulted in the revolutions of 1989 and the failed coup of 1991 are not unique to Eastern Europe or the U.S.S.R. The frictions and crises attendant on changes in global production are apparent in the private capitalist West. The process of restructuring is made more painful by the long period of relatively stagnant growth since the mid-1970s, punctuated by severe recessions. Levels of unemployment, bankruptcies, and poverty have all risen during the current recession to heights matched only by those of the early 1930s. In the face of these problems the scope of welfare-state activity is being cut back rather than extended. High unemployment, spreading poverty, and declining wages are as unlikely to be overcome by the next recovery as they were by the last one. Where recovery is already in evidence, as in the United States and Australia, it is proving weaker than that of the 1980s.

Nor has the end of the Cold War ushered in a period of international peace and harmony. Bush's phrase the "new world order" has more significance as unintentional black humor and an index of the delusions of the U.S. rulers than as a perspective that was ever plausible. Kolko has identified an underlying problem in U.S. foreign policy in "its repeated inability since 1949 to reconcile the inherent tension between its diverse aims in every corner of the earth with its very great but nonetheless finite resources."[45]

The pogroms in Yugoslavia and the Commonwealth of Independent States are fanned by nationalisms that both former Stalinists and Western powers have encouraged. The United Nations, now adding military adventures on behalf of imperialist powers to its previous role as ineffective cipher, presides over debacles in Somalia and Cambodia as well as Yugoslavia. Saddam Hussein, ex-ally of the United States, remains in power, despite the expenditures and, even by the standards of U.S. war aims, unnecessary bloodshed of the Gulf War. The stability of the international economy is threatened by longer-term economic stagnation, recession, and rising trade tensions. These developments point to an era of international instability and conflict beyond the control of any single state or group of states.

More important, the mass activity that brought down the despotisms of Eastern Europe is also apparent in the West. It has taken the form of incoherent riots against victimization and oppression by the selective police state in Los Angeles. In several Western European countries and Victoria in Australia there were general strikes against austerity packages during 1992 and 1993. Even former West Germany saw a sustained strike by public sector workers over wages. In former East Germany in 1993 metal industry employers broke a wage contract for the first time in the history of the Federal Republic. The resistance was moderately successful, due in part to the support by western workers, in defense of the 1991 agreement to progressively bring eastern wages up to western levels.

The end of the Cold War, through the end of Stalinism, bears an unpleasant message for capitalist regimes everywhere. They are not safe from economic crises. They are not safe from revolution. And the war between capital and labor—now hot, now cold—continues.

NOTES

1. A. Mayer, *The Dynamics of Counterrevolution in Europe, 1870–1956* (New York: Harper and Row, 1971), p. 9. Mayer, however, portrays this as a twentieth-century phenomenon, adopting the common but mistaken identification of Russian communism before, during, and after Stalin with the international labor movement. See below for a discussion of this conflation.

2. A. Farrell, *Crime, Class and Corruption: The Politics of the Police* (London: Bookmarks, 1992), p. 57.

3. Ibid., p. 69.

4. M. J. Heale, *American Anticommunism: Combating the Enemy Within, 1830–1970* (Baltimore, MD: Johns Hopkins University Press, 1990), p. 27.

5. See the classic accounts of L. Trotsky, *The History of the Russian Revolution* (London: Pluto, 1979); J. Reed, *Ten Days That Shook the World* (Harmondsworth, England: Penguin, 1974); and also more recent academic studies of the revolution such as S. A. Smith, *Red Petrograd: Revolution in the Factories, 1917–18* (Cambridge: Cambridge University Press,

1983) and D. Koenker, *Moscow Workers and the 1917 Revolution* (Princeton, NJ: Princeton University Press, 1981).

6. Cited in J. L. Gaddis, *The United States and the End of the Cold War* (New York: Oxford University Press, 1992), p. 21.

7. "It was not by accident that British and American military and political interests were greatest in those areas of Russia in which their economic interests were strongest." C. A. White, *British and American Commercial Relations with Soviet Russia, 1918–1924* (Chapel Hill: University of North Carolina Press, 1992), p. 36.

8. For the anti-Bolshevik campaign in Australia, see H. McQueen, "Shoot the Bolshevik! Hang the Profiteer! Reconstructing Australian Capitalism, 1918–21," in *Essays in the Political Economy of Australian Capitalism*, vol. 2, eds. E. L. Wheelwright and K. Buckley (Sydney: ANZ, 1978), pp. 185–206. The situation in the United States is dealt with in Heale, *American Anticommunism*, pp. 60–78; and in Canada by A. Angus, *Canadian Bolsheviks: The Early Years of the Communist Party of Canada* (Montreal: Vanguard, 1981), pp. 27–48. In Germany and Italy, not to mention eastern Europe, the campaigns against the working class and revolutionary left were even more virulent and violent.

9. Heale, *American Anticommunism*, p. 97.

10. V. I. Lenin, *Collected Works*, vol. 31 (Moscow: Progress Publishers, 1982), p. 397. Also see E. H. Carr, *The Bolshevik Revolution, 1917–1923*, vol. 3 (Harmondsworth, England: Penguin, 1977), p. 123.

11. See D. Hallas, *The Comintern* (London: Bookmarks, 1985); and T. Cliff, *Lenin*, vol. 4, *The Bolsheviks and World Revolution* (London: Pluto, 1979).

12. M. Reiman, *The Birth of Stalinism: The USSR on the Eve of the "Second Revolution"* (Bloomington: Indiana University Press, 1987), p. 119.

13. The original statement of this analysis is republished as T. Cliff, *State Capitalism in Russia* (London: Pluto, 1974).

14. For example, in the Russian cotton textile industry, as late as 1925, there was a strike which achieved some successes. From 1929 on any form of collective workers' activity was extremely dangerous for the participants and very likely to fail. See C. Ward, *Russia's Cotton Workers and the New Economic Policy* (Cambridge: Cambridge University Press, 1990), pp. 176–81, 259.

15. Stalin's "theory of socialism in one country, having become the theoretical foundation for Comintern strategy, signified, in the last analysis, that the world revolution, in all of its phases and episodes, was to be subordinated to the requirements of building socialism in the USSR." Hallas, *The Comintern*; F. Claudin, *The Communist Movement* (Harmondsworth, England: Penguin, 1975), p. 77.

16. Compare F. Halliday, who identifies the Cold War with efforts to defeat communism as a "social, economic and political system" ("The Ends of the Cold War," *New Left Review* 180 [March-April 1990]). This view emphasizes the unity of the entire post-1917 period in Russia and downplays the discontinuity between Lenin and Stalin and the continuity between prerevolutionary workers' movements and the young Soviet state. This Stalinist account of the Cold War was characteristic of large sections of the Left, some of whom, like Halliday, have been demoralized by the collapse of the Soviet empire and flipped over into an overestimation of capitalism and liberal apologetics for U.S. foreign policy.

17. L. Trotsky, *The Revolution Betrayed* (New York: Pathfinder, 1972), pioneered this analysis of the consequences of the degeneration of the Russian revolution.

18. K. Marx, " 'Provisional Rules' of the First International," in *The First International and After*, ed. D. Fernbach (Harmondsworth, England: Penguin, 1974), p. 82.

19. H. Draper, "The Two Souls of Socialism," in *Socialism from Below*, ed. H. Draper (Atlantic Highlands, NJ: Humanities Press, 1992), pp. 2–33.

20. A. Nove, *An Economic History of the USSR, 1917–1991* (Harmondsworth, England: Penguin, 1992), pp. 229–30.

21. Cited in ibid., p. 190.

22. D. Filtzer, *Soviet Workers and Stalinist Industrialization: The Formation of Modern Soviet Production Relations, 1928–1941* (London: Pluto, 1986), provides a detailed account of the implications of rapid Soviet accumulation for the working class.

23. C. Harman, "Glasnost Before the Storm," *International Socialism* 39 (summer 1988): 3–54; and "The Storm Breaks," *International Socialism* 46 (spring 1990): 3–93. Also see the arguments in C. Maier, "The Collapse of Communism: Approaches for a Future History," *History Workshop* 31 (spring 1991): 34–59.

24. Nove, *An Economic History of the USSR*, p. 232. See pp. 194, 228, and 278 for a statistical account of the pace of industrialization.

25. See C. Littler, "Soviet-Type Economies and the Labor Process," in *Work, Employment and Unemployment*, ed. K. Thompson (Milton Keynes, England: Open University Press, 1984), p. 89.

26. C. Harman, "The State and Capitalism Today," *International Socialism* 51 (summer 1991): 3–56, especially pp. 26–32.

27. Also see Nove, *An Economic History of the USSR*, p. 371.

28. A. Gwiazda, "Interview with Andrej Gwiazda," *Across Frontiers* 4, nos. 2–3 (spring-summer 1988): 45. For a more theoretical presentation of the impossibility of planning in an exploitative society, see D. Filtzer, *Soviet Workers and Stalinist Industrialization*, pp. 117–18.

29. K. Marx, *A Contribution to a Critique of Political Economy* (Moscow: Progress Publishers, 1977), p. 21.

30. "What Went Wrong at IBM: The Toughest Job in American Business," *The Economist*, January 16, 1993, p. 17; also see "To Save Big Blue," pp. 12–13. IBM's downgraded credit rating "is a strange fate for the company that in 1972 and again in 1982 was the world's most highly valued according to share market capitalization." B. Head, "Haemorrhage of a Blue Blood—$90,000 a Minute," *Australian Financial Review*, July 29, 1993, p.1.

31. See K. Marx, *Capital*, vol. 3 (Moscow: Progress Publishers, 1974), Part III; H. Grossmann, *The Law of Accumulation and Breakdown of the Capitalist System, Being Also a Theory of Crises* (London: Pluto, 1992); C. Harman, *Explaining the Crisis* (London: Bookmarks, 1984); R. Kuhn and T. O'Lincoln, "Profitability and Economic Crisis," *Journal of Australian Political Economy* 25 (1989): 44–69.

32. *Moscow News*, May 27, 1990. Also see S. Collins and D. Rodrik, *Eastern Europe and the Soviet Union in the World Economy* (Washington, DC: Institute for International Economics, 1991), pp. 4–10.

33. Nove, *An Economic History of the USSR*, p. 389.

34. P. Rutland, "Economic Crisis and Reform," in *Developments in Soviet and Post-Soviet Politics*, eds. S. White, A. Pravda, and Z. Gitelman (London: Macmillan, 1992), p. 204.

35. Gaddis, *The United States and the End of the Cold War*, p. 45.

36. A. Aslund, *Gorbachev's Struggle for Economic Reform* (Ithaca, NY: Cornell University Press, 1991), p. 15.

37. This is something that Gaddis and others who celebrated the U.S. "victory" in the Cold War missed. The "effort to 'roll back' Soviet influence" did not, on the contrary, involve "minimum cost and risk to the United States," as Gaddis claims in *The United States and the End of the Cold War*, p. 124. In terms of economic problems, domestic strife, racism, and a prolonged period of falling real wages for workers, the United States did not, as he asserts, avoid the danger which George Kennan identified in 1947: "The greatest danger that can befall us in coping with this problem of Soviet Communism is that we shall allow ourselves to become like those with whom we are coping." Cited in Gaddis, *The United States and the End of the Cold War*, p. 64.

38. D. Mandel, "Post-Perestroika: Revolution from Above v. Revolution from Below," in *Developments in Soviet and Post-Soviet Politics*, eds. S. White, A. Pravda, and Z. Gitelman (London: Macmillan, 1992), pp. 284–86, on bureaucratic resistance to *perestroika*.

39. J. Eyal, "Military Relations," in *The End of the Outer Empire: Soviet–East European Relations in Transition*, ed. A. Pravda (London: Sage, 1992), pp. 37–38.

40. For the state of the Soviet economy during the late 1980s and the emergence of a runaway budget deficit see Rutland, "Economic Crisis and Reform," pp. 204–5.

41. G. Khanin, "The Soviet Economy—From Crisis to Collapse," in *The Post-Soviet Economy in Soviet and Western Perspectives*, ed. A. Aslund (London: Pinter, 1992), pp. 9–24.

42. See C. Harman, *Bureaucracy and Revolution in Eastern Europe* (London: Pluto, 1974); B. Lomax, ed., *Eyewitness in Hungary* (Nottingham, England: Spokesman, 1981); P. Fryer, *Hungarian Tragedy* (London: New Park, 1986); C. Barker, *Festival of the Oppressed: Solidarity, Reform and Revolution in Poland, 1980–81* (London: Bookmarks, 1986); and V. Haynes, *Workers Against the Gulag* (London: Pluto, 1979), p. 14.

43. Mandel, "Post-Perestroika," pp. 290–92.

44. G. Hywood, "For Thanksgiving Bush Pledges an End to Cold War," *Australian Financial Review*, November 24, 1989, p. 3. The same is true of Western European governments; see A. Clark, "EC Leaders Discuss Aid to Bolster Falling Soviet Economy," *Australian Financial Review*, June 25, 1990, p. 3.

45. G. Kolko, *Confronting the Third World* (New York: Pantheon, 1988), p. 292.

IV

SYSTEMIC
GLOBAL CHANGES

11

Carrots Were More Important Than Sticks in Ending the Cold War

Kevin P. Clements

> Princes have always sought out soothsayers of one kind or another for the purpose of learning what the future holds. These hired visionaries have found portents in the configurations of stars, the entrails of animals and most indicators in between. The results, on the whole, have been disappointing. Surprise remains one of the few things one can count on, and very few princes have succeeded in avoiding it, however assiduous the efforts of their respective wizards, medicine men, counsellors, advisers and think tank consultants to ward it off.[1]

This quote reminds us that the predictive power of human beings is very slight indeed, and that no matter how fixed and predictable economic, political, and social relationships appear to be, they are capable of turning on a new hinge and moving in entirely unpredictable and unanticipated directions. The prospect of Yitzhak Rabin and Yasir Arafat shaking hands on the White House lawn would have seemed fanciful in 1992 and yet it became a reality by 1993. This serendipitous feature of human existence makes life interesting but poses fundamental challenges to the social sciences, since most social scientists are caught between narrow theoretical paradigms and the infinite complexities of a rapidly changing and dynamic world. To capture complexity, John Gaddis argues, requires "not just theory, observation and rigorous calculation, but also narrative, analogy, paradox, irony, intuition, [and] imagination."[2] In other words, it requires empathy, understanding, and wisdom as well as knowledge.

I would like to acknowledge the assistance of Wendy Lambourne and Chris Wilson in the production of this chapter. Chris in particular provided detailed editorial assistance and removed some glaring non sequiturs, for which special thanks.

This chapter seeks to explore what the end of the Cold War means, how best to explain it, and the lessons that might be drawn from its cessation.

WHAT HAS THE END OF THE COLD WAR ENDED OR CHANGED?

In their discussion, "Who Won the Cold War?" Daniel Deudney and G. John Ikenberry do not even bother asking this question.[3] They simply assert that "[t]he end of the Cold War marks the most important historical divide in half a century." For them and for most other commentators the end of the Cold War means primarily the cessation of military rivalry between the United States and the former Soviet Union. It means the breaching of the Berlin Wall, the emergence of democratic movements in Eastern Europe, the economic collapse of the former Soviet Union, and its consequent removal from superpower contention. All of these things happened, but this is not the complete story. The end of the Cold War *did* result in the cessation of direct military confrontation between the two superpowers, but it also stimulated a rather violent peace.

For strategists it is the cessation of direct military confrontation that epitomizes the end of the Cold War. This was what prompted the *Bulletin of the Atomic Scientists* to set the doomsday clock back, from five to seventeen minutes before midnight. In this view the end of the Cold War marks the end of a particular kind of bipolar interstate, political, military, and nuclear rivalry. It was this competition which provided the major organizing principle for international relations from 1947 onward and which legitimated many of the surrogate conflicts that took place in the Third World.

While military rivalry was the obvious outward and visible sign of the standoff between Moscow and Washington, there were other dimensions to the Cold War. For example, there was competition over economic and technological development and over the relative merits of both economic systems. What has the end of the Cold War brought about in this regard?

Many U.S. commentators argue that the rapid dissolution of the former Soviet economy and its speedy embrace of market principles represent a victory for capitalism. While it is true that the Soviet economy was inflexible and inefficient and that it has now collapsed, whether this indicates the victory of capitalism is a moot point. Those who argue that Soviet communism was "state capitalism" rather than "true socialism" underline the strong convergent elements in both economic systems. It was Russian technological prowess, for example, that stimulated the U.S. satellite program in the 1950s, and it was American industrial techniques (most particularly Taylorism and the school of scientific management) which underlay many of the heavy industry programs within the former Soviet Union. So what did the Cold War end in the economic realm? It catalyzed economic instability and chaos, which have now resulted in a dismantling of the central elements of the old command economy. State bureaucrats and old-style economic planners have been removed from key economic decision-making processes and are either assuming new roles as economic entrepreneurs or being replaced with a new breed of corporate managers/owners. In the United States the end of economic rivalry has refocused opinion on ways of stimulating national economic recovery.

The Cold War clearly distorted economic relations between and within both countries. Its ending provides an opportunity for thinking afresh about new and more fruitful economic directions for both countries. Whether policymakers and commentators are inclined to think imaginatively about these and other matters, however, hinges on the ideological starting point. This applies both to the Left and the Right of the political spectrum. (The chapters by Dow and Kuhn in this volume highlight some of the dilemmas faced by the Left in this regard.) In terms of economic direction and sustainable growth, long-term success will hinge on a willingness to move beyond the common logic of industrial capitalism. How this will happen is unclear at the moment; what *is* clear is that both economies are exhibiting signs of fatigue. While the U.S economy is manifestly stronger than that of Russia, it is premature to dismiss a Russian recovery at some stage in the future, a recovery which may result in a renewal of economic competition or even a revival of military competition.

In terms of ideological rivalry, what has the end of the Cold War meant? One result has been the complete delegitimization of Marxism-Leninism as an aspiration and as an acceptable world ideology. A corollary of this has been the global elevation of market capitalism, economic rationalism, monetarism, and democratization. What has not changed is Russian and U.S. nationalism and their own idiosyncratic conceptions of manifest destiny. While Russia is beset with internal conflicts and can no longer be termed a global superpower, Russian officials and commentators have warned that the world should not discount the possibility of a strong and united Russia emerging sometime in the twenty-first century. Similarly, the United States assumes that it is the only country capable of exercising a determinate effect on world politics in the last decade of the twentieth century and that this gives it special rights and responsibilities as the arbiter of world order. Thus in terms of ideological competition the balance sheet is mixed. The end of the Cold War has spelled an end to the nineteenth-century socialist project, but it has not substantially modified some of the deeper ideological tensions in Russian-U.S. relations.

In relation to political rivalry, the Cold War was a time of reasonably clear competition between authoritarian and democratic governments. The democratizing movements that swept across Europe in the 1980s represented an assertion of popular will in Poland, Hungary, Czechoslovakia, and the Baltic states. This time the former Soviet Union did not stand in the way of the diverse social and political movements. On the contrary, it encouraged reform. In East Germany, for example, the Soviet Union urged Erich Honecker to respond positively to the human rights and democracy movements (rather than in a draconian fashion) and eventually counseled him to resign rather than resist the popular will. The democratizing movements of Eastern Europe were both a cause *and* a consequence of the end of the Cold War. While it is too early to celebrate the triumph of democracy in Russia, democratic systems are being consolidated rapidly in the rest of Eastern Europe. In fact, while the old socialist–capitalist divisions have lost a lot of their meaning, nation-states can now be classified into those that are more or less authoritarian/totalitarian and those that are more or less democratic.

EXPLANATIONS FOR THESE DIVERSE CHANGES

With the advantage of hindsight it is clear that the twin policies of *glasnost* (openness) and *perestroika* (restructuring) were critical prerequisites for many of the internal and external developments outlined above. Without a willingness on the part of the Soviet Union to make some basic military, political, and economic processes more transparent and to embark on radical restructuring, it is highly unlikely that there would have been a thawing in the international relations between it and the United States or any of the equally dramatic domestic transformations that have occurred. The critical question is, What catalyzed this movement in favor of *glasnost* and *perestroika* nationally and internationally? Michael Salla's concluding chapter maps out a range of interpretive positions which help answer this question. Each one of these positions—the geopolitical, the cultural, the systemic, the economic, the ideational, the technological, and the mythological—has insights that help explain the tumultuous events of the 1980s, but each needs to be combined into a *processual* framework to explain the particular dynamic that ended the Cold War.

In 1990 Louis Kriesberg argued in a very prescient article that there are essentially four processual explanations for the end of the Cold War and that each one leads to different sorts of policy conclusions.[4] These four explanations are as follows.

The U.S. Hardline Explanation

In this view U.S. policymakers and their apologists argue that the Cold War ended and the Soviet Union changed as a consequence of tough U.S. foreign and defense policies and that it was only the stiff resolve of President Reagan, plus U.S. rearmament in the 1980s, that eventually persuaded the Russians to change direction. The end of the Cold War, therefore, is seen essentially as a victory for post–World War II global containment policies and for the demonstrated willingness of the United States to exert and project power all around the world. This triumphalist view argues that not only is the Cold War over but, more important, the United States won. (This view represents the sort of "orthodoxy" that Ralph Summy refers to in the introduction to this volume. It is the position expounded by Richard Lugar, Caspar Weinberger, and Zbigniew Brzezinski.) It was used as an ex post facto justification for all the billions expended on the U.S. military since 1947, and it gave rise to Fukuyama's premature judgment that history had ended.[5] As Kriesberg argues, however, this view fails to explain why the Soviet leadership decided to elect President Gorbachev and why he, in turn, initiated changes which transformed the system from which he benefited and which eventually resulted in his replacement by Boris Yeltsin. Nor does it provide a particularly adequate explanation for the specific path taken by the Commonwealth of Independent States (CIS) since 1990 and for the contradictory twists and turns that have characterized both domestic and Russian foreign policy over the past few years. It certainly does not help explain the current travails afflicting President Yeltsin as he tries to fashion a democratic system that enables him to exert old-style autocratic power while maintaining good faith with the West.

Soviet Domestic Factors Explanation

The second explanation is based on what Kriesberg calls Soviet domestic factors. In this argument, Gorbachev pursued a bolder foreign policy because the whole Soviet economy and society were in a state of collapse, reflected in declining life expectancy, rising infant mortality rates, and a general deterioration of the quality of life. There were escalating demands for a wide variety of consumer items, such as jeans, soap, and toilet paper, which the Soviet economy could not supply. Faced with these demands, Gorbachev and his colleagues had a stark choice, either to move in a more capitalist direction or to adopt the repressive path of his predecessors. Gorbachev chose not to take the latter course because he realized this would simply postpone the inevitable whirlwind of popular discontent and rebellion. The fact that he chose to move so rapidly toward market reform still has not been explained. In fact there is some evidence to suggest that Gorbachev wished to move in the direction of welfare capitalism with Sweden as his model.

The U.S. hardline explanation and the Soviet domestic economy argument, therefore, are only partial reasons for the internal and external transformations of Soviet policy.

World System Explanation

The third explanation described by Kriesberg argues from the perspective that the Soviet Union and the United States (while continuing to be crucially important) are simply not able to exercise a determining influence any longer, because there is a shift away from states as the major or only actors of significance and because the world as a whole is becoming highly interdependent. According to this explanation, both the former Soviet Union and the United States are challenged by Japan, the newly industrializing countries (NICs), transnational companies, and major financial institutions, not to mention a range of new international nongovernmental organizations and popular movements. Neither country can exercise decisive economic or political influence anymore. They remain (the United States more than Russia) important players, but they are no longer unassailable and are not always critical to outcomes. (For example, although President Clinton got recognition for bringing Rabin and Arafat together on the White House lawn, it was in fact the late Johan Joergen Holst from Norway who brokered the deal. This incident reflects some of the definite limits of military power and influence and the ways in which smallness and political integrity can be turned to political advantage.) Europe plus Japan, for example, represents economic and political power that neither the United States nor the Soviet Union can influence decisively.

From the perspective of this third explanation, it is the limits to power which determine critical changes, as politicians and big business seek alternative ways to enhance their influence and invulnerability. New opportunities flow out of the complex relations between state and civil society, state and the market.[6] These relationships determine not only economic well-being but also the amount of influence state and nonstate actors can exercise on social and political affairs. In this analysis the former Soviet Union acknowledged its economic dependence on the rest of the world and sought to expand a whole variety of economic and political relationships with those state and nonstate actors that could advance Russian national interests, a course which required fundamental changes to its internal political economy.

This helps explain why new organizations such as the Asia Pacific Economic Conference (APEC) are assuming so much direct political significance. They are developed to advance trade and investment and generate optimal conditions for business, but they also have very clear political and security implications as well and are undoubtedly challenging old and hard conceptions of national sovereignty.

Positive Relations Explanation

In the fourth and final explanation proposed by Kriesberg, he argues that the transformations of 1989–1990 were a consequence of the gradual improvement in East-West relations that had been occurring over the previous two decades. The Reagan years, he suggests, represent an aberration in the process. Events such as the conclusion of the Partial Test Ban Treaty in 1963, the Non-Proliferation Treaty in 1968, and various Soviet-U.S. grain or other economic agreements did more to encourage openness and restructuring than coercion and force. In this argument economic links, trade deals, and a variety of other functional relationships have more to do with social and political transformation than do negative or antagonistic relationships. Kriesberg notes that Western Europe has always been much more positively inclined toward maintaining a wide range of functional relationships with the Soviet Union than has the United States. For example, West Germany's pursuit of *Ostpolitik* and its maintenance of gas purchases and other commercial arrangements in spite of constant appeals from Washington to "turn the tap off" provided a positive model for former Soviet and Russian leaders. Similarly, the careful facilitation of East-West contacts under the auspices of such groups as the Quakers through the 1950s and 1960s, and the fostering of dialogue between European and Russian leaders in the discussions that led to the Conference on Security Co-operation in Europe, did much more to encourage multidimensional relationships between East and West than standoff confrontational tactics, the pursuit of "peace through strength," or the forlorn efforts to generate security at the expense of the Soviet Union.

In fact, there were two contradictory tendencies at work throughout the 1980s. On the one hand there was the "evil empire" rhetoric, which sat uneasily with Reagan's eventual concern to rid the world of nuclear weapons but which was absolutely vital for maintaining his coalition with the Right in the United States, and on the other hand there was a quiet enhancement of a variety of professional, scientific, and cultural contacts between the Soviet Union and other parts of the Western world over this period. These positive relationships were undoubtedly critical in helping the former Soviet Union overcome some of its national insecurity, acknowledge its own distinctive identity on the edge of Europe, and eventually challenge hard and arbitrary concepts of governance.

The new opportunities for dialogue and the emergence of a large number of popular movements, such as peace, ecology, and women's movements, resulted in a popular momentum in favor of change. By the mid to late 1980s this momentum had brought about a recognition that "win-win" rather than "win-lose" solutions were more likely to generate a stable peace between the Soviet Union and the United States. It must also be said, however, that this perception had wider currency in nonofficial than in official circles, with the result that nongovernmental actors operated on non-zero-sum assumptions and created opportunities for more official contacts later on.

If we accept Kriesberg's overall argument, it would seem that the Soviet Union did not transform itself because of fear of the United States but rather in anticipation of diverse rewards. In other words, as the title of this chapter suggests, it was carrots rather than sticks which generated a disposition within the former Soviet Union to contemplate international *glasnost* and *perestroika* and to enshrine the principles of common security as the guiding doctrine for Russian foreign policy.

Thomas Risse-Kappen, in an article analyzing the history of the INF Treaty (which many strategists see as a confirmation of the "peace through strength" policy), argues similarly that historical evidence does not support the conclusion that "peace through strength" ended the Cold War.[7] On the contrary, he asserts that it was a combination of major changes in the Soviet foreign ministry (particularly the advice of new thinkers such as Alexander Yakovlev) and "dovish coalitions" in Europe which was primarily responsible for the transformations in Eastern Europe and the end of the Cold War. Far from the United States winning the war, it was Gorbachev's desire to pursue common security, defense sufficiency, and more reassuring political and military strategies which countered coercive U.S. diplomacy. (This is the argument advanced by Galtung, too, in relation to the role of peace research and the peace movement.) The new policies advocated by Gorbachev were, literally, disarming policies that demanded bold solutions. They probably would not have advanced if the Soviet Union had been isolated by Europe and if no attempts had been made to cross the iron curtain and establish a whole series of positive functional relationships. But they probably would not have been advanced either had there not been a lot of new thinking about ways of solving security problems other than by confrontation.

Deudney and Ikenberry, for example, argue that a lot of Gorbachev's thinking was conditioned by his close aide and speechwriter Georgi Shaknaz-arov, who had worked closely with Richard Falk and Saul Mendlowitz in developing new conceptions of how to generate world order in the World

Order Models Project.[8] In fact, curiously for political scientists whose lives rest on ideas, theories, and explanations, the role of new ideas, new visions, and creative imagination in social and political transformation remains a rather underdeveloped area in post–Cold War political analyses. Invariably new ideas precede the altered action.

I personally have no doubt at all that the end of the Cold War owed much more to these positive, functional, reassuring, cooperative relationships than to isolating, coercive, and punitive relationships. A number of other studies bear this out. Fred Chernoff, for example, argues that there is no demonstrable relationship between U.S. military build-up and Soviet foreign policy reversal,[9] and even that liberal neorealist J. L. Gaddis asserts that historians are likely to argue that the Cold War tilted the balance toward integrative processes in world politics.[10] Although Gaddis cannot bring himself to follow the logic of his argument through to its conclusion, if he is right, these integrative processes require strategies of reassurance and incorporation, rewards rather than punishment, if they are to prevail against the fragmentizing tendencies.

POLICY IMPLICATIONS

It is clear that the end of the Cold War (whatever that means) does represent a fundamental turning point in world history and as such there is probably no end to the possible explanations for it. If the arguments by Kriesberg, Risse-Kappen, Chernoff, and myself are correct, however, and carrots are more important than sticks (i.e., cooperative approaches are more likely than competitive and coercive approaches to enhance peace and security), then this has very important implications for state and nonstate actors in relation to what might constitute appropriate and useful economic, political, military, and ideological policies.

In the first place it suggests that states, and major economic and social actors, have to spend much more time understanding and applying cooperative, nonviolent solutions to problems. Most state systems rest on competitive, adversarial principles and these internal principles are projected onto other states within the international system. If the "positive relationship" explanation provides a better understanding of the ending of the Cold War than the competitive, U.S. hardline explanation, then it is important that political actors start addressing the full implications of this in terms of developing alternatives to competitive confrontational politics.[11]

In particular, it is imperative that U.S. policymakers do not conclude that U.S. military strength alone was responsible for the collapse of the former Soviet Union and that therefore military power provides a solution to other problems confronting the world community. Much more attention needs to be directed (at all levels of political activity—national, regional, and global) to ways of enhancing cooperative relationships and generating genuine reciprocity. Recent international political events suggest that "bargaining from strength" is no guarantee of a successful political outcome. The Middle East breakthrough, as mentioned above, was brokered by a state which has little military power but a lot of political legitimacy because of its commitment to effective nonviolence and the just solution of problems. Only by concentrated world attention to the enhancement of positive rather than negative processes will virtuous rather than vicious circles become the norm in international relations. (The recent effort of the Australian foreign minister, Gareth Evans, to think beyond deterrence in his book *Co-operating for Peace* is an effort to develop more cooperative approaches to the solution of common problems. This is entirely consistent with the approach mapped out by Burton in this volume.)

If the "peace through strength" argument is flawed, it follows, therefore, that much more attention should be directed to an altered role for the military in international relations. If positive incentives and an orientation toward rewarding cooperative behavior were to become the preferred mode of operation in international relations, it should enable more accommodative behavior between states and peoples. Thus, the second policy implication that flows from this analysis is that national defense forces need to think much more consciously in terms of cooperative security arrangements which incorporate comprehensive, common, and collective security. The aim should be, as Gorbachev and his advisers spelled out very clearly indeed, common security and defense sufficiency. If this eventuates, there will be no need for the development of offensive capability in a system which is beginning to operate on alternative principles.[12] The time is ripe, therefore, for bringing nonoffensive defense principles much more directly into the mainstream of military thinking.

The economic collapse of the Soviet Union and its rapid embrace of capitalist free-market principles pose some interesting problems for policymakers. There is no room for triumphalism in relation to celebrating the conquest of communism. The Soviet Union is now afflicted by more fundamental problems than ever existed in the 1970s, or in the 1980s when Gorbachev initiated *perestroika* and *glasnost*. Corruption, organized crime, the subversion of the police and justice system, and an inability to deliver basic services in health, welfare, and education mean that the Russian economy and those of most of the republics are in a mess. It is by no means clear that the market will be capable of finding solutions for these complex problems, and, indeed, throughout Eastern Europe there is a recognition that the market is generating as many problems as it is solving.

The third policy implication of the end of the Cold War and the collapse of the Soviet economy, therefore, is not that capitalism is the instant solution, but rather that the world community has to start grafting social policy concerns back on to national and international political agendas. The U.N. Social Summit planned for 1995, for example, is an attempt to bring social and security concerns together and is based on an awareness that left to themselves, markets do not generate caring, responsive, and welfare-oriented societies. Rather, they generate competition, rivalry, and policies based on the survival of the fittest. While societies need some competitive and creative elements for survival, these need to be balanced by processes which generate stability and certainty. The end of the Cold War and the collapse of the command economy do not therefore provide an argument for unbridled capitalism and free-market forces; they are an argument for developing political systems which can judiciously balance market and welfare principles in response to popular demands and needs.

The end of the Cold War brought an end to a particular kind of ideological conflict, but there remain some underlying tensions between East and West. The fourth major area for policy analysis and concern, in my opinion, relates to ensuring that chauvinistic nationalism does not contradict more benign, integrative, and internationalizing tendencies. It is vital that the end of the Cold War should inspire intellectual endeavor aimed at ensuring that the cooperative principles at the heart of positive multilateralism assume a primacy over any residual atavistic tendencies. It is not only nineteenth-century socialist projects which must give way, but also vestigial elements of nineteenth-century nationalism as well. There is an urgent need for a new intellectual value framework to make sense of the interdependent world which constitutes the backdrop for most contemporary political and economic behavior.

In terms of political systems, the cessation of Cold War rivalry provides an opportunity for the enhancement of democracy and universal respect for human rights. Now that the Cold War is over, the major political cleavage dividing the world is between arbitrary and authoritarian systems which routinely violate human rights, and those committed to maximizing popular participation in decision making and which promote human rights. The major political dilemma facing the world community, therefore, is how to enhance the latter and reduce the influence of the former—how to ensure that all state systems guarantee the safety and security of all their citizens without fear or favor and work to ensure that all citizens are included in the key political processes. There are no simple solutions to this problem, and the experience of Russia is a salutary reminder of the difficulties confronting states and peoples wishing to move from authoritarian to democratic rule.

This question has clear global ramifications and needs to be addressed by the international community, since failed, fractured, and fissioning states generate a whole variety of problems for regional organization and the global community.

In all of this, the end of the Cold War has generated new possibilities for the United Nations. It is a sad twist of fate that, just at the moment when the United Nations has been freed from the paralysis that gripped it during the Cold War, it is confronted with major internal organizational and funding problems. Most member states are facing enormous problems balancing internal and external deficits and trying to stimulate growth, which means that attention is being directed to domestic rather than to international affairs. Yet if the above analysis is correct, this is exactly the moment when member states need to enhance the role of the United Nations and regional organizations so that they can help catalyze the social, economic, political, and military changes that will ensure the maintenance of international peace and security.

This particular task is also one that should be engaging the best minds and policymakers. It involves identifying problems that are tractable and capable of resolution and developing a range of responses to these problems. These responses should emphasize negotiated, nonviolent, cooperative, and creative solutions to problems. The solutions should be based on timely and accurate information; they should be oriented toward win-win solutions; and they should highlight early responses to conflicts at moments when the issues are still relatively clear and negotiable.

The end of the Cold War, therefore, whatever else it may be, is an invitation to think afresh about the frameworks within which all states and peoples relate to one another. It is an invitation to think afresh about the development of new national, regional, and global concepts of welfare and peace. The dramatic changes in the former Soviet Union have focused attention on the key issues facing the CIS and other states in Eastern Europe. These issues, however, cannot be confined to those states alone. They have a global scope and require new, altruistic, global solutions—solutions that emphasize rewards rather than punishments, carrots rather than sticks, and that enhance confidence and reassurance rather than produce insecurity and anxiety. This is the real lesson that flows from the end of the Cold War.

NOTES

1. John Lewis Gaddis, "International Relations Theory and the End of the Cold War," *International Security* 17, no. 3 (winter 1992–1993): 5.

2. Ibid., p. 58.

3. Daniel Deudney and G. John Ikenberry, "Who Won the Cold War?" *Foreign Policy* 87 (summer 1992): 123–38.

4. I am indebted to Louis Kriesberg's excellent paper for these four explanations. See "Explaining the End of the Cold War," in *New Views of International Security*, Occasional Paper Series No. 2 (Syracuse, NY: Syracuse University Press, 1990), particularly pp. 4–15.

5. Francis Fukuyama, "The End of History?" *The National Interest* 16 (summer 1989): 3–18.

6. For an illuminating analysis of some of these issues, see Joseph A. Camilleri, "Reflections on the State in Transition," paper prepared for the State in Transition Conference, Department of Politics, La Trobe University, Bundoora, Victoria, August 6–8, 1993.

7. Thomas Risse-Kappen, "Did 'Peace Through Strength' End the Cold War?" *International Security* 16, no. 1 (summer 1991): 162–88.

8. Deudney and Ikenberry, "Who Won the Cold War?" p. 135.

9. Fred Chernoff, "Ending the Cold War: The Soviet Retreat and the US Military Build Up," *International Affairs* 67, no. 1 (January 1991): 111–26.

10. J. L. Gaddis, "The Cold War, the Long Peace and the Future," in *The End of the Cold War: Its Meaning and Implications*, ed. M. J. Hogan (Cambridge: Cambridge University Press, 1992), p. 35.

11. For an elaboration of some of what this means, see John Burton, "From Strategic Deterrence to Problem Solving," in *Peace and Security in the Asia Pacific Region*, ed. K. P. Clements (Tokyo: UNU Press, 1992), pp. 365–77.

12. For a more detailed elaboration of some of these ideas, see Gareth Evans, *Co-operating for Peace* (Sydney: Allen and Unwin, 1993).

12

How the Cold War
Became an Expensive Irrelevance

Keith Suter

INTRODUCTION

There are various interpretations as to how the Cold War ended. As with the related questions of "why did the Cold War begin" or "when did the Cold War begin," it may be necessary for historians to agree to disagree on the various explanations. The answer to each of the three questions may contain several strands, and the dispute may be a matter of how much emphasis should be placed on each strand. In that same way, this chapter puts forward two strands of an explanation. It is not possible to determine the amount of emphasis that should be accorded to each.

This chapter argues, first, that the Cold War became too expensive to continue because of the economic and social costs of military expenditure and, second, that changes in the global system of nation-states made the Cold War irrelevant to the larger issues that were emerging.

In terms of Michael Salla's diagram in the last chapter, my argument straddles three interpretative positions: economic-historical (because of the cost of running the arms race), systemic-international (because of the change from the Westphalian System to a new global order), and politico-cultural (since there are references to nongovernmental organizations such as the peace movement).

THE ARMS RACE BECAME TOO EXPENSIVE

Concern over Military Expenditure

The two superpowers found the cost of running the arms race too expensive to continue.[1] President Gorbachev admitted in the late 1980s that this was the case for the U.S.S.R., and so he looked for ways of ending the arms race. This chapter endorses that view—and argues that the arms race also became too expensive for the United States.

There were warning voices at the time of the build-up that the cost would be too high. In February 1984, President Reagan submitted to Congress the first trillion-dollar budget in U.S. history: $1,006,538,000,000. This contained a $183.7 billion deficit. *Newsweek* magazine commented: "A consensus is forming that the US cannot afford as swift and sweeping a military buildup as Reagan proposes: a thirteen per cent increase in defense spending, after adjustment for inflation, in 1985 alone."[2]

In October 1981, two staff members of the Council on Economic Priorities had also sounded an early warning of the economic consequences of the military build-up:

> First, Reagan's proposed buildup is larger than the Vietnam War mobilization, while the economy is considerably weaker. Second, new weapons procurement comes at a time when military industries are already overheated. New demands will bid up prices in a sector presently experiencing 15 to 20 per cent inflation rates. And finally, Reagan's rearmament may "crowd out" new business investment as a result of increased demand for capital by defense contractors. Without new investment, U.S. firms will be hard-pressed to maintain their already declining position in the world marketplace, since our industrial allies are not undertaking similar "wartime" mobilizations.[3]

This concern over the high level of U.S. military expenditure was not new. Stephen Ambrose in his biography of President Eisenhower, commented:

> Aside from the basic question of war or peace, the most important problem any modern President faces is the size of the defense budget. Everything else—taxes, the size of the deficit, the rate of unemployment, the inflation rate, relations with America's allies and with the Soviet Union—is directly related to how much DOD [Department of Defense] spends. All of Eisenhower's major goals—peace, lower taxes, a

balanced budget, no inflation—were dependent upon his cutting the defense budget. He knew it and he was determined to do it.[4]

In his 1961 farewell address to Congress, Eisenhower warned about the "military-industrial complex." He was, in effect, collecting data on it throughout his eight years in the White House:

> "I'm damn tired of Air Force sales programs," Eisenhower told the Republican leaders [in 1953]. "In 1946 they argued that if we can have seventy groups [of aircraft], we'll guarantee security for ever and ever and ever." Now they come up with this "trick figure of 141. They sell it. Then you have to abide by it or you're treasonous." . . . "I will not have anyone in Defense who wants to sell the idea of a larger and larger force in being." The main Air Force spokesman on Capitol Hill, Senator Symington, was charging that Eisenhower's program would leave the United States open to a Russian strategic bombing campaign. Eisenhower thought that too was "pure rot."[5]

There is nothing new when it comes to inventing reasons why there should be an increase in U.S. defense expenditure. After the "bomber gap" in the 1950s (when it was alleged that the U.S.S.R. had more bombers than the United States and could inflict a devastating surprise attack on the U.S.), there came the "missile gap" in the late 1950s and early 1960s, and then there was the "window of opportunity" that Reagan claimed the U.S.S.R. had in the late 1970s.[6]

Jimmy Carter was a slow learner on the economic cost of the arms race. As president, he gave an argument similar to that soon to be adopted by his successor: "Another myth is that our defense budget is too burdensome, and consumes an undue part of our Federal revenues. National defense is, of course, a large and important item of expenditure, but it represents only about five per cent of our gross national product, and about a quarter of our current Federal budget."[7] But he adopted a different attitude when he wrote his memoirs:

> I have pointed out to the other members of the National Security Council that the demands for defense expenditure comprise a bottomless pit which we can never fill. One of the most serious problems we have, as I have said many times to this group, is the inclination on the part of our military leaders—the Joint Chiefs of Staff and the civilian leaders as well—to seek more money by savaging ourselves, constantly denigrating America's formidable military capability. This hurts our own

country and our allies' confidence in us, and might lead the Soviet leaders to make a suicidal misjudgment based on the chorus of lamentations from the Pentagon and defense contractors that we are weak and impotent.

We all agree that a major continuing commitment to arms control will be imperative—not only for us and our reputation as a peaceful nation, but for our relations with the Soviets as well. The nation's total budget will be increasingly limited in the years ahead, no matter who might be serving as President.[8]

Assessing the Cost of the Arms Race

The cost of the arms race is more than just the amount of money spent on weapons, personnel, and so on. President Carter in the earlier quotation gave the standard comparison: the amount of money spent on defense compared with the total federal budget or as a percentage of gross national product (GNP).

This assessment is a measure of inputs and not outputs. A motor car manufacturer, for example, does not measure its efficiency by the cost of making a car (the input), but by the number of cars sold. Defense forces are not subject to the same regular market test since they are not constantly at war. Therefore, it is easier to focus any defense debate on the need to acquire extra weapons and to spend extra money—with the implication that extra dollars buy extra security—rather than looking at the output of such expenditure.

This focus on inputs distorts the perception of a nation's true security. Power and security are seen narrowly in terms of the amount of defense expenditure—rather than how it is used or where else that amount of money could be spent. For example, Peter Calvocoressi noted the source of the British empire's "power": "British power in its heyday rested ultimately not on the Royal Navy but on the industry which fashioned the ships and guns and paid for them; and the prosperity of this industry was itself derived from a worldwide primacy in invention and a worldwide market for its products."[9] Therefore, three other ways of looking at the cost of U.S. military expenditure are as follows: the way in which the United States became a debtor nation partly to fund the military expansion; the "opportunity cost" of military expenditure whereby a dollar spent on the military cannot be spent elsewhere, such as on social welfare or rebuilding the infrastructure; and the diversion of skilled personnel into the military and away from civilian research and development.

The Debt

The United States began the 1980s as the major lending nation. It ended the 1980s as the world's main borrowing nation. President Reagan embarked upon the largest and most expensive peacetime military expansion in U.S. history. The president, who was ironically committed to reducing U.S. government budget deficits, borrowed more than all his predecessors combined. In the middle of 1985 (despite the economic recovery then under way), the United States became a net debtor internationally for the first time in seventy years. Debt has destroyed empires in the past, and it is now eroding the United States. Lloyd Dumas in 1986 set out the details of the U.S. debt:

Whereas the interest-bearing public debt of the United States stood at about $530 billion in 1975, by 1985 it had more than tripled to over $1.8 trillion. More than $900 billion of that debt has been added since 1981, despite reductions in federal social programs in the service of expanded military spending. In September 1985, the president of the Federal Reserve Bank of New York estimated that *interest* payments on the federal debt would amount to some $130 billion that year—roughly equal to the total personal income taxes paid by every taxpayer living west of the Mississippi River.[10]

A nation is not rich because it has a large military force; it has a large military force because it is rich and can afford it. Paul Kennedy in his *Rise and Fall of Great Powers*[11] has examined the rise and fall of major European nations since 1500. They each started out small and efficient, but then became big and overly ambitious and suffered from imperial overstretch; they acquired too many foreign commitments. Great Britain was the most recent nation to succumb to this cycle. Kennedy argues that the United States is now going the same way.[12]

A nation in debt has limitations on how it may act. Its creditors may require it to carry out certain tasks (such as working off the debt) rather than embarking upon foreign adventures. Indebted Third World nations are vulnerable to pressure from international financial institutions, which insist on economic restructuring. The United States was not at the Third World's level of vulnerability to financial pressure. But some U.S. businesspeople argued that the United States should get out of the arms race and start rebuilding itself.[13]

B. A. Santamaria has joined the ranks of people concerned about where debt is leading the United States; he wrote in July 1992:

As Henry Kissinger pointed out during the course of the Gulf War, to finance that campaign the United States had to take the hat around, and at the same time use plenty of "persuasion" to raise the necessary $50 billion, of which some $13 billion came from Japan and $5 billion from Germany. Even Australia, which is close enough to bankruptcy, was pressured into writing off $200 million of the debt owed to it by Egypt so as to reduce American commitment to that country.

America's internal debt is now approximately four trillion dollars. The deficit on the present budget is $400 billion, more than one billion dollars a day, of which half is taken up by interest, which must further compound. Many Europeans have noted Kissinger's statement that a nation that had to take the hat around to finance a Gulf War was hardly in a position to enforce a "new world order."[14]

Domestic Decline

Military power is not an end in itself: it is a means to an end. The overall end is the betterment of one's own citizens (if not the rest of humankind). While the United States has been so busy overseas, it has neglected the well-being of its own citizens. James Reston (formerly of the *New York Times*) has called for the creation of a "New American Order" to address the problems back home:

Yet many people, I among them, think we are holding on too long to militaristic policies, as we clung too long earlier in the century to the policies of isolation. I believe that the threats to the nation's security after the Cold War are coming not from abroad but from the neglected problems at home. No country has ever been so rich, but at the beginning of the nineties the bipartisan National Commission on Children reported that America's infant mortality rate was higher than those of 21 other industrial countries; that one fourth of all births in the United States were to unmarried mothers; that one in every four children was being raised by a single parent; and that 40 per cent of all children in school were in danger of failing.[15]

Reston is particularly concerned about the fate of black Americans:

In the nation as a whole, two thirds of black babies are born to unmarried mothers, and unemployment among blacks was 10.5 per cent at the beginning of the nineties, twice that for whites. Though there is a developing black middle class, almost half of the black teenagers in

Chicago fail to graduate from high school; in Washington DC, four times as many blacks are jailed as graduate from the public schools.[16]

There is no automatic trade-off between reduced military expenditure and increased social welfare expenditure. In other words, there is no guarantee that reduced military expenditure would be converted into increased social welfare expenditure; the reduction could be manifested, for example, as a tax cut. But a continued high rate of military expenditure gives an excuse to provide fewer resources to social welfare—since "national security" has to come first.

Seymour Melman has been a consistent critic of the high rate of military expenditure.[17] In 1989, he speculated on what could be done with the "peace dividend" now that the Cold War was over:

> As a result of years of neglect, our nation's infrastructure is failing to support a modern industrial society. Examples of the decay are every-where. In New York City alone two water mains rupture every day. The scale of the problem is vast: estimates for repairing our nation's infra-structure—its roads, bridges, highways, waterways and so forth—are between $3 trillion and $5 trillion. . . . From 1947 to 1987, according to the Federal Government's own estimates, the United States spent $7.6 trillion on the military, a sum roughly equal to the total value of the nation's plant and equipment, plus the value of its civilian infrastructure. This means that since 1947, our military has used up resources sufficient to rebuild nearly everything that is manmade in the United States.[18]

These are examples of the "opportunity cost" of the arms race: a dollar spent on the military cannot be spent on social welfare or rebuilding bridges.

The Relative Economic Decline of the United States

The Cold War is over. Japan won it.

A third way of looking at the impact of military expenditure is to see what the expenditure has done to civilian research and development. As the United States—and the U.S.S.R.—were building more sophisticated weapons sys-tems, so other nations (especially Japan and West Germany) were making money from the far larger civilian market.

Seymour Melman spent three decades warning against the diversion of trained personnel from the civilian sector to the military sector. He wrote in 1989:

The military budget represents an enormous capital fund that could be put to productive civilian use. Military spending is 6 per cent of GNP, but it pays for the services of 25 to 30 per cent of all our nation's engineers and scientists, and accounts for 70 per cent of all Federal research and development money, $41 billion in 1988. These are resources that can be far more productive if used in the civilian sectors of the economy.

As a result of our military expenditures, by the close of the 1970s, the United States was no longer a first-class industrial economy with respect to productivity growth, research and development, the quality of infrastructure, average wages, competitiveness and standard of living. From this second-rate condition, the United States is headed for further decline.[19]

Details of the relative decline of the United States (along with that of the U.S.S.R. and the United Kingdom) have been published in the surveys by Ruth Leger Sivard in *World Military and Social Expenditure*.[20]

To sum up so far, the United States and the U.S.S.R. eroded their national economies in running their arms race. The difference between Gorbachev and Reagan is that Gorbachev recognized this danger—while Reagan left office still blind to it.

A NEW GLOBAL ORDER

While the two superpowers were so focused on their own arms race, a new global order started to emerge.[21] This is replacing the Westphalian System (which was based on the nation-state), and instead, power is being diffused among international organizations (most notably the United Nations), transnational corporations, and nongovernmental organizations.

This part of the chapter looks at the changing global order. It is derived from what I believe is taking place—and not necessarily what I hope will take place. I have, for example, grave concerns about a global consumer culture based on McDonalds and Madonna! In my own subjective way, then, I think it beneficial when, for example, nongovernmental organizations use the global mass media for social justice (such as the use of the mass media by Eastern European groups to help end the Cold War), but I am less keen when the global mass media are used to sell Western consumer goods to Eastern Europeans (or anyone else).

Several examples are taken from the environmental crisis. First, these illustrate very well the erosion of the Westphalian System; acid rain, for instance, does not recognize national boundaries. Second, the crisis also illustrates the irrelevance of the Cold War: while the U.S. and Soviet governments were politically opposed to each other, some of their scientists were working together on joint solutions to the environmental crisis. Third, with the Cold War over, greater attention now needs to be given to ending the real "war" on this planet—that of humankind versus the environment.

The Westphalian System

The Westphalian System began in 1648, at the end of Europe's Thirty Years' War and the destruction of the Holy Roman Empire. It is the present international order—namely, one based on nation-states. The previous international order was based on tribes and city-states and the imperial ambitions of some tribes and city-states (such as Athens and Rome).

One characteristic of the nation-state system is the centralization of power in some form of ruler. Because of improvements in technology, such a person can govern large areas of land. Clear boundaries are very important for the Westphalian System since the globe is divided up into a neat patchwork of nation-states.

Second, there is uniformity. Nation-states have many similarities in, for example, their political institutions (even though they may operate differently) and this similarity enables governments to cooperate with one another. For example, there was no specific ministry for the environment thirty years ago. Government departments handling internal affairs also covered environmental matters. The 1972 U.N. Conference on the Environment was the incentive for governments to create specific ministries for the environment. Environmental protection has since became a governmental growth industry.

But can the Westphalian System cope with, for example, global environmental problems? Here are three instances of the limitations of the nation-state system. First, pollution is not new but its global character certainly is. For example, acid rain is generated in one nation and falls in another; a nuclear disaster in the U.S.S.R. results in radioactive contamination going across Europe. As for the alleged global warming, here is one global problem which is being created by many nations but which will have different impacts. Australia, on a per capita basis, is a major contributor to this problem, and yet the rising sea (if it takes place) will hurt Australia's neighbors in the South Pacific and Indian Ocean islands far more than Australia itself. In other words, people in one nation will suffer because of the life-styles of people in other nations. Additionally, diseases such as AIDS can now sweep more easily from one nation to another because of improvements in transport which permit people to travel from one continent to another.

Second, each nation-state is a sovereign entity: it cannot be forced into accepting international obligations. President Bush at the 1992 U.N. Conference on Environment and Development (UNCED) said that the U.S. standard of living was not up for debate. The United States refused to accept some of the Rio agreements—which were (in any case) weak—and there was nothing that could be done to coerce the United States into accepting the agreements against its will.

Third, national governments think in the short term: up to the next election or palace coup. Environmental problems, by contrast, build up over the years. They do not necessarily manifest themselves within the lifetime of a government.

Governmental authority is being eroded. The Westphalian System is being undermined. This process is being accelerated by the environmental crisis— among other crises. The nation-state will not disappear entirely. National governments will remain but will not be as important as the mass media like to imply (especially at election time). Instead, a new global order is evolving in which national governments are having to share their authority with international organizations (especially the United Nations), transnational corporations, and nongovernmental organizations.

The United Nations

The United Nations was established in 1945. Its charter is both prenuclear and preenvironmental. In other words, the charter was finalized (in June) before the explosion of the atomic bombs in Japan (in August). If the charter had been finalized a few months later, it would probably have given far more attention to disarmament. Similarly, environmental problems in 1945 received little attention. The only such problems then seemed to be filthy air and rivers, and the preservation of national parks and historic buildings. There was little speculation about the planet running out of nonrenewable resources.

The United Nations is not a world government. It is a clearing house for governmental action on common problems. It can move only as quickly as governments would like—which on disarmament and environmental matters is often very slowly! The United Nations has many limitations. For example, it is weak financially. UNCED considered a global plan for protecting the environment that would cost US$125 billion to implement—only US$3 billion was pledged at UNCED. But the Gulf War cost the allies a total of $60 billion—and the money was easily found. The world can find money for war but not for peace. The problem is not the shortage of money but shortage of vision. Meanwhile, Greenpeace, one of the world's major environmental groups, has a larger international budget than the U.N. Environment Program (UNEP).

However, national governments are having to work with the United Nations. They may not like to do so and still try to pretend at national elections that national governments have control over the national destiny. But the transnational character of the environmental crisis means that they have to find ways of working together. For example, with the Regional Seas Programs, UNEP has brought together nations (some of them political enemies) to help clean up the seas. Governments realize that they either cooperate together or their coasts perish separately. About 80 percent of U.N. personnel and finances have been devoted to economic and social cooperation. This percentage has changed since the end of the Cold War owing to the renewed interest of the United States in using the United Nations for peacekeeping purposes.

Disarmament, the Middle East, and South Africa may attract publicity for the United Nations. But until the recently revived interest in peacekeeping, most of the work has been done through the specialized agencies, such as the World Health Organization (WHO), Food and Agricultural Organization (FAO), and the International Maritime Organization (IMO). The agencies are helping to create an interdependent globe.

This element of international cooperation added to the irrelevance of the Cold War. The United States and the U.S.S.R. were arming against each other in the highly publicized arena of world politics, while their scientists and technicians worked together—out of the media spotlight— to solve common problems. U.S.-Soviet cooperation helped, for example, to eradicate smallpox: the first time that a major disease had been removed from the planet. Good news is not news. The mass media were not interested in the success stories of superpower cooperation, such as the eradication of smallpox. Confrontation—rather than cooperation—sells newspapers.

Transnational Corporations

Transnational corportations (TNCs) are the major global economic actors. They have greater liquid assets than all the major central reserve banks combined. With the deregulation of the international financial system in the 1980s, TNCs can move money around the globe even more easily. They are the major units of manufacturing and are increasingly dominating agriculture ("agribusiness").

Thus, the world is moving into a new global era. Governments are no longer the masters of their national economic destiny. TNCs have eroded the notion of a national economy. There is now only a global one. For example, almost all Western nations follow the ideas from the early part of this century of the British economist John Maynard Keynes. He said there should be some government intervention in the economy; during a recession, therefore, governments should put money into circulation to stimulate economic activity. In today's global economy, however, an injection of money into a national economy does not necessarily stay in that economy. About half of what is called "international trade" is actually trade conducted within different components of the same corporation. An attempt to stimulate a national economy by traditional Keynesian methods will not necessarily work—as governments are finding out.

Another example of the influence of transnational corporations is the ability of television to shape political and social priorities. Communications corporations may one day be viewed by historians with the same importance as the railway barons of a century ago are seen today. They created a new way of enabling people to move around. Once a town was connected to a railway line, its life was transformed. Once people get a television set, they are also transformed. Television brings tragedies right into our homes. People can have dinner and watch "live" as Somalians die of hunger. American viewers were so distressed at Somalia that they insisted President Bush intervene. He did not want to deploy U.S. forces, but television coverage mobilized a nation to insist that this happen. Viewers were not interested in the niceties of international law and the restrictions of the Westphalian System. They wanted action. The same process took place in Australia.

Therefore, the Westphalian System is being eroded. As in 1648, it is not a matter of a new world order being created overnight in a deliberate fashion. Instead, it is happening in a series of small steps. Global television coverage is part of that process. It has created a new era of transparency. Stalin could get away with his mass murders because they were done out of the mass media spotlight. Gorbachev's U.S.S.R., by contrast, could not be so easily hidden from foreign view. For example, the U.S.S.R.'s first nuclear disaster (in the Urals in 1957) was hidden from Soviet and foreign view for about two decades,[22] whereas the 1986 Chernobyl disaster was known within hours overseas and was well televised (including by foreign satellite coverage). Television's impact also includes—for better or worse—the development of a global consumer culture. This is currently based on such items as Coca Cola, Big Macs, and Madonna. Big Macs are the global fast food, and Coke supplies the global soft drink.

The grass-roots nongovernmental organizations in Eastern Europe which campaigned for an end to the Cold War and the free movement of people throughout the continent were partly motivated by the desire to gain access to the "good things" in Western life. Revolutions go better with Coke.

Nongovernmental Organizations

Nongovernmental organizations (NGOs) are the most important way of mobilizing public opinion and focusing attention on a problem. The 1972 U.N. Conference on the Environment arose largely from the way in which NGOs argued that there was an environmental crisis. NGOs acted—and governments reacted. Similarly, NGOs publicized the Brundtland Report[23] and encouraged governments and the U.N. to create UNCED.

NGOs are, then, a growing force in global politics. They are adept at attracting media coverage; they appeal to people who are disenchanted with the usual party political process; and they provide a sense of vision and continuity which outlasts the short-term perspective of governments. As some of the other authors in this book have claimed (such as Johan Galtung), "people power" within Eastern Europe helped to end the Cold War. Ordinary people were suddenly given the opportunity to change the flow of political events—especially when their work was publicized by the global mass media.

Robert Cullen traveled extensively in Eastern Europe as the Soviet bloc crumbled. He recalled the role of the Reverend Laszlo Tokes in galvanizing public opinion against the Ceausescu regime in Romania. Tokes and his congregation were in the Hungarian minority in western Romania (Transylvania):

> The discipline of the Warsaw Pact had for years stifled Hungarian resentment over the loss of Transylvania [in 1918] and the mistreatment of its Hungarians by the Romanian regime. But as *glasnost* expanded the limits of political expression, the fate of Transylvania became a major issue in Hungary. Word of Tokes's plight leaked out to Hungary, and in July 1989 a Hungarian television crew managed to get to Tokes and film an interview. He spoke of his own situation and, more generally, about repression in Romania. . . . The interview also made its way to Radio Free Europe, the BBC and other Western radio stations that transmitted to Romania. Foreign broadcasts over Romania's borders, bypassing the state media, played a major role in the revolution and the Tokes interview was one of the first instances of the phenomenon.[24]

Global Governance

Global governance is the emerging issue for the 1990s. First, the replacement for the Westphalian System will not be created overnight. No one in 1648 set out specifically to create a new global order. The global order evolved and people bit by bit noticed that it had emerged. The same process is under way today. The Westphalian System is in decay. But there is a debate both as to what will replace it and, indeed, whether it is in decay at all. Some politicians and scholars claim that the nation-state system is here to stay and that ways need to be found to strengthen it. For example, some critics of TNCs claim that the best way of controlling TNCs is to strengthen the powers of national governments. My view is that this approach is now too late.

Second, therefore, the post-Westphalian global order will need to find formal ways of drawing TNCs and NGOs into global decision making. There has to be dialogue and cooperation, rather than confrontation. For example, TNCs benefit greatly from U.N. peacekeeping operations. Why not impose global taxes on TNCs to help finance the United Nations? This could be accompanied by giving TNCs a role in U.N. decision making: no taxation without representation.[25]

THE COLD WAR AND THE NEW GLOBAL ORDER

While the two superpowers were so busy running the arms race, a new global order emerged. This may be seen in two ways. First, as outlined above, TNCs and NGOs became more important in world affairs and transcended national borders, while the United Nations provided a forum for cooperation. Second, a new global agenda emerged in which military expenditure was part of the problem and not part of the solution.

TNCs are helping to create—for better or worse—a new global culture. The citizens of the former U.S.S.R. may have been militarily loyal to Moscow but their hearts were in Hollywood and New York.

The United States made a fundamental mistake in implementing its policy of containment. It opposed the U.S.S.R. on the U.S.S.R.'s grounds rather than on its own. A centrally planned economy can make weapons but it has much more difficulty in making consumer goods; it is itself the market for the first (and therefore knows what it wants) but its citizens are the market for the second. The U.S.S.R. was able to keep in the arms race—though the United States overestimated the U.S.S.R.'s strength.[26] It could not match U.S. production of consumer goods. The U.S.S.R. could put people into space but could not put food on the shelves.

Cold War politicians and scholars saw the arms race as the key component of the Cold War. But they ignored the everyday basics of life. Few predicted the collapse of the U.S.S.R. from within.[27] The Soviet citizens were yearning for the good things of life and recognized that the Soviet system could not produce Coke, Big Macs, and Madonna. The Red Army could resist a NATO invasion into Eastern Europe but not the televised transmission of *Dallas* and

Dynasty. Thus, while President Reagan regarded the U.S.S.R. as the "evil empire," TNCs saw Soviet citizens as potential customers. Soviet citizens were disturbed by such presidential rhetoric—but still yearned for the American way of life.

Now that the Cold War is over and the iron curtain—made, incidentally, in France since East European barbed wire was not as rust-resistant—has been removed, TNCs are moving into Eastern Europe. NGOs also cut across national borders. Citizens' diplomacy enabled U.S. and Soviet citizens (such as those in peace groups) to meet and discuss the Cold War and ways of ending it. They focused on what united humankind rather than what divided it. NGOs in other walks of life enabled citizens to discuss, for example, scientific and cultural matters. There was never a Cold War at the South Pole—scientists either worked together or froze separately.[28]

The United Nations also brought the United States and the U.S.S.R. together. Smallpox was eradicated; a global telephone dialing service was created based on numbers (rather than letters) leading to international subscriber dialing; radio and television airwaves were apportioned out; a common bill of lading was created for merchant vessels; and a global network was created for exchanging data on weather patterns. These are examples of both U.N. work and the value of "functionalism," whereby Mitrany argued that it was better initially to get cooperation on specific tasks rather than political unity.[29]

Thus there was a growing sense of the irrelevance of the Cold War. It froze the governmental relations between the United States and the U.S.S.R. but the chill did not reach all areas of the lives of their respective civilians. Along with the growing importance of TNCs, NGOs, and the United Nations, a new global agenda also emerged. For example, the "national security state"[30] that emerged at the outset of the Cold War had a narrow military-dominated perception of "national security." A broader definition of "national security" should include environmental concerns:

> The erosion of soils, the deterioration of the earth's basic biological systems, and the depletion of oil reserves now threaten the security of countries everywhere. Ecological stresses and resource scarcities have already given rise to economic stresses—inflation, unemployment, capital scarcity and monetary instability. Ultimately, these economic stresses will translate into social unrest and political instability.[31]

Military expenditure could do little to help protect the environment. Once again, then, the Cold War was perceived as an irrelevance. Defense expenditure was diverting money away from (in this example) environmental renewal.

To conclude, the Cold War was overtaken by events. It became an expensive irrelevance. It dominated global politics for almost half a century. But eventually other concerns took priority. Now it is necessary to address the issues the world should have addressed in 1945—before it was diverted by the Cold War.

NOTES

1. Material in this section is taken from Keith Suter, "Creating the Political Will Necessary for Achieving Multilateral Disarmament: The Need for a Peace-Industrial Complex" (Ph.D. diss., Deakin University, 1986); and Keith Suter, *Peaceworking: The United Nations and Disarmament* (Sydney: United Nations Association of Australia, 1985).

2. "That Monster Deficit," *Newsweek*, March 5, 1984, p. 37.

3. Robert DeGrasse and Paul Murphy, "The High Cost of Rearmament," *Bulletin of the Atomic Scientists* 37 (October 1981): 16.

4. Stephen Ambrose, *Eisenhower: The President* (London: George Allen & Unwin, 1984), p. 88.

5. Ibid., pp. 88–89.

6. See Robert Scheer, *With Enough Shovels: Reagan, Bush and Nuclear War* (New York: Random House, 1982).

7. Jimmy Carter, "America's Position in a Changing World," US Policy Statement Series—1978 (Washington, DC: International Communication Agency, 1978), p. 3.

8. Jimmy Carter, *Keeping the Faith: Memoirs of a President* (Sydney: Bantam, 1982), p. 588.

9. Peter Calvocoressi, *The British Experience, 1945–75* (London: Penguin, 1979), p. 199.

10. Lloyd Dumas, "The Military Burden on the Economy," *Bulletin of the Atomic Scientists* 42 (October 1986): 22.

11. Paul Kennedy, *The Rise and Fall of Great Powers* (London: Fontana, 1989).

12. Kennedy's book has generated considerable debate. For example, see Samuel Huntington, "The US—Decline or Renewal?" *Foreign Affairs* (1989): 76–96; Samuel Huntington, "The Errors of Endism," *National Interest* (fall 1989).

13. Harold Willens, *The Trimtab Factor* (New York: Morrow, 1984).

14. B. A. Santamaria, "Don't Look to Uncle Sam to Solve the Family Quarrels," *The Australian*, July 11, 1992, p. 22.

15. James Reston, *Deadline* (New York: Random House, 1991) p. 459.

16. Ibid., p. 460.

17. Seymour Melman, *The Permanent War Economy: American Capitalism in Decline* (New York: Simon & Schuster, 1974).

18. Seymour Melman, "What to Do with the Cold War Money," *New York Times*, December 17, 1989.

19. Ibid.

20. Ruth Leger Sivard, *World Military and Social Expenditure* (Washington, DC: published annually by World Priorities and distributed in Australia by the Australian Council of Churches).

21. The material in this section is taken from Keith Suter, *Global Change: Armageddon and the New World Order* (Sydney: Albatross, 1992).

22. Zhores Medvedev, *Nuclear Disaster in the Urals* (New York: Norton, 1979).

23. World Commission on Environment and Development, *Our Common Future* (Oxford: Oxford University Press, 1987).

24. Robert Cullen, *Twilight of Empire: Inside the Crumbling Soviet Bloc* (London: The Bodley Head, 1991), pp. 77–78.

25. For example, Marc Nerfin has suggested that TNCs and NGOs be given greater roles at the United Nations. See his "An Introduction to the Third System," in *Dossier*, ed. Marc Nerfin (Nyon, Switzerland: International Foundation for Development Alternatives, 1986), pp. 3–30.

26. Anne Hessing Cahn and John Prados, "Team B: The Trillion Dollar Experiment," *Bulletin of the Atomic Scientists* 49 (April 1993): 23–31.

27. A good piece of predictive writing was a novel: Donald James, *The Fall of the Russian Empire* (London: Granada, 1982).

28. See Keith Suter, *Antarctica: Private Property or Public Heritage?* (London: Zed, 1991).

29. David Mitrany, *The Functional Theory of Politics* (London: Martin Robertson, 1975).

30. See Daniel Yergin, *Shattered Peace: The Origins of the Cold War and the National Security State* (London: Penguin, 1977).

31. Lester Brown, *Building a Sustainable Society* (New York: Norton, 1981), p. 362.

V

EMERGING PARADIGMS
AND LESSONS LEARNED

13

The Continuing Cold War

John W. Burton

The Cold War was, of course, a term used to describe the critically tense relations between the former U.S.S.R. and the Western democracies led by the United States. Now that one of the parties has disintegrated, it is reasonable to argue that this particular Cold War has ended.

However, this limited conception of the Cold War is of relevance only to those persons whose concern is with the particular and the immediate, and not with the future prospects of conflict and its avoidance—for example, media reporters and strategists. In the broader context of global relationships this particular Cold War has not ended. It has been transformed into many wars, cold and hot. Not only are there wars among autonomies within the former Soviet Union, some of which have a nuclear capacity, but in addition its so-called ending has allowed widespread leadership battles, ideological and ethnic conflicts, and territorial disputes to surface, both within the former Soviet Union and elsewhere. No longer are the former Cold War powers motivated or able to intervene in the conflicts taking place in and between smaller countries. These seemingly separate wars become linked as parties having shared ideologies and belief systems seek mutual support. In this perspective the Cold War has merely changed some of its features. The threat of major global thermonuclear conflict has given place to many actual conflicts which together result in the actuality of high levels of death and destruction, and also to rivalries between one of the Cold War actors and other rising major powers.

In systemic terms nothing has changed except the actors and increased levels of violence. If one examines this particular Cold War in a wider historical and global context, it becomes clear that its nature and sources were no different from those of many other wars, including the hot ones of 1914 and 1939 and the many current wars, cold and hot, between and within countries. In this sense it is not very informative to think of the end of the Cold War as implying some major shift in international relations, some "new world order," as U.S. presidents would have us believe. On the contrary, if the perceived new world order leads to unchallenged demands by the remaining superpower, the United States, on others to observe so-called human rights (a cultural notion not to be confused with human needs that are universal), particular trading policies, and forms of government, the Cold War will spread beyond Russia and its associated autonomies, to China, Japan, and other countries, large and small.

Let us go back in time. After World War I there was a continuing cold war until it became a hot one in 1939. There were deprivations imposed on Germany by the peace agreements after World War I, accompanied by massive unemployment, giving rise to popular leaderships intent on reclaiming territories. Germany may have been the aggressor in a military sense, but it was not necessarily the cause of World War II, for the aggression was a seemingly inevitable response to nonmilitary aggressions, that is, economic and related conditions imposed by others.

It was at this point in time that the Cold War involving the U.S.S.R. commenced. The Soviet Union was fearful of aggression from its unwelcomed inception, and indeed Germany invaded it despite a nonaggression pact. For ideological reasons there were many in Britain and elsewhere who welcomed this, and even some who advocated joining Germany in invading Russia. Indeed, Winston Churchill's Second Front did not take place until Germany was defeated in its attempts to invade the Soviet Union, the latter paying heavy costs. During this time he sent messages to Commonwealth countries saying not to refer to the Soviet Union as an ally. Australia responded to this instruction or request saying that in the light of the tremendous role the Soviet Union had played in defeating Germany, it could not go along with the request.[1] The Soviet Union was therefore reasonably fearful, on the basis of past experience, of Western interventions that were seemingly motivated by ideological beliefs, and it was accordingly cautious in subsequent postwar relationships.

Because of the Depression, Western powers, Great Britain especially, had been pursuing since the early 1930s domestic economic policies that protected their textile industries and deprived, in particular, Japan, an island economy dependent on sources of raw materials and markets, of access to Britain and its Asian and African colonies. Thus, as a response to conditions imposed by the domestic interests of the then more powerful countries, another cold war was created, which was soon to become a very hot war involving nuclear weapons.

It is interesting to note that on the eve of war with Germany there was an international conference of scholars in Bergen, Norway, presided over by John B. Condliffe, then the professor of international relations at the London School of Economics. It was attended by two Japanese economists who presented papers warning of the inevitable, unless immediate changes in Western economic policies took place. In anticipation of war with Germany, Australia was negotiating contracts with Britain for the supply of wheat and other commodities. War with Japan, then not contemplated, would threaten supply lines. I was at that conference, and was also involved with this contract work at Australia House. When these Japanese papers were brought to the attention of Stanley M. Bruce, then high commissioner in London, he sent a message to the Australian prime minister, Robert G. Menzies. The reply was to the effect, "Do not insult our former loyal allies." Both were right. Japan would have preferred not to be at war with its former allies, but had no option. Today, of course, as a result of war, it has its sources of raw materials and its markets. Let us hope that the new world power, intent on using its position to protect its industries, does not repeat Britain's mistakes.

In a similar way we could examine sources of conflict in relation to North Korea and Vietnam, and in Central and Latin America. In each case domestic politics in the United States and attempts by more powerful nations to impose their will on the less powerful were essential sources.

Vietnam provides an instructive case study. There were clear domestic reasons for U.S. interest, especially the domestic politics of anticommunism. In Australia there was a debate as to whether the internal Vietnamese conflict was the pursuit of communism or a struggle for independent nationalism.[2] Records now show that those who took the communist-threat or domino line did so largely for domestic political reasons and also to keep on the side of the United States and win its support in the region.[3] Richard Casey assured parents that unless the spread of communism were stopped, their children would be pulling Chinese about in rickshaws.[4] Paul Hasluck, then foreign minister, took a similar power politics stance.[5] But Casey went home and recorded something quite different in his diary, accepting the nationalist motivation as being important.[6] The people of Australia supported the tough line, there being available no insightful analysis of the postwar, postcolonial Asia, except by a few Canberra scholars who were denigrated for their efforts.[7]

In short, if one stands back from particular events and situations and looks at the sources of conflicts, it is quite superficial to refer to the end of the Cold War as though it were a significant or historically important event. The personal and political domestic conditions that contributed to it remain and are global.

These need spelling out. It is not for any one person to do this, for we are dealing with varied and complex influences. But attempts to do so need to be encouraged to offset the dominance, since Hans Morgenthau and Georg Schwarzenberger in the 1950s, of simplistic power political and strategic deterrence theories that ignore human and behavioral influences.

I list some of the causes of cold wars that persist and seem to be relevant.

Political Leadership Ambitions

We have had in recent years so many examples of this that documentation seems unnecessary. It is a general phenomenon, not confined to the United States despite glaring examples there. Political leaders, including some of our own, seem to be prepared to sacrifice lives for personal political purposes. Scholars have not given due attention to the problem of leadership. Libraries have many biographies and autobiographies, but few books on the problem of leadership. This is a major problem, perhaps the most important problem in contemporary conflictual relationships. An important contribution has recently been made by Paul Kennedy in his *Preparing for the Twenty-First Century*.[8] He is also the author of *The Rise and Fall of the Great Powers*, which is very relevant to our topic.[9] Until we arrive at a consensus that leadership is a facilitating role and bring different viewpoints together, encouraging an analytical rather than an adversarial approach, the popular support of aggressive leaders will become a source of many conflicts.

Ignorance of Behavioral Inputs

Why do leaders and governments fail accurately to assess the consequences of their policies? Why are wars started and lost? The answer has to be ignorance of human responses and a belief that the threat and use of military power can reliably alter behaviors. The United States, according to a senior State Department official talking to students at George Mason University after the Gulf War, did not contemplate any response from Iraq except withdrawal. The theory that deterrence deters still dominates academic and political thinking, despite empirical and theoretical evidence that there are certain human needs that *will* be pursued, regardless of consequences—separate identity and autonomy being among them. Nor was the State Department, according to the same official, fully aware of the ethnicity problems being faced by Iraq.[10] We have been so power-oriented in our thinking that knowledge of human responses and of the consequences of the use of force has been limited; failure has been put down simply to not enough force being employed.

Adversarial Political Institutions

The Western political system is characterized by adversarial institutions. Legal institutions are adversarial, as are those governing industrial relations. The party political system is adversarial and leads to decisions designed to promote leadership and party political interests. These are the institutions that are called "democratic," even though they effectively exclude minorities and the less privileged. It is time societies reexamined these adversarial institutions, realizing they are historically a recent development of we/they feudal systems. They are the source of aggressive foreign policies and behaviors, such as have already been noted.

Interest Groups, Especially the Arms Industry

This hardly needs spelling out. Societies seem to have come to terms with the realities of arms promotion, believing that nothing can be done about it, especially in conditions in which interest groups can determine political decisions. It is significant that, despite the belief that the Cold War has ended, the arms trade is at a record high level. Once again, means of control is a field that academics have not taken up. On the contrary, strategic studies have, over the years, played into the hands of arms producers and exporters.

The Availability of Weapons

Disputes which in the past did not reach high levels of violence are now between parties that are armed with modern weapons. In many cases these are made available by Western governments, including our own. Under Ben Chifley the Australian government had a policy of not exporting weapons, as the Dutch found when trying to export arms to Indonesia.[11] Today, for party political and leadership reasons, short-term industrial and financial expediency overshadows longer-term national interests.

Trade and Commerce Deprivations

Great powers have gone through their own protectionist phases, but now demand that small states conform with their free-trade interests. There are good economic and cultural reasons for production diversity, and demands made on other countries have to be resisted. This is becoming an important source of dispute and conflict, even between major powers such as the United States, China, and Japan.

Boundaries

The global society is still in the postcolonial phase so far as boundaries are concerned. The newly independent states have been reluctant to make changes in their sovereign possessions.[12] Hence there are many ethnicity and autonomy problems, and there is a reluctance by greater powers to tackle them.[13]

Unrepresented Nations

The United Nations comprises states that seek to defend their existing boundaries, despite demands in many of them for separate autonomies. There are many nonrepresented peoples, some of whom have formed their own organization. The United Nations at first comprised fifty nations; now there are four times that number. The real explosion has yet to come, and the United Nations will be seen to be wholly irrelevant in global society.

U.N. Interventions

The United Nations has not been able to tackle conflicts at their source. There is a strong resistance to any analytical conflict-resolution process, for this would necessarily raise questions of territorial sovereignty and ethnicity. The United Nations has rested on "peacekeeping" by military means, leaving the core problems unresolved. Such interventions probably do more harm than good in the longer term. To the Secretariat and members of the United Nations, intent on defending their sovereignties, problem solving means preservation of the status quo and peacekeeping by military means.[14]

Intelligence Organizations

Intelligence organizations are not known for the broad training of their members. Yet they argue that they exist "to save democracy from itself," to use a phrase of the founder of the Australian Security Intelligence Organization (ASIO).[15] They assume a political and philosophical knowledge greater than that of politicians and scholars. They are the institutions that can unseat governments and demolish persons whose policies they disagree with. They have representatives at diplomatic missions, thus forming an international network pursuing its own ideological goals, regardless of government policies.

For example, in Australia, ASIO sought successfully to prevent a Labor government coming into office in order to prevent, in particular, the diplomatic recognition of China, thought at the time to be important to the United States.[16]

Deceptions by Governments

Related to all these causes are the deliberate deceptions that governments promote for their own domestic and leadership reasons. The deceptions relating to the Vietnam War are now well documented. The postwar independence movements of Asia were described as evidence of communist aggression, and the domino theory was used to attract support for the Vietnam War and the extreme anticommunist policies in the United States and elsewhere. Far worse, and not yet documented because the relevant documents have been withheld or destroyed both in Washington and Canberra, was the assertion that the Korean War was started from the North. My own knowledge based on experience is that the U.N. border commission reported that patrols were being sent from the South to the North to attract patrols south over the border, giving an excuse for invasion. The United States was sure it could defeat the North in a few days and reunite Korea. Such deceptions and manipulations of public opinion are not unusual, and they become a major source of escalated tensions and conflict.

One could go on with many other conditions that promote cold and hot wars. Until these conditions are dealt with, cold wars—frequently leading to hot wars—will continue. Until these conditions are dealt with, there cannot be an end to any cold war. Such conditions are not likely to be removed by governments acting separately or together. On the contrary, they are becoming more and more entrenched in defense of the nation-state and its existing boundaries. The question that needs to be posed is not why the Cold War ended, but how existing hot wars can be ended and future cold wars prevented.

It is, in my view, high time that the academic community gave priority to this question. It may seem overly ambitious, even merely idealistic, to tackle such fundamental questions that touch on the essence of our contemporary systems. But the reality is that either societies do so, or societies have no civilized future. Environmental destruction is understandable as there are current gains to be had, even at the expense of the future. With conflicts, there are in practice only costs. The problem is in thought systems which one would think are alterable.

Let us face the fact that thinking, and the assumptions that are the basis of academic disciplines, have not kept pace with social and political realities. Are our institutions democratic in practice? The U.S. president and Congress are elected on the positive votes of less than 25 percent of the total population. Can there be one-person-one-vote democracies in societies that contain economic, cultural, and religious minorities and that have come to be the global norm? Is multiculturalism other than a recipe for disaster as in the former Yugoslavia, and should we not be pressing for unicultural societies that discourage foreign nationalisms, regional ethnic clusters, and factions at schools and encourage the incorporation of imported cultures into the national culture?

In particular, the time has come to recognize the reality that deterrence does not deter, which has been the basic assumption of power politics and strategic studies, and to focus on means of conflict *provention*.[17] The empirical evidence is that peacekeeping and similar power politics attempts to prevent conflict are self-defeating. But unlike the 1960s and 1970s, when power politics and strategic studies dominated the study of international relations, we now have theoretical explanations of why deterrence does not deter and of known options to deterrence strategies.[18] Why are the legal and social science communities so reluctant to face challenges to practices and thinking?

There are known and tested means by which parties can be helped to be analytical about their conflicts so that there can be accurate costing of the consequences of their policies.[19] These need to be pursued in respect of particular conflicts. In a global setting in which conflict is almost universal, resolving or avoiding a particular conflict is of little significance. More important is the pursuit of policies that anticipate and avoid conflict. It is these costing processes that are most likely to change perceptions of conflict and shift parties away from threat and deterrence strategies.

The two, resolution and avoidance, are in practice related. It is insights that are gained from facilitated conflict-resolution processes that give clues to the hidden causes of conflict and, by deduction, to positive policies. It is this kind of facilitated interactive experience—and the accurate costing of consequences of policies—that could lead disputants to those changes that are required to avoid cold and hot wars.[20]

The United Nations is not in a position to do this. It seeks to preserve its sovereign constituents and to resist pressures for separate autonomies and altered boundaries. A nongovernmental organization is required, and only the academic community can take the necessary initiatives.

There are a growing number of university degree-giving institutions that have this focus. They cannot be departments because they cut across all behavioral disciplines in dealing with the real person and the real society.

Separate disciplines focus on institutions and imply that human behavior should conform with institutions, and not the other way around. To be scientific, "the economic person" and its unidimensional equivalents in other social science disciplines, including psychology, have been invented. Conflict resolution and *provention* look to institutional change as the means of satisfying human requirements.[21] In this sense they are a challenge to separate disciplines, and not always welcome.

Perhaps the main lesson of the disintegration of the former U.S.S.R. is that prediction of important events, whether they be political or environmental, is almost impossible. To the extent that this is so, preventive policies are limited. This points to the need for processes built into institutions, at all social levels, that allow for constant reassessments and adjustments to emerging conditions. This is not happening in industrial relations, in legal processes, in parliamentary processes, and least of all in relations between sovereign states, despite the globalization of economic relationships. On the contrary, adherence to the past is claimed as a duty and a desirable goal, while innovation and advocacy of change are regarded as subversive. The opposite is the truth.

The academic community has here a great responsibility. Until it rethinks, politicians and the media cannot be blamed for cold and hot wars. The Cold War is still alive and well. We academics are the culprits.

NOTES

1. I have not traced back files to this date. My memory is that the inward telegram was marked as from Churchill.

2. The debate in Australia and events that led up to the Vietnam War have been well described and documented by John Murphy, *Harvest of Fear—A History of Australia's Vietnam War* (Sydney: Allen & Unwin, 1993). This book provides more than a history in that it describes by implication how domestic and foreign politics mix and how governments are prepared to be involved in wars for ideological and domestic political purposes.

3. See, in particular, ibid., Chapter 4.

4. See ibid., p. 40.

5. See ibid., pp. 103, 111.

6. See ibid., pp. 40, 63.

7. See ibid., p. 63.

8. Paul M. Kennedy, *Preparing for the Twenty-First Century* (New York: HarperCollins, 1993).

9. Paul M. Kennedy, *The Rise and Fall of the Great Powers: Economic Change and Military Conflict from 1500 to 2000* (London: Unwin Hyman, 1988).

10. These discussions with a senior State Department official took place at the George Mason University Institute for Conflict Analysis and Resolution shortly after the Gulf War.

11. During the Chifley government the Dutch attempted to purchase and send weapons to Indonesia. Waterside workers seemed to be aware of this and allowed crates of "medical supplies" to drop and open. Chifley took a firm line with the Dutch ambassador, making it

clear that he was not preventing the shipment of arms to Indonesia in particular. He was opposed to all arms exports.

12. For example, the Organization of African Unity from its first meeting resolved not to alter boundaries, even though they were established as a result of colonial invasions and frequently cut across tribal and racial boundaries.

13. At a seminar, the U.S. government's Institute of Peace reported in their "In Brief" (No. 42, September 1992), there was a discussion on "Does any group of citizens have an inherent right to secede—even forcefully—from an internationally recognized state?" Ambassador Max Kampelman took the shared view that "self-determination is a limited human right encompassing cultural independence . . . but it does not include the right to change boundaries at will because that is destabilizing."

14. A group of ten ambassadors of middle-power countries met in 1989 at George Mason University to explore the possibilities of forming a group that could act as problem-solving mediators in the absence of any desire or ability by the U.N. Secretariat to do this. They concluded that this would undermine the United Nations. They did not state, but did imply, that many disputes before the United Nations were disputes involving minorities seeking separate autonomies.

15. This phrase was used by then Colonel Charles Spry during some discussions I had with him during the Lapstone conference in 1948. We related well to each other and I respect his commitment. But it is an approach that is likely to cut away constitutional rights and the foundations of constructive criticisms of society. See Laurence Maher, "The Lapstone Experiment and the Beginning of ASIO," *Labour History* 64 (May 1993): 103–18.

16. In 1954, Vladimir Petrov, a ministry of state security official at the Soviet embassy, sought political asylum in Australia. He claimed the existence in Australia of a Soviet espionage system that involved members of the opposition leader Dr. H. V. Evatt's staff. Evatt's defense of the staff and subsequent criticism of the Royal Commission investigation created a furor that brought about his party's defeat at the next general election. Various books on the Petrov affair, including that of Nicholas Whitlam and John Stubbs, *Nest of Traitors: The Petrov Affair* (Brisbane: Jacaranda Press, 1974) leave little doubt that the Petrov defection just prior to an election was an ASIO attempt to prevent the Australian Labor Party under Evatt from coming into office.

17. The term *prevention* has the connotation of containment. The term *provention* has been introduced to signify taking steps to remove sources of conflict, and more positively to promote conditions in which collaborative and valued relationships control behaviors.

18. There are now available theories of behavior that explain why deterrence does not necessarily deter. See in particular a book of articles, John Burton, ed., *Conflict: Human Needs Theory*, vol. 2 of *The Conflict Series* (New York: St. Martin's Press, 1990).

19. There have been many problem-solving interventions on an exploratory basis, and some reference has been made to them in Burton, *Conflict: Human Needs Theory*. Essential to the process is confidentiality; otherwise there could not be an in-depth analysis of the problem.

20. The procedures of conflict analysis are set out in John Burton and Frank Dukes, eds., *Conflict: Practices in Management, Settlement and Resolution*, vol. 4 of *The Conflict Series* (New York: St. Martin's Press, 1990).

21. It is important to make a distinction between human values and human requirements, which may be culturally determined, and human needs that are inherent and universal.

14

In the Shadow
of the Middle Kingdom Syndrome:
China in the Post–Cold War World

C. L. Chiou

INTRODUCTION

Since 221 B.C. when the first emperor of China, Qin Shi Huang, defeated other states, thereby ending the long Warring States period of ancient Chinese history and unifying the land of the Yellow River and the people of the Yellow Emperor, the centrist, irredentist, and unitary Middle Kingdom syndrome has continued to dominate Chinese political culture and political behavior.[1] Reinforced by Qin Shi Huang's construction of the Great Wall and more importantly by the installation of Confucianism as its national ideology by the Han emperors (196 B.C.–A.D. 167), a Sinocentrist superiority complex has been so integrated into the psyche of the Chinese people that it has become a sort of "total ideology," as defined by Karl Mannheim.[2] Thus one of the most famous statements exemplifying the Middle Kingdom superiority complex was made by the third emperor of the last imperial dynasty of China, the Qing dynasty, Qian Long (1736–1795), a contemporary of George Washington, in his edict to King George III: "Our celestial empire possesses all things in prolific abundance and lacks no product within its own borders. There is therefore no need to import the manufactures of outside barbarians."[3]

Superiority and inferiority complexes are, of course, often twin brothers. Their twin brotherhood has been manifested vividly in both China and Japan since the West began to knock on their doors in the eighteenth century. In China, since the 1840 Opium War, in spite of one humiliation after another at the hands of Western imperialists which created an

increasing inferiority complex among the Chinese people, the twin brothers have continued to haunt the citizens, particularly the ruling mandarin
class of the Middle Kingdom. The twins have caused havoc in China's
domestic politics as well as foreign relations, for example, the 1900 Boxer
Rebellion, the 1958 invasion of Tibet, the Sino-Soviet dispute in the
1960s, Mao Zedong's Cultural Revolution of 1966 to 1976, and Deng
Xiaoping's 1989 Tiananmen massacre.

On October 1, 1949, Mao Zedong stood at Tiananmen (gate of heavenly
peace) and declared, "The Chinese people have stood up." On the one hand
he was reasserting the sinocentrist position of the Middle Kingdom; and on
the other, he was continuing the Yellow Emperor's tradition, signaling his
intention to create another "cultural China" dynasty.[4] If under the weak
Chiang Kai-shek dynasty the Chinese people suffered an extreme inferiority
complex, under the messianic revolutionary Maoist dynasty, the Chinese
people's ego was artificially inflated to such an extent that in the 1959 Great
Leap Forward, they believed China's economic and political might would
overtake that of the United Kingdom and catch up with that of the United
States in fifteen years. During the ten-year Cultural Revolution, they really
thought they were doing something much more superior than their counterparts in the former Soviet Union had ever done. Mao's anti-U.S. and then
anti-Soviet foreign policies between 1956 and 1976 were so clearly anti-
foreign that they looked more like Emperor Qian Long's edict to King George
III than part of a Marxist attempt to create a new China—a new and better
classless society.

When Mao died in September 1976, the Chinese people were forced to
wake up from a nightmare, discovering that Mao was just another Han Gao
Zu (206–195 B.C., first emperor of the Han dynasty) or Tang Tai Zhong
(712–756, first emperor of the Tang dynasty). The superiority complex Mao
had successfully cultivated and raised to such a great height among the
Chinese people was just another self-deceiving, or rather self-indulging, ego
trip. Immediately after the great helmsman's death, they were shocked to
discover their Middle Kingdom was still one of the poorest countries in the
world. An inferiority complex set in again among many Chinese, and Deng
Xiaoping felt compelled to embark upon another aggrandizing scheme, the
so-called four modernizations, to restore the centrist position of the Middle
Kingdom.

The economic modernization road—called a "socialist market economy"
and "building socialism with Chinese characteristics"—taken by Deng has
been pragmatic and realistic and, despite the serious setback of June 4, 1989,
has been fairly successful. However, as indicated by the June 4 massacre,
Dengist China is still an ethnocentrist Middle Kingdom that will not tolerate

"foreign intervention" in its internal affairs. Moreover, as the ongoing dispute with Hong Kong's Governor Chris Patten over democratic reform, and the semiofficial contact between Beijing and Taipei in April 1993, have shown, "economics in command" can only go so far. Once it threatens Beijing's "politics in command," the maintenance of the "mandate of heaven" invariably takes precedence over the economic well-being of the subjects of the "Central Plains."

Thus in the post–Cold War multipolar international politics—although Dengist China has tried hard to push its socialist market economy in order to raise people's living standards and avoid the catastrophic fate of the former Soviet Union—it has not been able to break out of the two-thousand-year straitjacket of the Middle Kingdom syndrome of anti-Western, Cold War attitudes and policies. For China, its anti-Western imperialist war started much earlier than the end of the World War II. It began in the mid-nineteenth century, continued in the Republican period, especially in the May 4 Movement, and—with some change of protagonists—persisted into the Cold War period. Moreover, with the collapse of European communism, together with further adjustments in threat perception, it has continued into the post-1990 new world order.

HONG KONG, TAIWAN, AND TIANANMEN

During the height of the dispute over Hong Kong in February-March 1993, although the modest political reforms proposed by Governor Patten would only make Hong Kong's legislature more representative of the will of the people, on several occasions Beijing warned it might ignore the 1984 Sino-British joint declaration on the future of Hong Kong. Beijing threatened to set up a "shadow government" that would not abide by the promises made in the 1983–84 Sino-British negotiations. It might even take over Hong Kong before the agreed-upon 1997 deadline. China's director of the Hong Kong and Macau Affairs Office, Lu Ping, called Patten a *jian-gu zui-ren* (eternal villain, historic sinner).[5] The vocabulary used by Beijing during this period was in the mode of Qian Long's imperial edict, full of ultranationalist, Han chauvinistic overtones.

Just as ominously, Beijing also threatened to withdraw cooperation with British and Hong Kong authorities on vital infrastructure projects, such as the construction of the new international airport, thus damaging the colony's economic development. China's foreign trade minister, Li Lanqing, also indicated that Sino-British commercial ties could be disrupted. Chinese officials said this could see British companies excluded from lucrative contracts, in much the same way as Beijing had shut out French firms following

Paris's decision to sell Mirage fighters to Taiwan in late 1992. The threats rocked the Hong Kong stock market and drove away foreign investors. Although very important to the Chinese economy, the economic stability and prosperity of a Western imperialist colony were less important, if not totally inconsequential, in terms of the nationalist pride of the Middle Kingdom.[6]

On the year-long attempt at realizing the Beijing-Taipei talks of April 27–29, 1993, in Singapore, Taiwan's pragmatic economic stance was consistently challenged by China's "one China" political maneuver.[7] While Taipei authorities wanted protection for their businessmen and investors on the Chinese mainland—thereby encouraging more Taiwanese investment on the mainland—the Beijing regime was more interested in creating a "one China" Middle Kingdom image than in merely solving pressing economic matters.

The pro-democracy movement of April 15 to June 4, 1989, at Tiananmen was the most critical test for the Dengist regime. On May 19 when martial law was declared and on June 4 when the People's Liberation Army (PLA) troops were sent in to clear the square, Deng Xiaoping was shown to be just another Oriental despot, a traditional Chinese emperor.

Just as unfortunately for Dengist China, in late 1989 the Berlin Wall fell and there followed in quick succession the total collapse of Soviet and East European communism. With the dramatic end of the European Cold War and the condemnation of the Tiananmen massacre by the West, China found itself again a target of "Western imperialist" intervention, especially in the area of human rights. China was forced to retreat behind its Great Wall fortress.

Of course, the post–Cold War new world order had arrived and Deng was no Mao. Thus after two years of "consolidation and restructuring," Deng reached the conclusion that without economic development and improvement of people's living standards, his attempt at building socialism with Chinese characteristics could not succeed. In 1992, he reinstated his economic "reform and open-door" policy, and in 1993, he removed all pretenses of a centrally planned economy and called China's present-day economic system a "socialist market economy." However, if the West believes that the disappearance of central economic planning and state ownership of the means of production in China means that the Leninist-Confucianist party dictatorship has been shaken loose and that Beijing's economic open-door policy has led to a political open-door foreign policy, it is, of course, sorely mistaken.

On the economic front, 1992 and 1993 saw China's annual growth rate of 12 percent top the world, particularly in southeastern China, with Guangdong province leading the field—its growth rate reached more than 20 percent. The impression was created that in this part of China, a capitalist, rather than a socialist, market economy was the dominant force. It would, however, be misleading to interpret China's political power center as having shifted from Beijing to Guangzhou (Canton) or Shanghai. It has not and will not in the foreseeable future. Thus on the political front, it must be borne in mind that Chinese perceptions of the world in Beijing are very different from those in Shanghai or Guangzhou. In an interesting discussion of relations between nationalism and modernization, Lucian Pye points out the fundamental differences and contradictions between interior and coastal China. He explains that the huge population of interior China was cursed with poverty and corrupt government, while in the coastal enclaves there was an environment where the Chinese could prosper and realize the spirit of modern life.

He adds: "Interior China was thus seen as the real China, but it was a flawed and, in modern terms, a disgraced China. For the Chinese in the enclaves there was an inescapable sense of guilt as they became more nationalistically conscious. For the Chinese of the interior there was shame and humiliation as they became more conscious of modernization."[8] Since the reformist movements of the late nineteenth century, the Chinese cultural and political elite has followed a *ti-yong* modernization formula in which Chinese values are at the core and Western technology is merely utilitarian. The formula set the stage for checking the political power of technically trained people in Shanghai and Guangzhou. As Pye puts it: "The rationale of the formulation was that those who specialize in useful knowledge should yield authority to those who claimed to speak for essential Chinese values."[9] Thus, politically, Shanghai has never become the center of power and has always been subordinate to Beijing.[10]

Beijing has been a capital city for roughly a thousand years, and as Fairbank explains, "foreign potentates or their envoys have turned up practically every year, as regularly as the winter solstice or the fall equinox. They have come for a variety of motives, most to present tribute in order to profit from trade, some to have their legitimacy confirmed, others to ask for military help, and not a few to demand payoffs to keep quiet."[11] Both Jiang Zemin, general secretary of the Chinese Communist Party (CCP), and Zhu Rongqi, vice-premier, are former mayors of Shanghai. What they said and what they did in Shanghai are very different from what they have been saying and doing in Beijing since they moved to the CCP center in Zhongnanhai, the former imperial palace. In Shanghai, both sounded like pragmatic capitalists, while in Beijing they act like Confucian paternalistic leaders and Maoist ideologues. In a recent convention of the CCP propagandists, the even more pragmatic Zhu was heard praising "ideological and political work among the proletariat" as "a powerful weapon" for building a socialist market economy.[12]

Although Deng, Jiang, and Zhu have accepted the end of the bipolar international system, and thus the end of the U.S.-Soviet-dominated Cold War, they have not really come to terms with the fact that East-West relations have also substantially changed. From Beijing's Sinocentrist perspective, the capitalist West, led by the only superpower, the U.S., is still perceived as an anti-Chinese cultural, economic, ideological, political, and to a lesser extent, military threat. To the Beijing-based political leadership, such a Western "imperialist" regime has been continuously trying to pull down the Middle Kingdom since the 1840 Opium War. The collapse of European communism and the end of the Cold War have not really altered that basic historical, or rather cultural, condition.[13]

Patten's democratic reforms; sales by the United States and France of jet fighters to Taiwan; Clinton's support of the Dalai Lama; accusations of China selling nuclear technology to Pakistan and chemical weapons ingredients to Iran; demands for improvements in China's human rights condition; U.S. pressure on North Korea not to develop nuclear bombs; and the support of many Western countries for Taiwan's membership in the General Agreement on Tariffs and Trade (GATT) have all been seen by Beijing as parts of an anti-China conspiracy.[14] Thus Beijing ordered the French consulate general in Guangzhou to be closed,[15] accused the U.S. of being the obstacle to the resolution of the Taiwan question, forced the United Nations to withdraw its invitation to the Dalai Lama to attend the June 1993 human rights conference in Vienna,[16] and pressured the GATT council to change the name and admission time of Taiwan's observer membership.

THE GENERALS' LETTER

According to the fairly authoritative Hong Kong monthly, *Cheng Ming*, in mid-April 1993, 116 People's Liberation Army (PLA) generals, including the chief of the general staff (Zhang Wangnian), the director of the political department (Yu Yongbo), and the head of the logistics department (Fu Quanyu), coauthored a letter to Deng Xiaoping and Jiang Zemin asking them to convene an enlarged Politburo meeting to revise China's foreign policy toward the United States.[17] They stressed that Beijing's patient, compromising, and conciliatory U.S. policy needed to change. They said that unilateral concessions made by the Chinese government toward the Americans were hurting the "dignity of the Chinese people, self-reliance image of the Chinese race and glorious tradition of the PLA" and "were adversely impacting on the fighting capability and morale of the PLA."

The letter pointed out that since the normalization of relations between the People's Republic of China (PRC) and the United States, the Americans have never stopped interfering in China's internal affairs and carrying out subversive activities to overthrow the Chinese government. Especially after the collapse of the former Soviet Union, the United States has perceived China as its "strategic enemy" and actively and openly stirred up anti-Chinese actions. The United States has broken the agreements in the three Sino-U.S. communiqués signed in 1972, 1978, and 1982 by selling advanced weaponry to Taiwan and supporting Taiwan's independence movement. The United States has also supported the Dalai Lama's separatism and other anti-Chinese activities in the "neighboring" countries.

The anti–United States and anti-West stance has been supported by none other than the late Chen Yun, the second most powerful elder statesman in China. In the eyes of Chen Yun and his faithful followers, the East-West Cold War not only did not end with the collapse of European communism, but it has become more dangerous for the East because the demise of the former Soviet Union has left the United States the sole superpower in the world. Chen was reportedly quite explicit on the point that with the disintegration of the former Soviet Union, China would inevitably become the number one strategic target of U.S. military might, and it would be wishful thinking to contemplate the United States wanting China to become strengthened and reunified with Taiwan.

On May 14, 1993, Jiang Zemin told a CCP Politburo meeting basically the same thing. He commented on the May 11–12 meeting between the U.S. assistant secretary of state, Winston Lord, and the Chinese deputy foreign minister, Liu Qinghua, and warned that the "U.S. ultimatum" on China's human rights violations and sales of nuclear technology and advanced weaponry to Pakistan, Iran, Saudi Arabia, and others was a clear threat to China. He said that since China wanted cooperation, it was not seeking confrontation and was willing to work within the principles laid down in the three Sino-U.S. communiqués; China would not bow to hegemonism and compromise with power politics; and it would be ready to face any threat and challenge to protect the motherland's sovereignty, independence, and dignity.

THE OFFICIAL LINE

The above views represent very strong Cold War rhetoric. Of course, they could not be officially pronounced. Officially, Beijing has been more constrained. Nevertheless, a careful reading of what CCP leaders have said since 1989 reveals a basically similar anti-West, Middle Kingdom mentality.

After Clinton agreed on May 28, 1993, to give China the most-favored-nation (MFN) trade status with a sort of probationary period of one year to improve its human rights record, the PRC foreign ministry responded sternly on May 29 by declaring that Clinton's "conditional granting of the MFN status to China for the 1994–95 period is an act openly in violation of the principles of the three Sino-US communiqués and the trade agreements between the two countries, and is a serious interference in Chinese internal affairs. The Chinese government strongly objects to the US action and protests against the US government."[18] The spokesperson also warned that if the United States continued to *yi-yi gu-xin* (stubbornly go it alone), it would severely damage Sino-U.S. relations. He emphasized: "We all know that Chinese and American social systems, thoughts, and historic and cultural backgrounds are different, and thus on the concepts of human rights and other matters the two countries have different views."

In his "Report of the Work of the Government" to the fifth session of the seventh National People's Congress on March 20, 1992, Premier Li Peng stated:

> The old world structure has come to an end, while the new one has yet to take shape. The world is moving in the direction of multipolarization. Forces are disintegrating, their elements are being realigned, and new contradictions are being interwoven with the old. The world we live in is still far from tranquil. International economic competition is growing bitter. Contradictions between North and South are becoming more pronounced. Some ethnic feuds have touched off new regional conflicts. . . . Hegemonism and power politics are the root cause of turmoil in the international situation, and China is opposed to them both.[19]

He then proceeded to assert that China should continue to strengthen its traditional friendship and cooperation with North Korea and its solidarity and cooperation with other developing countries. He pointed out that China has maintained close contacts with many developing countries in Asia, Africa, and Latin America.

In his lengthy report to the fourteenth CCP National Congress on October 12, 1992, Jiang Zemin, though in greater detail, basically repeated what Li had said. The general secretary talked about the "great change" in the world system: the movement toward multipolarization, the turbulent current international situation, the emerging new contradictions and conflicts between nations, and the widening gap between North and South. He condemned "hegemonism and power politics" as the main obstacles to peace and development and as the main threat to independence and sovereignty of the poor countries. He urged the developing nations to seek solidarity and cooperation together. Then he repeated the two policy lines that had been made by Mao

Zedong and Zhou Enlai at the height of the Cold War in the 1950s and 1960s:

> On questions involving our national interests and state sovereignty, we shall never yield to any outside pressure. China will always stand firm as a strong defender of world peace. It will not enter into alliance with any country or group of countries and will not join any military bloc. China will never seek hegemony and expansion; it is opposed to hegemonism, power politics, and aggression and expansion in any form.[20]

He then declared that the founding of the PRC had put an end to the "Chinese people's tragic history of suffering from long aggression, oppression and humiliation" and had "fundamentally changed the situation of human rights in China." He concluded, "In the final analysis, the question of human rights is a matter within each country's sovereignty; China is absolutely opposed to the use of human rights to interfere in other countries' internal affairs."[21]

MILITARY PROWESS

Despite the demise of the former Soviet Union and the increasing withdrawal of the U.S. military presence in Asia, China has continued to increase its military expenditures and buy new advanced weapons systems for the last four years.

According to the *Far Eastern Economic Review,* China's military budget in 1990 increased 15.2 percent over 1989.[22] According to *Remin Ribao,* China's military budget was $6.1 billion in 1991, $6.7 billion in 1992 (an increase of 12 percent), and $7.3 billion in 1993 (an increase of 14.8 percent). The 1993 military expenditure accounts for 8.99 percent of the total national budget, the highest percentage since 1975.[23]

In the immediate aftermath of the collapse of the Soviet Union, China enlisted numerous former Soviet technical personnel and purchased military supplies and technology to make the PLA the strongest military force in the Asian region. Moreover, the PLA Headquarters of the General Staff and the Chinese Institute of Military Science oversaw the prompt re-formation of various military organizations and services into a Center for the Research of Foreign Military Equipment Procurement, a body expressly charged with looking into the feasibility of purchasing advanced weaponry from the former Soviet Union and enticing former Soviet experts in military technology to work in China.[24]

While Beijing, according to *Remin Ribao*, downplayed its military build-up in the post–Cold War years as insignificant and much less than the military expenditures of the United States, Japan, Germany, and the United Kingdom,[25] Japan's *Yomiuri Shimbun* asserts that the figures do not tell the whole story.[26] Western military analysts hold that some overlapping occurs throughout the Chinese military budget, so that the actual defense budget is closer to three times higher than the officially announced figure. Funding for a significant majority of such items as advanced military technology research, advanced weaponry and technology procurement, and so on, is not contained in the national defense budget.

After signing an agreement worth more than $1 billion for twenty-four SU-27 fighters in mid-1991, the Chinese air force began taking delivery of the aircraft and by the end of 1992 all the SU-27s had been delivered.[27] More purchases of SU-27s are expected soon and military analysts also have confirmed that a contract was signed in 1992 for the purchase of MIG-31 fighters. There are indications the SU-27 and MIG-31 deals may include the transfer of assembly facilities to enable the aircraft to be produced in China. In addition, the Russians may be willing to provide other important technologies, including powerful engines for fighter aircraft and even radar-evading stealth technology for China's next generation of F10 fighters.

As well as fighters, China has ordered six Ilusin-76 long-range military transport planes. In December 1992, China used the occasion of President Boris Yeltsin's visit to Beijing to finalize secret arms deals with Russia.[28] These include the purchase of twenty-seven SU-27 fighters between 1993 and 1995, four long-range bombers, eighteen S-300 guided missile anti-aircraft systems with around one hundred anti-aircraft missiles, seventy modified G-72 M-class tanks, and three conventional submarines.

According to a Radio Moscow report,[29] additional arms negotiations, including talks over MIG-31 fighter production technology transfers, the purchase of ninety MIG-29s, and the sale of an aircraft carrier, have been carried out. Recently, the Chinese navy has actively lobbied Ukraine in the hope of procuring one 67,000-ton aircraft carrier currently under construction. While these talks have broken down over price, China has by no means scrapped its plan to obtain an aircraft carrier, and has turned to Russia, hoping to purchase two 38,000-ton light aircraft carriers currently in service. China also wants to obtain the thirty-plus vertical takeoff and landing fighters and antisubmarine helicopters on board these vessels.

According to *China Times*,[30] there were already more than 1,500 Russian technicians in Guiyang, Yunan, working with Chinese counterparts in the technical transfer of manufacturing several hundred MIG-31 fighters. Another 700 Russian military scientists and technicians were working in Shanghai in advanced surface-to-air missile production. The report cites a Chinese document on Beijing's ambitious "blue-water plan," in which the PRC wants to become a global naval power with its warships "reaching every corner of the world" by the year 2040. Currently, China's navy counts among its possessions over sixty medium- and large-sized guided missile destroyers, nearly one thousand small vessels, 181 submarines (including two nuclear submarines equipped with nuclear missiles and five nuclear submarines armed with conventional missiles), and more than seven hundred fighter planes and helicopters.

For General Liu Huaqing's blue-water navy plan, naval intelligence analysts report that shipyards in Shanghai and other port cities have rarely been so busy. At present, several new types of warships are close to completion in Shanghai, including a new class of destroyer known as the Luhu, a new Jiangwei-class frigate, and logistic support ships that will help the Chinese navy's efforts to become a blue-water force.[31] The Chinese navy is currently hard at work developing advanced weaponry including electronic cannons and neutron bombs. From the military build-up described above, one can infer that the Chinese navy and air force have evolved from a defensive configuration hugging the mainland coast to a blue-water, long-range fighting force with offensive capability. With China's expanding strength and international prominence, a blue-water navy with aircraft carriers would coincide with China's self-perceived image as a major world political, economic, and military power.[32]

MARX, MAO, DENG, AND CONFUCIUS

Deng Xiaoping is reported to have said at a CCP meeting: "I have always hoped that the Cold War would end, but I am sorely disappointed that another Cold War is picking up where the first one has left off."[33]

To Deng, Jiang Zemin, and Li Peng, not to mention the old guard Chen Yun, the Cold War has continued uninterrupted since the end of World War II. To them, although the collapse of communism in Europe has changed the roles of the main players in the power game equation, East-West contradictions continue to divide the world and to challenge the Sinocentrist position of the Middle Kingdom. However, is it still a Cold War mortal struggle between socialism-communism and capitalism? In Maoist China it was never very clear, and in Dengist China it has become even more difficult to answer the question. Was Mao basically a Marxist revolutionary or a Confucian emperor? Is Deng still a socialist-communist or basically another Confucian autocratic ruler?

In China after June 4, 1989, these questions have had totally different meanings for the Chinese as well as the Sinologists. During the Cold War,

Marx played a dominant role in the bipolar international system, but in China it was Confucius rather than Marx who fundamentally determined Mao's as well as Deng's worldview, although the rhetoric may have sounded otherwise. As a functional political ideology, Marxism-Maoism has certainly played an important role in Chinese politics. However, as a deep-rooted two-thousand-year-old political culture, Confucianism has been a "total ideology," a way of life, that has not really been substantively dented by Marx or Lenin. It has continued to determine the fundamental psychocultural outlook and sociopolitical behavior of the Chinese people.

From Mao's Great Leap Forward to Deng's condemnation of the Cultural Revolution and rejection of "continued revolution under the dictatorship of the proletariat," and from a Dengist socialist planned commodity economy to a socialist market economy, the economic, political, and ideological transformations are critical. They do make substantive differences. The question that needs to be asked and answered is that if communism has died in the former Soviet Union and Eastern Europe, have Maoist communism and then Dengist socialism also died—probably a slower death in China? As has already been pointed out, from Shanghai's and Guangzhou's hectic and expanding market economy, some may argue that socialism has died. However, from the perspective of centrist imperial Beijing, the picture is very different and no one should be rushing to the deathbed of this key area of socialism-communism.

Not only is Chen Yun's "bird-cage" economic theory still popular among the CCP rank and file, if not among the "neo-authoritarian" economic modernizers, but Deng's, Jiang Zemin's, and Li Peng's constant adherence to the "four cardinal principles"—the socialist road, the people's democratic dictatorship, leadership by the CCP, and Marxism-Leninism and Maoist thought—has not really been questioned. Either as a functional ideology or a committed belief system, the four principles are the justification and rationalization of the very existence of the CCP regime.

In his political report to the fourteenth National Congress of the CCP, Jiang Zemin stated quite clearly that "China's socialist system has withstood severe tests and shown great vitality in the face of drastic changes in the world situation."[34] Then he linked the old China with the new China:

> The semi-colonial and semi-feudal China of the past, which for over a hundred years had suffered from foreign aggression and bullying, was turned into a new and independent socialist China in which the people were the masters. This revolution, the greatest China had ever seen, ushered in a new era in the history of our country. This new revolution [Dengist program of building socialism with Chinese characteristics] is

designed to turn our underdeveloped socialist country into a prosperous, strong, democratic, culturally advanced and modern socialist country, so as to fully demonstrate the superiority of socialism in China. It is based on our earlier revolutionary victory and on our great achievements in socialist construction, and it is being carried out step by step, in good order, under the leadership of the Party. This revolution is not intended to change the nature of our socialist system but to improve and develop it.[35]

This is what he called a "vigorous socialism." He also insisted that members should recognize the importance of the role Mao had played in Chinese history and reaffirm the value of Mao's thought as a guide to action.

CONCLUSION

As John King Fairbank has indicated, Maoism became more plainly nationalistic and romantic after the 1960s Sino-Soviet dispute. Mao's attempts to go it alone and capture the leadership of the communist world revolution, although clothed in Marxist-Leninist-Maoist terminology, was never "a Hitlerite blueplan for conquest abroad, but instead reminded one of the ancient theory of tributary relationships of neighboring states to Peking—the theory that China was a model that other countries should follow, but on their own initiative."[36]

In comparison with Mao's efforts to line up the amorphous Third World against the two superpowers in the 1960s and 1970s, Deng's independent foreign policy in the post–Cold War era is even more Sinocentrist—thus less expansionist-imperialist in terms of its traditional Middle Kingdom perspectives—than Mao's "people's wars of liberation." Despite the fact that since 1990 China has forcefully pursued an ambitious blue-water military plan and acquired an in-flight refueling technology to extend the range of its fighter-bombers and other weapons systems to nearly 800,000 square kilometers of "survival space,"[37] Deng's "new Cold War" is just as defensive, if not more so, in practice than Mao's "people's wars" theory. Its principal goal is to reclaim the Sinocentrist position for the Middle Kingdom, rather than to realize any sort of "Hitlerite master plan."

Thus, Mao's antisuperpower "people's wars" of the Cold War era and Deng's anti-Western, anti-U.S., "new Cold War" of the 1990s are fundamentally the same. They are the continuity of the Sinocentrist "cultural China" of the Boxer Rebellion, the May 4 Movement, and the anti-Japanese war. Although the forms, the expressions, or the functional ideologies (such as Confucianism and Maoism) are sometimes different, the substance, the essence, is basically the same.

In the post–Cold War era of multipolarity, Deng's China has been forced to refocus on a new set of threats to continue a new Cold War against the West. Although the new Cold War has extended into the vast new realm of international economy where military and political considerations no longer primarily prevail, China still feels the need to be militarily and politically powerful in order to dominate its Asian neighbors and defend itself against any military threats from outside the Great Wall and across the oceans. The need has not really changed since the Opium War.

In the revised edition of his 1948 classic, *The United States and China*, Fairbank states:

> Foreign models and foreign activities in China, whether Japanese, Western, or Soviet, could serve only as stimuli, not as substance. To say that the new order under the PRC is the latest phase of China's response to the outside world would omit the heart of the matter, which is the Chinese people's great mass, inertial momentum, and native genius for creating their own culture.[38]

The first edition of this book in 1948, at the onset of the Cold War, concluded that "the disintegration of the old order in China leaves that country open to reorganization under the dominant influence" of either the U.S.S.R. or the United States as superpowers. What nonsense! China has always gone its own way.

In a recent theoretical treatise, Samuel Huntington asserts that the ideological conflicts between communism and Western democracy have ended with the end of the Cold War, and that new clashes have begun to emerge among the world's seven or eight major civilizations.[39] He says the fault lines between civilizations are replacing the political and ideological boundaries of the Cold War as the flash points for crisis and bloodshed. However, Huntington's new theory is not new for the Middle Kingdom. Unlike Europe or the Middle East, the fault line between China and its antagonists, especially the West, has been—since at least the mid-nineteenth century, if not much earlier—the civilization boundaries between Han (Confucian) Chinese and non-Han ("barbarian") civilizations.

In other words, Huntington is agreeing that "[w]ith the Cold War over, the underlying differences between China and the United States have reasserted themselves in areas such as human rights, trade and weapons proliferation. These differences are unlikely to moderate. A 'new cold war,' Deng Xiaoping reportedly asserted in 1991, is underway between China and America."[40]

NOTES

1. John King Fairbank, *The United States and China*, 4th ed. (Cambridge, MA: Harvard University Press, 1979), pp. 53–170; Lucian Pye and Mary W. Pye, *Asian Power and Politics: The Cultural Dimensions of Authority* (Cambridge, MA: Harvard University Press, Belknap Press, 1985), p. 184.

2. Karl Mannheim, *Ideology and Utopia* (New York: Harcourt Brace; London: Routledge & Kegan Paul, 1936).

3. Fairbank, *The United States and China*, p. 8.

4. Tu Wei-ming, "Cultural China: The Periphery as the Center," *DAEDALUS* 120, no. 2 (1991): 1–32.

5. Tai Ming Cheung, "Turning on the Heat: Second Power Centre Threatened by China," *Far Eastern Economic Review* (*FEER*), February 18, 1993, p. 18; Tai Ming Cheung, "Changing Signals: China Stayed Out of Reach on Talks Issue," *FEER*, March 4, 1993, pp. 12–13; Jonathan Karp, "Through Train Slows Down: China Hits Back As Patten Gazettes His Reforms," *FEER*, March 25, 1993, p. 12; Tai Ming Cheung, "Front Assault," *FEER*, April 1, 1993, pp. 10–11; for an interview with Chris Patten, see "Question of Honour," *FEER*, April 1, 1993, pp. 11–12.

6. "Question of Honour," pp. 11–12.

7. C. L. Chiou, "Relations with Taiwan," in *China Review 1993*, eds. Joseph Cheng Yu-shek and Maurice Brosseau (Hong Kong: Chinese University Press, 1993).

8. Lucian W. Pye, "How China's Nationalism Was Shanghaied," *Australian Journal of Chinese Affairs* 29 (1993): 114.

9. Ibid., p. 125.

10. During the Cultural Revolution, Madame Mao, Jiang Qing, and her "gang of four" did try to make Shanghai into their revolutionary center but failed and lost the power struggle to the Beijing party elders.

11. John King Fairbank, *China Watch* (Cambridge, MA: Harvard University Press, 1987), pp. 127–28.

12. Lincoln Kaye, "Role Reversal," *FEER*, May 27, 1993, pp. 10–11.

13. Samuel P. Huntington, "The Clash of Civilizations?" *Foreign Affairs* 73, no. 2 (1993): 22–41.

14. Susumu Awanohara, "Lukewarm Welcome: Dalai Lama Gets Cautious Reception in Washington," *FEER*, May 6, 1993, p. 13; Helen Trinca, "Storm over Dalai at Human Rights Conference," *The Australian*, June 14, 1993, p. 8; Susumu Awanohara, "China Consensus: Clinton and Congress Converge on MFN Issue," *FEER*, April 22, 1993, p. 13.

15. Lincoln Kaye, "Rapped Knuckles: China Punishes France for Mirage Sale," *FEER*, January 14, 1993, p. 17.

16. Trinca, "Storm over Dalai," p. 8.

17. *Cheng Ming*, June 1993, pp. 14–16.

18. "Power Game," *FEER Asia Yearbook 1991* (Hong Kong: FEER, 1991) p. 15.

19. Li Peng, "Report of the Work of the Government," *Beijing Review* 35, no. 15 (1992): 1–16.

20. Jiang Zemin, "Accelerating the Reform, the Opening to the Outside World and the Drive for Modernization, So As to Achieve Greater Successes in Building Socialism with Chinese Characteristics," *Beijing Review* 35, no. 43 (1992): 26–28.

21. Ibid.

22. "Power Game," 1991, p. 15.

23. Mu Huiming, "The Theory of Chinese Military Threat Is Completely Devoid of Factual Basis," *Remin Ribao,* April 20, 1993, p. 6, overseas edition.

24. Yue Jia, "Beijing in the Market for Advanced Soviet Weaponry," *Front Line Monthly* (April 1993): 32–33.

25. Huiming, "The Theory of Chinese Military Threat," p. 6.

26. *Yomiuri Shimbun,* April 2, 1993, p. 1.

27."Power Game," *FEER Asia Yearbook 1993* (Hong Kong: FEER, 1993) p. 19.

28. Radio Moscow Chinese broadcast, April 16, 1993. The broadcast is translated by *Inside China Mainland* 15, no. 6 (1993): 64–66.

29. Ibid.

30. *China Times,* July 12, 1993, p. 9.

31. *FEER Asia Yearbook 1993,* p. 20.

32. Radio Moscow, April 16, 1993.

33. Liao Zhaobao, "Arms Races and Regional Cold War," *Trend Monthly,* April 1993, pp. 31–32.

34. Jiang, "Accelerating the Reform," p. 10.

35. Ibid.

36. Fairbank, *China Watch,* p. 126.

37. *FEER Asia Yearbook 1993,* p. 110.

38. Fairbank, *The United States and China,* p. 470.

39. Huntington, "The Clash of Civilizations?"

40. Sheng Lijun, "Chinese Foreign Policy 1978–84: From Anti-Hegemonic United Front to the Independent Foreign Policy" (Ph.D. diss., University of Queensland, 1993), p. 34.

15

The Cold War . . . and After:
A New Period of Upheaval in World Politics

Joseph A. Camilleri

Though the end of the Cold War represents a dramatic turn in contemporary history, the full significance of these events cannot be grasped unless they are placed within a wider historical context, which means taking full account of the continuities as well as discontinuities between the Cold War and post–Cold War periods. A macrohistorical perspective, however, can do more than just establish the connections between the events of the late 1980s and early 1990s and those which immediately preceded them. By going beyond the confines of the post-1945 period, it can help to identify longer-term historical trends which have their origins in the nineteenth century.

CHARACTERIZATION OF THE COLD WAR

At its simplest, the Cold War may be understood as the conflict arising from the concerted attempts of the United States and the Soviet Union "to divide the world into two opposing camps, to impose bipolarity on a global scale."[1] In line with this interpretation, the Cold War was characterized by increasing political and military discipline within each camp, the establishment of integrated military alliances, and a tendency for the locus of decision making to shift from the nation-state to the bloc.

Though there is much to be said for this commonsense characterization of this unique period in modern history, there is good reason to delve a little more deeply. Numerous interpretations have been offered at different times, each with its distinctive analysis of structures, agencies, and processes. It is nevertheless possible to classify the majority of available explanatory models into three main clusters. Within the first cluster would be included those explanations, resting largely on balance-of-power theory, which viewed the bipolar conflict as a contest between two superstates. By virtue of their economic resources, geographic position, and military capabilities, these two states now enjoyed unchallenged preeminence over all other states. Only Washington and Moscow could now pursue global policies; only they could shape the central balance of power.

A closely connected but conceptually distinct explanation has stressed the functionality of the Cold War—that is, its instrumental role in entrenching the dominance or hegemony of two superpowers within their respective camps. Viewed from this perspective, both the American and Soviet blocs operated on the principle of limited sovereignty, at least so far as junior allies were concerned. The Cold War offered the necessary legitimation for the maintenance of order within each alliance system. To use Halliday's words, the Cold War provided "a diversion, a ritual, an excuse" masking the reality or potential for disorder within and between states of both camps.[2]

A third view, certainly one which had considerable currency in official discourse in the West as in the East, attached much greater priority to the role of ideology. The Cold War was likened to a contest between two opposing social and economic systems, where the function of ideology was, at least in part, to stabilize and legitimize the capitalist and communist orders respectively. The ideological claims and counterclaims emanating from Moscow and Washington reflected sharply conflicting interests and a tendency on the part of the Soviet and U.S. policy-making elites toward interventionism, particularly in the Third World. The United States had by the early 1950s arrogated to itself a global policing role, not only as the keeper of the peace in Third World conflicts but as the guarantor of international stability and capitalist prosperity. As for the Soviet Union, it presented itself as the model of the proletarian state in the making and the self-proclaimed embryo of the universal proletarian state. To this extent, the conflict between these two major centers of power and the strategy of nuclear deterrence could be viewed as the outcome of political pressures endogenous to the two systems. As this explanation underwent further refinement, it was argued that both sets of interests benefited from intersystemic or interbloc conflict. There was as much collusion as collision.[3] E. P. Thompson took this argument to its logical conclusion by developing the thesis that the Cold War was not just a competition between two systems but a system in its own right with a logic and a dynamic of its own.[4]

While each interpretation highlights different aspects of the conflict and attaches different weights to particular factors, all three point in different ways to the globalization of the East-West conflict and to the interconnectedness of the political, economic, and military spheres of action. To appreciate the full import of these two tendencies, it is necessary to place them in a macrohistorical setting. Here we can perhaps do no better than turn to the illuminating analysis offered by Yoshikazu Sakamoto, who suggests that the Cold War can be best understood as a function of three polarities central to modern history: capitalism versus socialism, state nationalism versus internationalism, and democracy versus authoritarianism.[5] As we shall see, the great merit of this conceptualization, despite a degree of oversimplification, is that it gives due weight to the role of ideology but by relating it, at least implicitly, to the two dominant institutions ushered in by the industrial revolution, namely, the market and the nation-state.

THE SAKAMOTO THESIS

The two world wars, Sakamoto argues, were the decisive test of strength between the capitalist/nationalist/liberal-democratic systems (which he designates as the early-developed core empires) and the capitalist/nationalist/authoritarian systems (or the late-developed industrial empires). Lacking the economic, financial, and military capabilities to match the British and French empires, Germany and Japan resorted to penetration of "peripheral old empires," namely, Russia and China, thereby helping to create conditions conducive to socialist revolution.[6] Following their defeat in World War II at the hand of the liberal democracies, the Axis powers were incorporated into the global liberal-democratic capitalist order constructed primarily under the umbrella of U.S. power and leadership. A new antithesis, however, soon emerged as the capitalist/nationalist/democratic core was subjected to a wide-ranging challenge by the socialist/nationalist/authoritarian core composed of the Soviet Union and China.

Though socialism was an important factor in the politics of Western Europe, especially in the aftermath of World War II, socialist or social democratic parties were gradually co-opted by the capitalist nation-state, while Communist parties were effectively marginalized. In the East, socialist movements captured the state only to be co-opted by it. Nowhere was this more strikingly evident than in Stalin's Russia where, under the slogan of "socialism in one country," a repressive bureaucratic apparatus attempted to accelerate the process of industrialization with minimal regard for the socialist ethic.

There were significant similarities between the political trajectories of East and West, but also significant differences. In the West, capitalism captured the state and became the dominant factor in the organization of economic and political institutions, though social democracy and the labor movement generally were able to extract a number of concessions, particularly with respect to wages and working conditions. In the East, socialism held state power, but in practice the state co-opted socialism, stifled its international ethos, and became the dominant factor in the socialist/nationalist/authoritarian complex. In this sense, state socialism became a contradictory and ultimately self-defeating exercise. State socialism, it is true, kept alive, at least rhetorically, the aspiration for equality and equity on the part of marginalized classes (both nationally and internationally), but its capacity to give effect to these aspirations was severely limited by the internal (sociocultural) and external (geopolitical) environment within which it operated.

The Cold War was no doubt a multidimensional phenomenon, but one of its defining characteristics was the clash between state-centric authoritarian socialism and a capitalist liberal-democratic order which, though outwardly wedded to nationalist sentiment and institutions, was engaged in a process of rapid and profound globalization.

SYSTEMIC CONTEXT OF THE COLD WAR

As has been argued elsewhere, the rival nationalisms which collided in the two world wars were themselves the product of a global competition for power, status, and markets, which greatly exceeds the explanatory potential of the state-centric conception of international relations.[7] The argument applies with even greater force to the stark confrontation between communism and capitalism in the aftermath of World War II. Each of these contests was a symptom of, but also a vehicle for, the internationalization of conflict, characterized by the deepening interconnection of different regions on the one hand and between those regions and the global economic and strategic system on the other.

The internationalization of economic activity underpinned by rapid technological change has been a distinguishing feature of the twentieth century. The net effect has been the increasing mobility of capital across national boundaries, the interpenetration of national economies, and the subjection of even advanced capitalist states to the competitive logic of the world market and the requirements of transnational trade, production, and finance.[8]

The trend has been especially pronounced in the case of peripheral states, which, though having achieved political independence, were nevertheless effectively incorporated into the structure of the world market through strategic aid programs, counterinsurgency and low-intensity warfare strategies, and, more recently, the structural adjustment policies of international institutions, notably the International Monetary Fund (IMF) and the World Bank.

According to the conventional wisdom the command economies, which proliferated after 1945 to form the socialist bloc, detached themselves from this hegemonic internationalization, otherwise referred to as the growth of a world economy. Indeed, they were seen by many as posing a direct threat to global capitalism. But it is also possible to interpret the quasi-autarkic development attempted by communist regimes in the Soviet Union, Eastern Europe, and China as at best a temporary and partial withdrawal on the part of the semiperiphery.[9] The socialist bloc is perhaps best understood as that region which escaped complete domination by the U.S. hegemon, partially developed its capacities, and subsequently reentered the capitalist system. There is some validity to the claim that Russia left the capitalist world with a largely peasant society only to return seventy years later with a developed, scientific, and industrial infrastructure. As Wallerstein and his associates have argued, communist states, though involved with strikingly different economic and political institutions, had to operate within a strategic diplomatic and economic framework whose modus operandi derived largely from the logic of the world market.[10] Placed in this context, "socialism in one country" becomes part of the dynamic of the capitalist world system rather than an alternative to it.

There is more, however, to globalization than the internationalization of economic activity. One of the most important functions of the Cold War was precisely the internationalization of security. By the late 1940s a global security system had emerged that rested on the twin pillars of strategic deterrence and collective security. Ideological bipolarity provided the framework and justification for the construction of two opposed military systems in which the nuclear peace coexisted with the internationalization of local and regional conflicts. Extended nuclear deterrence and limited sovereignty (which applied as much to the Western as to the Eastern bloc) became the twin pillars of alliance integration and a vehicle for a policy of global military intervention, enabling the two superpowers to penetrate not only the boundaries of their respective allies but those of a host of Third World states.

THE COLD WAR AND THE DYNAMICS OF DETENTE

The Cold War gave effect to important superpower interests, yet it was at best a mixed blessing. While it encouraged allies to toe the line, it also heightened their fears about a possible nuclear exchange, and to that extent curbed their enthusiasm for nuclear deterrence. In any case, the United States and the Soviet Union were themselves vulnerable to the risks of nuclear brinkmanship. As for their interventionist policies, the diplomatic, economic, and military costs were often greater than the anticipated gains. In short, the Cold War entailed a range of negative consequences, the cumulative weight of which could not be indefinitely ignored. Detente thus proved to be a useful safety valve, helping to set limits to the nuclear arms race and to adjust strategic doctrine and deployments to changing economic and technological circumstances. More specifically, detente provided opportunities for negotiation which were reassuring to allies and often quite useful for the containment, if not resolution, of regional conflicts. The frequent fluctuation between the Cold War and detente—there were as many as five main periods of detente: post-1945, mid-1950s, early 1960s, early 1970s, and mid to late 1980s—indicates an ambiguous and spasmodic process. The simple fact is that neither detente nor the Cold War was capable of satisfying the rapidly evolving and often contradictory interests of the two superpowers and their allies.

THE END OF THE COLD WAR

What, then, were the factors which precipitated the end of the Second Cold War and ushered in this most recent and decisive phase in the relaxation of East-West tensions? To rephrase the question: What exactly ended or changed with the end of the Second Cold War?

The short answer to the question is that the end of the Cold War meant the end of the Soviet-U.S. geopolitical confrontation. With it came a series of disarmament and arms control agreements (e.g., the INF Treaty, and START), progress in the resolution of several regional conflicts (e.g., Afghanistan, Namibia, and Cambodia), and a less paralyzed U.N. system with enhanced peacekeeping and "peacemaking" functions. As for the existing alliance systems, they were either dissolved (e.g., the Warsaw Pact) or substantially revamped (e.g., NATO). The end of the Cold War had its most dramatic impact on the European geopolitical landscape, putting an end to the division of Europe and contributing with remarkable speed to the reunification of Germany. An integral part of this process has been the establishment of an extensive framework of pan-European security cooperation and a major transformation in the political economy of Eastern Europe. Perhaps the most striking indicator of change has been the decline of ideological conflict in particular between the ideology of central planning and that of the free market. That decline may be partially attributed to the slow but steady convergence of these two industrial systems, but the more decisive factor was the collapse of the communist system of power in Russia and East Europe.

[handwritten annotations in margins: "Western papers — primary sources", "put in Gorby", "chapter to why Gorbachev is under-rated."]

EXPLAINING THE END OF THE COLD WAR

A popular account of the end of the Cold War, certainly one which gained widespread currency in the West, not least among U.S. policymakers, was that which emphasized the triumph of capitalism over communism.[11] The more sophisticated versions of this account speak of the decline of Soviet hegemony, often interpreted as the outcome of imperial overstretch.[12] Several factors are often cited as contributing to this outcome:

1. the growing burden of Eastern Europe (associated with the recurring political instability faced by communist regimes; the economic subsidy entailed in the supply of Soviet energy sources; the disproportionate cost of military defense borne by the Soviet Union; and the unreliability of the Warsaw Pact's alliance arrangements)[13]

2. the high and rising cost of military competition with the West exacerbated by the Reagan policy of "peace through strength"[14]

3. the domestic and international penalties arising from foreign entanglements (e.g., Afghanistan)[15]

4. the heavy toll of continuing economic stagnation in the Soviet Union, resulting in growing political disaffection[16]

This last factor is regarded by many as the most telling, certainly the one which weighed most heavily on Gorbachev's mind and provided the impetus for his attempts at political and administrative reform (*glasnost* and *perestroika*). This is not to argue that the Soviet economy had failed in an absolute sense or that the population was in revolt. The supply of goods remained adequate if somewhat limited, both qualitatively and quantitatively. The levels of economic inequality, though rising, were still manageable. Yet the economy was in gridlock with falling rates of economic growth,[17] a stunted capacity for technical innovation, severe ecological degradation, and a rapidly decaying industrial and social infrastructure, all of this exacerbated by bureaucratic shortsightedness, bordering at times on paralysis, the inevitable result of which was the growing technological gap between East and West.

The failure of the domestic economy severely constrained the Soviet state's external conduct, for it reduced the resources available to foreign policy, weakened the legitimacy of the Soviet regime, and tarnished the attractiveness of the Soviet economic and political model. To put it differently, economic stagnation resulted in the gradual but steady exhaustion of Moscow's inter-

[handwritten annotation at bottom: "Afghan."]

national political credit. Change was clearly needed, but the obstacles to it were immense. Because state socialism had developed in the near absence of civil society, there was no simple strategy of harnessing the social forces needed to breathe new life into the socialist project. The "revolutionary" strong state resting on the ideology of the "dictatorship of the proletariat" had deprived itself of the democratic impulse necessary for mass mobilization. The Gorbachev revolution may be interpreted as a belated attempt at democratization from above, with all the risks and limitations that such a project inevitably implied.

To these domestic sources of Soviet conduct must be added the impact of the international environment and most important of economic globalization. Despite the protective shield which Soviet planners had erected around the Soviet economy, they could not insulate it from the powerful pressures exerted by the world economy, and in particular by the transnationalization of production, trade, and finance. Two other important dimensions of the international environment are worth noting: the growing acceptance of human rights norms, a trend greatly facilitated by the Helsinki process, and the expanding web of cultural, technological, and organizational linkages, which implicated a significant cross section of Soviet professional and intellectual life. The net effect of these mutually reinforcing trends was to multiply the incentives and opportunities for greater Soviet integration into the Western-centered system of international decision-making processes and institutions.

These, then, were some of the conditions which prompted and shaped Gorbachev's multifaceted response to Soviet decline, namely, his attempts to restore economic growth, maintain political stability, and create the more relaxed international climate needed for the achievement of his domestic goals.[18]

Glasnost, or democratization from above, was designed to create the necessary space for civil society, regarded as the sine qua non for a more open and efficient political system. *Perestroika*, on the other hand, was intended to restructure the economy through gradual marketization and privatization, which, it was hoped, would result from the introduction of greater economic incentives and the more rapid integration of the Soviet Union into the capitalist world economy.[19]

The objectives of growth, stability, and security that were central to the Gorbachev revolution were predicated on the gradual contraction of the Soviet empire. This would involve a conscious effort to reduce support for allies in Eastern Europe and pro-Soviet governments and movements in the Third World (e.g., Afghanistan and Vietnam). In time, the process would involve another, largely unforeseen, and certainly less palatable dimension, namely, the fragmentation of the Soviet Union itself.

The state of the Soviet economy and the need for access to Western capital and technology were decisive considerations, yet they do not fully explain the Gorbachev revolution in foreign and defense policy. For during this period there occurred a radical transformation in Soviet perceptions of security and of the importance of territory as a buffer against aggression.[20] It was this changed mind-set which gave rise to notions of common security and, in particular, to the idea of a common European home. Under the rubric of "new thinking" the Soviet leadership was now willing to explore new concepts of global governance which went beyond the already established agenda of arms control, confidence-building measures, and even nuclear disarmament. There was now a readiness to entertain various forms of institutional innovation, including a commitment to global monitoring and inspection, an enhanced role for U.N. peacekeeping, and an international response to ecological degradation.

In all of this Gorbachev and his associates were responding to forces from below as much as to changes in the global balance of power, although the external environment undoubtedly offered significant opportunities and constraints which could no longer be ignored. Here the objective of Soviet policy was to reach accommodation directly with Western governments but also to tap the considerable pressures emanating from Western civil society for denuclearization, disarmament, human rights, and pan-European cooperation. The aim was to shape a new set of international expectations which Western governments could not ignore. Significantly, Gorbachev made relatively little headway in his long-term objective of economic transformation, but was remarkably successful in his immediate priority, which was to change the climate of East-West relations.[21]

The question immediately arises: To what extent was the Gorbachev phenomenon attributable to U.S. policy, and in particular to the ideological and military assertiveness of the Reagan presidency? Here there is reason to think that U.S. pressure was a more negligible factor in shaping Soviet conduct than is often assumed. Putting rhetoric aside, many of Reagan's practical initiatives were effectively diluted by the opposition of other Western governments or by public and congressional opinion within the United States itself, which preferred economic cooperation to sanctions, and diplomatic accommodation to brinkmanship and arms control. Foreign policy under the Reagan administration was also blunted by intellectual inconsistencies and a good deal of bureaucratic inertia. There is little evidence to suggest that the emphasis on technological competition, or even the Strategic Defense Initiative, did much to tilt the military balance decisively in favor of the West,[22] which may help to explain the failure of the Star Wars program to gain the necessary momentum within the United States or to substantially derail the arms control process. The Intermediate Nuclear Forces (INF) Treaty is perhaps a case in point.[23] The tough bargaining posture adopted by the United States made little headway prior to 1985. The treaty was made possible largely as a result of the leadership change in Moscow and by domestic developments in Western Europe and to a lesser extent in the United States.[24] These interacting trends led the United States and NATO to adopt the zero option, which Moscow soon matched by proposing the double zero option.

There was, then, more to the end of the Second Cold War than the decline of Soviet hegemony. No less significant was the contraction of U.S. power and influence. Indeed, the Second Cold War reflected in part an attempt by the United States to reassert its dominant role within the Western alliance system and to use its strategic primacy as a lever with which to extract economic concessions from its allies. But the strategy, which became apparent in the latter part of the Carter presidency, had limited success in part because of growing European resistance to the extension by the United States of its domestic jurisdiction, especially in the area of East-West trade. U.S. actions, particularly under Reagan, were predicated on the assumption that military capability (i.e., technical prowess in the military sphere) could compensate for declining economic performance, or to put it differently, that higher levels of spending on sophisticated military technology would play to the comparative advantage of the United States. In practice, military muscle could only partially offset the downward curve of U.S. economic health. The United States was now the world's largest debtor nation (as was reflected in its large and rising trade and budget deficits); its proportion of global manufacturing, which stood at 65 percent in 1945, had fallen to 25 percent in 1988; U.S. productivity in the 1970s and 1980s lagged behind that of its chief competitors;[25] and rather ominously, the United States was now falling behind in nonmilitary developments and microelectronics and was on the verge of losing its lead in fiber optics, computers, and biotechnology. Most important, it could no longer afford to finance its global military system, hence the emphasis on burden sharing. In the Gulf War, the United States needed billions of dollars from Germany, Japan, and the Arab oil-producing nations to finance the war, in sharp contrast to the situation which had obtained at the time of the Korean War. The high cost associated with the global projection of military power and the widening perception that others, notably Europe and Japan, were growing rich courtesy of American taxpayers had exacerbated American frustration and resentment and given added weight to the conviction that the time had come for others to bear the costs of global security and perhaps for Washington to abandon or at least reduce its global policing role.

Rapidly changing U.S. economic circumstances were an important factor in the shift from Cold War to detente, which is not to say that the linkage was direct or entirely devoid of ambiguity. The dismantling of the elaborate U.S. military-industrial complex has been gradual and uneven. The military and political structure created by Cold War policies continues to perform three interconnected functions:

1. the retention of an elaborate alliance system (including the incorporation of a unified Germany into NATO)

2. continuing pressure on Cuba, Vietnam, North Korea, and even China to conform to U.S. strategic and other priorities

3. the ability to exercise leverage in relation to a greatly weakened Russia

So far as the United States is concerned, the end of the Cold War and the Gulf War itself may be viewed as transitional steps toward a new universal alliance framework, operating with at least tacit Russian support, legitimated by U.N. actions and resolutions, and underpinned by a number of formal and informal coalitions constructed to serve specific objectives in specific circumstances. Such a coalition strategy, premised on the need for periodic coordination with Japan, Western Europe, and Arab oil-rich states, is designed to deter Third World upstarts likely to endanger the peace, and reassure allies that U.S. leadership remains firm and effective. However, it is by no means clear that these various actors (i.e., U.S. allies, Arab states, Russia, United Nations) will continue to play the role allocated to them by this script and that the relative decline of U.S. power can be arrested, let alone reversed.[26]

The end of the Cold War represents above all a shift from bipolarity to multipolarity. It did not result from, nor did it give rise to, U.S. hegemony. Gorbachev's reforms, in close interaction with other international trends (e.g., German reunification and pan-European institutionalization), have themselves accentuated the polycentric tendencies on a global scale. Since the early 1970s power has gradually diffused outward in a multipolar direction and shifted qualitatively from the military to the economic sphere. The Europeans, in particular, who are one of the principal beneficiaries of this shift, have asserted an increasingly independent stance in international affairs, resisting U.S. pressures for increased defense spending, just as they resisted the strident anti-Sovietism of the early Reagan period. By the early 1980s, Western Europe was preoccupied with the challenges posed by political and economic integration on the one hand, and the need for a more durable

relationship with Russia and Eastern Europe on the other. The primary focus
was on putting the European house in order rather than on winning the Cold
War. It is worth noting in this connection that it was the Kohl-Gorbachev
agreement of 1988 rather than any Soviet-U.S. understanding which paved
the way for German reunification. It cannot be stressed enough that the great
appeal of Gorbachev's reforms, particularly so far as the Europeans were
concerned, was precisely the removal of the Soviet threat, which in turn held
the prospect of greater pan-European cooperation and greater independence
vis-à-vis the United States.

In a rapidly evolving polycentric world, not only Europe but also Japan
and other emerging centers of power (i.e., China, Association of Southeast
Asian Nations [ASEAN], India, in due course resurgent Russia, and even an
Islamic coalition) were likely to demand an increasing share in international
decision making. The progressive diffusion of power had preceded but also
hastened the end of the Cold War.

THE AFTERMATH OF THE COLD WAR

With the end of the Second Cold War came the relaxation of international
tensions, a more flexible European security framework, and a more cooperative relationship between the United States and Russia. Far-reaching though
they were, however, these changes did not mean the dissipation of the many
antagonisms which had characterized the Cold War period. At best they
meant the alleviation of some, but also the intensification of others. The
post–Cold War period does not signify the end of ideology, much less the
end of history. It is at best a transitional period marked as much by
continuities as by discontinuities. Communism as a political system, though
greatly modified by the introduction of market principles, remains a political
force to be reckoned with in much of Asia (Communist parties remain in
power in China, Cuba, North Korea, and Vietnam and continue to exercise
varying degrees of leverage in Cambodia and the Philippines). We may even
be witnessing a partial revival of the fortunes of Communist parties in parts
of Eastern Europe and the former Soviet Union. Other axes of conflict, it is
true, now occupy center stage—none more so than the West-West struggle
for economic ascendancy, characterized by deepening trade rivalries and the
incipient formation of regional blocs. To this must be added the unresolved
North-South tensions and in particular the issues of debt and structural
poverty. The risks of horizontal nuclear proliferation are, if anything, assuming greater importance. So long as deterrence strategy remains the bedrock
of U.S. and Russian nuclear policy and a comprehensive test ban treaty fails
to materialize, other states will remain attracted to the nuclear option,

whether in South Asia, Northeast Asia, the Middle East, or the former Soviet Union.

The post–Cold War era is perhaps best characterized as a period of flux and indeterminacy with numerous states on the verge of disintegration under the cumulative impact of renewed ethnonationalist sentiment, economic recession, and civil disorder.[27] Side by side with these subnational tensions are the pressures emanating from the twin processes of regional integration and economic globalization. The long-term political and cultural implications of the homogenizing influence of the world market have yet to be fully evaluated either in theoretical or practical terms. There is, however, mounting evidence that an increasingly integrated economy, precisely because it involves the rationalization of production through the restructuring of labor processes and the introduction of labor-displacing technologies, often gives rise to domestic fragmentation, with not only wealth but also race, religion, gender, and ethnicity emerging as important instruments of division.

Notwithstanding the ambiguities surrounding the present conjuncture, it has been argued that the end of the Cold War is part of a worldwide trend toward democratization and increasing attention to human rights, at least of the civil and political variety, in line with the priorities of the liberal-democratic tradition. There is much validity to this analysis if one is to judge by recent attempts to introduce multiparty politics in parts of Eastern Europe and even Africa and Latin America. Yet it would be unwise to interpret the trend as simple affirmation or celebration of capitalist democracy.

Here we need to return to one of the key themes in our analysis. If it is true that the Cold War represented in part a conflict between capitalist/nationalist/democratic states and socialist/nationalist/authoritarian states, and if it is true that state-centric socialism has given ground or been substantially transformed by the powerful tide of capitalist globalization, it is equally true that the tide is creating havoc within capitalism itself. The accelerating inequalities of wealth and income between core and periphery as well as within the core, combined with the diminished efficacy of the traditional instruments of national economic management, have sharply accentuated the contradictions between capitalism and democracy. Within capitalist-liberal societies, the democratic process is institutionalized largely within the framework of the national state and constrained by a relatively narrow definition of the political, whereas in practice the most crucial areas of policy are increasingly governed by the structures and processes of economic transnationalization. We are thus faced with the unanswered question: how can democracy effectively function within this elusive, fluid, borderless terrain? Any durable, viable answer to the question, whether the emphasis is on the decentralization of power and authority or on global institutionalization or some combination of the two, will ultimately involve a transformation of the political landscape of capitalist societies, which may prove as far-reaching as anything we have recently witnessed in the communist societies of Eastern Europe and the Soviet Union. Far from inaugurating the end of ideology, let alone the end of history, the passing of the Cold War may prove to be no more than one episode in a much longer story, the full implications of which we have scarcely begun to unravel.

NOTES

1. J. A. Camilleri, "Towards an Understanding of the International System," in *Powers and Policies: Alignments and Realignments in the Indo-Pacific Region*, ed. Max Teichmann (Melbourne: Cassell Australia, 1970), p. 17.

2. Fred Halliday, *The Making of the Second World War* (London: Verso, 1983), p. 42.

3. See Anatol Rapaport, *The Big Two: Soviet-American Perceptions of Foreign Policy* (New York: Pegasus, 1971).

4. E. P. Thompson, "Notes on Exterminism, the Last Stage of Civilization," in *Exterminism and Cold War*, ed. New Left Review (London: Verso, 1982), pp. 1–33.

5. Yoshikazu Sakamoto, "Perspective on Changing World Order—A Conceptual Prelude," paper delivered to the International Symposium on Sources of Innovation in Multilateralism, Lausanne, Switzerland, May 1994.

6. This aspect of the Sakamoto thesis is supported by Thesa Skocpol's analysis in "States and Revolutions: France, Russia and China," in *States and Societies*, eds. David Held et al. (Oxford: Basil Blackwell, 1985), pp. 151–69.

7. J. A. Camilleri and Jim Falk, *The End of Sovereignty? The Politics of a Shrinking and Fragmenting World* (Aldershot, England: Hants, Elgar, 1992), p. 147.

8. See Susan Strange, *Casino Capitalism* (Oxford: Basil Blackwell, 1986); United Nations Centre on Transnational Corporations, *Transnational Corporations in World Development: Trends and Prospects* (New York: United Nations, 1988); also Camilleri and Falk, *The End of Sovereignty?* pp. 69–77.

9. Immanuel Wallerstein, *The Capitalist World-Economy* (Cambridge: Cambridge University Press, 1979), pp. 108–18.

10. For a nuanced answer to this question see Fred Halliday, "The Ends of Cold War," *New Left Review* 180 (March-April 1990): 5–24.

11. For a standard triumphalist account, though one couched more in geopolitical than ideological terms, see Zbigniew Brzezinski, "The Cold War and Its Aftermath," *Foreign Affairs* 71, no. 4 (fall 1992): 31–49.

12. This argument is reminiscent of the theoretical perspective in Paul M. Kennedy, *The Rise and Fall of the Great Powers: Economic Change and Military Conflict from 1500 to 2000* (New York: Random House, 1987). See also Robert Gilpin, *War and Change in World Politics* (New York: Cambridge University Press, 1981).

13. See Valerie Bruce, "The Empire Strikes Back: The Evolution of the Eastern Bloc from a Soviet Asset to a Soviet Liability," *International Organization* 39 (winter 1985): 1–46.

14. See J. Einhorn, *Negotiating from Strength: Leverage in U.S.-Soviet Arms Control Negotiations* (New York: Praeger, 1985); John Lewis Gaddis, "Hanging Tough Paid Off,"

Bulletin of the Atomic Scientists 45, no. 1 (January 1989): 11–14; Jonathan Haslam, *The Soviet Union and the Politics of Nuclear Weapons in Europe, 1969–87* (London: Macmillan, 1989).

15. See Valerie Bruce, "The Soviet Union under Gorbachev: Ending Stalinism and Ending the Cold War," *International Journal* 46 (spring 1991): 226.

16. See Marshall J. Goldman, *The USSR in Crisis: The Failure of an Economic System* (New York: Norton, 1983).

17. Daniel Deudney and G. John Ikenberry, "The International Sources of Soviet Change," *International Security* 16, no. 3 (winter 1991–92): 99.

18. For an incisive interpretation of Gorbachev's "new thinking," see Andrew C. Janos, "Social Science, Communism, and the Dynamics of Political Change," *World Politics* 44, no. 1 (October 1991): 100–101.

19. For an analysis of the failure of *perestroika*, see Leo Panitch and Ralph Miliband, "The New World Order and the Socialist Agenda," in *Socialist Register 1992*, eds. Leo Panitch and Ralph Miliband (London: Merlin Press, 1992), pp. 3–4.

20. This argument is developed in Deudney and Ikenberry, "The International Sources of Soviet Change," pp. 89–94.

21. See Daniel Deudney and G. John Ikenberry, "Soviet Reform and the End of the Cold War: Explaining Large-scale Historical Change," *Review of International Studies* 17, no. 3 (July 1991): 225–50.

22. See Barry R. Posen and Stephen van Evera, "Defense Policy and the Reagan Administration: Departure from Containment," *International Security* 8, no. 1 (summer 1983): 3–45; also Farced Zakaria, "The Reagan Strategy of Containment," *Political Science Quarterly* 105, no. 3 (fall 1990): 373–95; Fred Chernoff, "Ending the Cold War: The Soviet Retreat and the US Military Build-up," *International Affairs* (London) 67, no. 1 (January 1991): 111–26.

23. Thomas Risse-Kappen, "Did 'Peace Through Strength' End the Cold War?" *International Security* 16, no. 1 (summer 1991): 162–88.

24. Reference here is primarily to the rise of antinuclear sentiment during the late 1970s and early 1980s. See Thomas Rochon, *Mobilizing for Peace: The Anti-Nuclear Movement in Western Europe* (Princeton, NJ: Princeton University Press, 1983); Frances B. McRea and Gerald E. Markle, *Minutes to Midnight: Nuclear Weapons Protest in America* (Newbury Park, CA: Sage, 1989).

25. See Camilleri and Falk, *The End of Sovereignty?* pp. 89–94; Kennedy, *The Rise and Fall of the Great Powers*, pp. 458–71, 514–40; Lester Thurow, *Head to Head: The Coming Economic Battle among Japan, Europe, and America* (New York: William Morrow, 1992), pp. 153–202.

26. For an examination of the ambiguities surrounding the U.S. role in the international security system, see J. A. Camilleri, "Alliances and the Emerging Post–Cold War Security System," in *The Post-Cold War Order*, eds. Richard Leaver and James L. Richardson (Sydney: Allen & Unwin, 1993), pp. 81–94.

27. Halliday, "The Ends of Cold War," pp. 21–22.

Conclusion

The End of the Cold War:
A Political, Historical, and Mythological Event

Michael E. Salla

Why did the Cold War end? This question unifies the contributions to this anthology but invites diversity in underlying assumptions over what the Cold War means, what the end of the Cold War refers to, and finally in the answers given. Before one can provide an overall framework for analyzing explanations given for the end of the Cold War, some conceptual housecleaning is needed. Two assumptions will be made that will facilitate understanding the question and classifying the contributors' responses to it. Though both of these assumptions underlie many of the responses given in this book, they cannot be made without some debate.

The first assumption is that the Cold War was a conflict dating from shortly after World War II involving two military alliances based on rival social, political, and economic systems led by the United States and the U.S.S.R., respectively. This assumption is not held by all the contributors. For Johan Galtung, "the Cold War started in 1917. Challenging the Western formulation based on the expansion of capitalism, democracy, human rights, and Christianity, the communists introduced planning instead of market forces; dictatorship and terror instead of democracy and human rights; and scientific atheism instead of God and Christianity."[1] For Rick Kuhn, the cold war refers to an even earlier conflict between labor and capital dating from at least the nineteenth century, one that is still occurring despite the end of the Cold War between the United States and the U.S.S.R.[2] For C. L. Chiou, on the other hand, the Cold War is viewed by the Chinese political establishment

I wish to thank my coeditor, Ralph Summy, for his help and suggestions in writing this chapter.

as originating shortly after the "barbarian west" began to seriously impact upon Chinese culture and politics:

> For China, its anti-Western imperialist war started much earlier than the end of World War II. It began in the mid-nineteenth century, continued in the Republican period, especially in the May 4 Movement, and—with some change of protagonists—persisted into the Cold War period. Moreover, with the collapse of European communism, together with further adjustments in threat perception, it has continued into the post-1990 new world order.[3]

Finally, April Carter points out that the "Cold War has been used to denote the period of acute tension between the U.S.S.R. and the West between 1947 and 1953 . . . [and it] was in this sense that commentators began to identify the 'Second Cold War' of 1979 to 1984."[4]

The second assumption is that the phenomenon called the end of the Cold War is a sequence of political milestones, for example, ratification of the INF Treaty, rejection of the Brezhnev Doctrine, destruction of the Berlin Wall, the East European revolutions of 1989–90, and the Gulf War coalition. Again, agreement does not exist here over exactly when the sequence both started and ended. Galtung, for example, argues that the end of the Cold War began in "December 1979 and August 1980. In this period two movements sprang up. For the first time the dissident movement became a mass movement in Poland, and the peace movement became a mass movement in the Netherlands and Germany."[5] Joanne Wright, on the other hand, believes that the sequence began with a speech by Mikhail Gorbachev: "If anything can be said to have triggered the end of the Cold War, it must be Gorbachev's speech to the United Nations in December 1988 announcing significant troop withdrawals. It was this above all that signaled to the East Europeans that maybe the tanks were going home to stay."[6]

Views on the end of the sequence range from the fall of the East German government and the opening of the Berlin Wall on November 9, 1989,[7] to the final dissolution of the Soviet Union in 1991. Nevertheless, there is widespread agreement that the end of the Cold War in terms of the U.S.-U.S.S.R. direct confrontation does involve a sequence of political milestones that include, at the very least, the events of 1989–90 in Eastern Europe and the Soviet Union.

The political milestones in the sequence collectively constitute a political event. Explaining this political event, then, involves applying interpretive frameworks common to international relations. While there are a variety of frameworks that may be applied here, I will limit my discussion to three which I believe are paradigmatic in international relations.

First, the end of the Cold War can be explained in terms of political realism.[8] Political realism has its conceptual origins in Hobbesian assumptions over individuals' quest for security and the rational desire to dominate others in a "state of nature." For political realists the international system is analogous to Hobbes's state of nature and is characterized as a conflict between states where each seeks to further its national interest and maximize power. For example, Hans Morgenthau writes: "The concept of the national interest presupposes neither a naturally harmonious, peaceful world nor the inevitability of war as a consequence of the pursuit by all nations of their national interest. Quite to the contrary, it assumes continuous conflict and threat of war to be minimized through the continuous adjustment of conflicting interest by diplomatic action."[9]

Critical international events such as the end of the Cold War, then, are ultimately explained in terms of policy successes, shifts, or failures in a global competition for maximizing state power. Joanne Wright, for example, argues that the rejection of the Brezhnev Doctrine was a trigger mechanism for the end of the Cold War. Joseph Camilleri, Kevin Clements, and Ralph Summy explain how orthodox policymakers in the West saw the policy of containment, and/or Reagan's policies of renewed military expansion and an ideological offensive, as successful insofar as it/they led to an awareness among Soviet strategic thinkers of the ultimate failure of Soviet policy: "The massive US defense build-up of the early 1980s—including the decision to proceed with the Strategic Defense Initiative—both shocked the Soviets and then strained their resources. Its scale, momentum and technological daring had been totally unexpected . . . [and] it dawned on Soviet leaders that they could neither match nor even keep up with the American efforts."[10]

Second, the end of the Cold War can be explained in terms of political events being driven by political-cultural forces such as mass protest movements, migration, or political consciousness. The underlying theme here is that social and political power ultimately resides in collective human action and shared consciousness, that is, "people's power." David Cortright, Johan Galtung, Robert Elias, and Jennifer Turpin, for example, argue that the U.S and West European peace movement and the East European dissident movement were critical factors in ending the Cold War because of the collective action they could harness to challenge state power and the shared political consciousness they mobilized regarding U.S. militarism, a nuclear-free Europe, and a common European home. This is paralleled by Kevin Clements's argument that the positive relations fostered between states and their citizens ultimately led to the end of hostilities between East and West:

"[N]ew opportunities for dialogue, and the emergence of a large number of popular movements, such as peace, ecology, and women's movements, resulted in a popular momentum in favor of change. By the mid to late 1980s this momentum had brought about a recognition that win-win rather than win-lose solutions were more likely to generate a stable peace between the Soviet Union and the United States."[11] Alternatively, examining the critical state of East Germany, Ulf Sundhaussen posits that the mass migration of East Germans to the West and the overwhelming desire to adopt West German life-styles led to German reunification and to the end of the Cold War. On a similar note, Keith Suter argues: "Cold War politicians and scholars saw the arms race as the key component of the Cold War. But they ignored the everyday basics of life. . . . The Soviet citizens were yearning for the good things of life and recognized that the Soviet system could not produce Coke, Big Macs, and Madonna. The Red Army could resist a NATO invasion into Eastern Europe but not the televised transmission of *Dallas* and *Dynasty*."[12]

Third, changing systemic features of the international system, such as a transition to a more interdependent world, can be used to explain the end of the Cold War. Clements believes that there "is a shift away from states as the major or only actors of significance and [that] the world as a whole is becoming highly interdependent."[13] In a similar vein, Suter argues: "While the two superpowers were so focused on their own arms race, a new global order started to emerge. This is replacing the Westphalian System (which was based on the nation-state), and instead, power is being diffused among international organizations (most notably the United Nations), transnational corporations, and nongovernmental organizations."[14] The assumption here is that systemic factors largely determine political, social, and economic relations between states and peoples. Thus the emerging transition of the international system from a Westphalian model of nation-states competing against one another, to an interdependent model where international governmental and nongovernmental organizations (INGOs and NGOs) and transnational corporations (TNCs) largely influence global events, makes states simply one actor among many in an interdependent global system. Consequently, the Cold War "became an expensive irrelevance."[15]

The difficulty with solely applying the preceding frameworks for explaining the end of the Cold War as a self-contained political event is that it is also a dynamic historical event. The assumption here is that the end of the Cold War is part of a much larger sequence of historical events that contextualize it—we are thus entering historiography. For example, the Cold War may be seen as a renewed challenge to liberal democracies by totalitarian/authoritarian regimes. It is thus a version of the cold wars in the 1930s between Nazi

Germany and its allies on the one hand, and France, Britain, and their allies on the other; and prior to World War I, between the Hapsburgs and imperial Germany, and France and Britain. Consequently, conclusions drawn from these earlier conflicts regarding their causes and effects can be used to interpret the end of the Cold War. Interpreting the end of the Cold War as a historical event, then, involves different interpretive frameworks. Again, there are a number of frameworks that might be used. However, the discussion will again be limited to three.

First, history can be interpreted as a procession of powerful city-states, nation-states, and empires that rise and fall in the international system in terms of territory, prestige, and regional power. The determining factor in this procession is the economic resources that political units can draw upon. A clear example of this interpretive position is given by Paul Kennedy: "[T]he historical record suggests that there is a very clear connection in the long run between an individual Great Power's economic rise and fall and its growth and decline as an important military power (or world empire)."[16] If a state or empire falls relative to others (or in absolute terms), this is explained in terms of failing to match the resources that its rivals can draw upon. Dennis Phillips argues, for instance: "The condition of the Soviet economy made the U.S.S.R. look increasingly like 'Upper Volta with rockets.' . . . The Stalinist model of the economy, whatever purposes it may have served in the past, simply was not appropriate as a strategy for economic growth in a late twentieth century global marketplace."[17] Similarly, Geoff Dow argues that the Soviet Union started from a much lower level of capital formation than the capitalist West: "As a mode of production, socialism is not something that can be constructed through will, from a low base of prior development, before capitalism has done the dirty work."[18] Thus he argues that the Soviet Union should have been aided in its development efforts rather than drained in a debilitating Cold War and associated arms race. For Rick Kuhn, "The arms race compelled the Soviet Union to attempt to match the military build-up of the United States. Its economy was much smaller and . . . by the 1970s, much less efficient than that of the United States. It got less rockets for its rubles than the United States got bang for its bucks."[19] This led to Kuhn's and Clements's argument that the strain on Soviet resources led to domestic difficulties:

[T]he whole Soviet economy and society were in a state of collapse, reflected in declining life expectancy, rising infant mortality rates, and a general deterioration of the quality of life. There were escalating demands for a wide variety of consumer items, such as jeans, soap, and toilet paper, which the Soviet economy could not supply. Faced with these demands, Gorbachev and his colleagues had a stark choice, either to move in a more capitalist direction or to adopt the repressive path of his predecessors.[20]

Of course, Gorbachev decided to move "in a more capitalist direction" and introduced the policy of *perestroika* so as to reform the Soviet economy. Nevertheless, *perestroika* failed to reverse economic decline with the result that the "failure of the domestic economy . . . weakened the legitimacy of the Soviet regime and tarnished the attractiveness of the Soviet economic and political model."[21] Finally, Suter argues that the arms races depleted the economies of both the United States and the U.S.S.R., thereby forcing them to end the Cold War if they were to compete successfully with the expanding economies of other industrialized nations.

Second, history can be seen as a procession of universal ideas, values, or principles that are embodied by individuals, communities, nations, and empires and that compete on the international stage. The whole of human history, then, is a dialectic of universal ideas that are the ultimate determinants of human affairs. Thus the English revolution was a battle between the universal ideas of absolute monarchy and constitutional government; the French revolution developed this further into a battle between absolute monarchy and republicanism; World War II and the Cold War made it a battle between different forms of totalitarianism and liberal democracy. This leads to Fukuyama's celebrated thesis about the victory of the idea of liberal democracy and the end of history: "What we may be witnessing is not just the end of the Cold War, or the passing of a particular period of postwar history, but the end of history as such: that is, the end point of mankind's ideological evolution and the universalization of Western liberal democracy as the final form of human government."[22] According to this view, the Cold War ended because of a widespread recognition by citizens and governments of the universal worth of liberal democracy as an organizational idea and value system. Sundhaussen and Galtung present explanations that are variations on this theme. Similarly, Clements argues that the end of the Cold War resulted in "the complete delegitimization of Marxism-Leninism as an aspiration and as an acceptable world ideology. A corollary of this has been the global elevation of market capitalism, economic rationalism, monetarism, and democratization."[23] This explanation is contested by Kuhn, who attempts to disassociate, somewhat ingenuously, the ideological significance of the end of the Cold War from the ongoing cold war between capital and labor. With regard to "new thinking" in Soviet domestic and foreign policy, this simply represents the end-of-history view of "a world dominated by economic concerns, in which there are no ideological grounds for major conflict between nations, and in which, consequently, the use of military force becomes less legitimate."[24]

Third, historical change may be viewed as determined by "innovations that alter the optimal scale of organizations."[25] Arguably, two of the most important are innovations in information processing and military technology. Such innovations allow political units first, to gain revenue from taxes; and second, to use military force to control territory. As Leonard Dudley puts it, "an increase or decrease in scale economies of information processing will change the willingness of citizens to pay taxes. On the other hand, an increase or decrease in military scale economies will alter the cost of controlling territory."[26] This explanation is identified by April Carter, who suggests that "faced with the 'third military revolution' of microelectronics and lasers in the 1970s [the Soviet Union] began to fall inexorably behind."[27] Accordingly, the Cold War ended first, because of the technological breakthroughs the United States was perceived to be ready to exploit in its Star Wars program and second, because of the information processing advantage the United States enjoyed as a result of its silicon chip technology.

Finally, in addition to being simultaneously a political and a historical event, the end of the Cold War has also become a mythological event. That is to say, it has entered a mythological sphere where human actors become heroes or catalysts for momentous global changes. The assumption here is that human civilization is shaped or steered by heroic personalities and/or human instruments of divine forces. This is exemplified by Georg Hegel's description of "world-historical individuals": "The great individuals of world history . . . are those who seize upon . . . [the] higher universal and make it their own end. . . . To this extent they may be called heroes. . . . They are the most far-sighted among their contemporaries; they know best what issues are involved, and whatever they do is right. The others feel that this is so, and therefore have to obey them. Their words and deeds are the best that could be said and done in their time."[28] Ralph Summy identifies one strand of the emerging orthodoxy on why the Cold War ended—represented by Zbigniew Brzezinski—as congratulating the architects and heroes of the "visionary" policies that led to the end of the Cold War: "[T]he historical credit for fashioning the winning strategy and for forging the victorious coalition must go to one man above all: Harry Truman. He committed America because he understood the stakes."[29] Similarly, Ronald Reagan is identified by Summy and Clements as the crux of the second strand of the emerging orthodoxy, which claims that his heroic ideological crusade stemming from a passionate religious conviction and his "visionary" policy of Star Wars and massive rearmament ultimately led to the collapse of the "evil empire" and ensured global peace. In a similar vein, Gorbachev is identified as the catalyst for the end of the Cold War by Phillips, Galtung, Turpin, and Wright: Gorbachev "served simultaneously as symptom, catalyst, producer, and product of forces for change."[30]

Seven interpretive frameworks have been offered for explaining the end of the Cold War either as a political, historical, or mythological event.[31] These appear in summary form in Table 4. These frameworks are not intended to be mutually distinct since there is some overlap in the explanations they each offer. If we are to construct meaning from the end of the Cold War as simultaneously a political, historical, and mythological event, we are obliged to adopt a holistic perspective and steer away from explanations, no matter how attractive, that limit the end of the Cold War to a single interpretive framework.

Such a restrictive attempt to explain the end of the Cold War was earlier argued to be the danger with the emerging orthodoxy that the United States won the Cold War because of "the relentless application of the West's military superiority and the dynamism of its ideas and economic system."[32] The "near universal acceptance"[33] enjoyed by such an orthodoxy threatens to become an unchallenged theoretical perspective that will shape foreign policy making in the West for decades to come. Such an outcome would prove disastrous in that first, it would ignore the "underlying sources of conflict" that John Burton succinctly identifies as remaining unaddressed by the conduct of cold or hot wars[34]; and second, it would threaten the repetition of similar foreign policy mistakes and assumptions and in the future could perhaps take the form of a confrontation between Chinese/Confucian civilization and the West, as C. L. Chiou intimates. If single or restrictive explanations for the end of the Cold War are avoided, we are much more likely to eliminate the twin dangers of imbibing the wrong lessons and therefore enhancing the prospects of future cold wars.

Table 4
Frameworks for Why the Cold War Ended

Interpretive Framework	Analytical Focus	Assumptions	Explanations for Why the Cold War Ended
Political realism	States, policies	Policy making is all about maximizing power; the national interest is the primary concern of states	Containment Reagan's ideological crusade Star Wars program and rearmament End of the Brezhnev Doctrine
Political-cultural	Mass movements, political consciousness	Social and political power resides in mass collective action and the harnessing of political consciousness	Role of the U.S. and West European peace movements Role of the East European dissident movement Positive relations Desire to emulate Western life-styles
Systemic-international	Systemic features of the international system	All political, social, and economic relations are shaped by underlying structures; global interdependence creates new international structures	A new global order based on the influence of INGOs, NGOs, and TNCs replacing the Westphalian State System Cold War became an expensive irrelevance
Historical-economic	Economic resources, markets	Power and influence in international relations is ultimately determined by economic capacities of societies	Imperial overstretch Arms races depleted U.S.S.R. and United States Inherent weakness of Soviet economy *Perestroika*
Historical-ideas	Universal ideas, values, and principles	Human history is shaped by the influence of universal ideas, values, and principles	Liberal democracy "End of history" "New thinking"
Historical-technological	Innovations in information and/or military technologies	History is determined by technological breakthroughs in the optimal scale of organizations	Star Wars Silicon chip and advanced informational technologies
Mythological-transcendent	Heroes, catalysts, world-historical individuals	Major global events are ultimately shaped by heroic personalities and catalysts/ instruments for global change	Harry Truman Ronald Reagan Mikhail Gorbachev

NOTES

1. "Europe 1989: The Role of Peace Research and the Peace Movement," Chapter 6 of this volume, p. 95.

2. For a discussion of Kuhn's distinction between the cold war and the Cold War, see "Whose Cold War?" Chapter 10 of this volume, pp. 153–69.

3. "In the Shadow of the Middle Kingdom Syndrome: China in the Post–Cold War World," Chapter 14 of this volume, p. 219.

4. "Did Reagan 'Win' the Cold War?" Chapter 1 of this volume, p. 20.

5. Galtung, "Europe 1989," p. 95.

6. "The End of the Cold War: The Brezhnev Doctrine," Chapter 3 of this volume, p. 59.

7. See Galtung, "Europe 1989," p. 92; Ulf Sundhaussen, "The Erosion of Regime Legitimacy in Eastern European Satellite States: The Case of the German Democratic Republic," Chapter 7 of this volume, pp. 117–18.

8. For a discussion of political realism and its principal exponents, see James Dougherty and Robert L. Pfaltzgraff, Jr., *Contending Theories of International Relations: A Comprehensive Survey*, 2nd ed. (New York: Harper & Row, 1981), pp. 84–133.

9. Hans Morgenthau, "Another 'Great Debate': The National Interest of the US," *American Political Science Review* 46, no. 4 (1952): 978.

10. Zbigniew Brzezinski, "The Cold War and Its Aftermath," *Foreign Affairs* 71, no. 4 (1992): 42.

11. "Carrots Were More Important Than Sticks in Ending the Cold War," Chapter 11 of this volume, p. 180.

12. "How the Cold War Became an Expensive Irrelevance," Chapter 12 of this volume, pp. 200–201.

13. Clements, "Carrots Were More Important Than Sticks," p. 178.

14. Suter, "How the Cold War Became an Expensive Irrelevance," p. 194.

15. Ibid., pp. 187, 202.

16. Paul M. Kennedy, *The Rise and Fall of the Great Powers: Economic Change and Military Conflict from 1500 to 2000* (London: Unwin Hyman, 1988), p. xxv.

17. "Upper Volta with Rockets: Internal Versus External Factors in the Decline of the Soviet Union," Chapter 8 of this volume, p. 126.

18. "Marxism, Capitalism, and Democracy: Some Post-Soviet Dilemmas," Chapter 9 of this volume, p. 142.

19. Kuhn, "Whose Cold War?" p. 162.

20. Clements, "Carrots Were More Important Than Sticks," p. 177.

21. Joseph A. Camilleri, "The Cold War . . . and After: A New Period of Upheaval in World Politics," Chapter 15 of this volume, p. 239.

22. Francis Fukuyama, "The End of History?" *The National Interest* 16 (summer 1989): 4.

23. Clements, "Carrots Were More Important Than Sticks," p. 175.

24. Fukuyama, "The End of History?" p. 17.

25. Leonard Dudley, *The Word and the Sword: How Techniques of Information and Violence Have Shaped Our World* (Oxford: Basil Blackwell, 1991), p. 320. Also quoted in Ralph Summy, "Book Review," *Australian Journal of Politics and History* 39, no. 1 (1993): 136.

26. Dudley, *The Word and the Sword*, p. 9. Also quoted in Summy, "Book Review," p. 136.

27. Carter, "Did Reagan 'Win' the Cold War?" p. 22.

28. Georg Hegel, *Lectures on the Philosophy of World History*, trans. H. B. Nisbet (Cambridge: Cambridge University Press, 1975), pp. 82–84.

29. Ralph Summy, "Challenging the Emergent Orthodoxy," introduction to this volume, p. 5; Brzezinski, "The Cold War and Its Aftermath," p. 45.

30. Jennifer Turpin, "Gorbachev, the Peace Movement, and the Death of Lenin," Chapter 4 of this volume, p. 79.

31. For another analytical approach, see Louis Kriesberg's four explanations for the end of the Cold War outlined in Clements, "Carrots Were More Important Than Sticks," pp. 176–80.

32. Summy, "Challenging the Emergent Orthodoxy," p. 3.

33. Ibid., p. 4.

34. "The Continuing Cold War," Chapter 13 of this volume, pp. 207–16.

Selected Bibliography

Allan, P., & K. Goldmann, eds. *The End of the Cold War—Evaluating Theories of International Relations.* Dordrecht, the Netherlands: Nijhoff, 1992.

Allen, E., & F. Schurmann. "Neo-Nationalist Fallacies." *Foreign Policies* 87 (summer 1992): 105–22.

Armstrong, D., & E. Goldstein, eds. *The End of the Cold War.* London: Frank Cass, 1990.

Artaud, D. "The End of the Cold War: A Skeptical View." *Diplomatic History* 16, no. 2 (1992): 256ff.

Balzer, H., ed. *Five Years That Shook the World: Gorbachev's Unfinished Revolution.* Boulder, CO: Westview, 1991.

Bergh, G. V. B. *Nuclear Revolution and the End of the Cold War: Forced Restraint.* Basingstoke, England: Macmillan, 1992.

Beschloss, M. R., & S. Talbott. *At the Highest Levels: The Inside Story of the End of the Cold War.* Boston: Little, Brown, 1993.

Blackburn, R., ed. *After the Fall: The Failure of Communism and the Future of Socialism.* London: Verso, 1991.

Bowker, M., & R. Brown, eds. *From Cold War to Collapse: Theory and World Politics in the 1980s.* Cambridge: Cambridge University Press, 1993.

Brzezinski, Z. "The Cold War and Its Aftermath." *Foreign Affairs* 71, no. 4 (1992): 31–49.

——— . "Is the Cold War Over?" *International Affairs* 11 (1989): 32–37.

Bush, G. "America—The Last Best Hope for Man on Earth: A World in Which the Rule of Law Prevails." *Vital Speeches of the Day* 59, no. 7 (1993): 194–201.

——— . "State of the Union." *Vital Speeches of the Day* 58, no. 9 (1992): 258–63.

Charlton, M., ed. *Footsteps from the Finland Station: Five Landmarks in the Collapse of Communism.* New Brunswick, NJ: Transaction Publishers, 1992.

Chernoff, F. "Ending the Cold War: The Soviet Retreat and the US Military Build Up." *International Affairs* 67, no. 1 (1991): 111–26.

Christian, D. " 'Perestroika' and the End of the Soviet Experiment, 1982–1991." *Teaching History* 27, no. 1 (March 1993): 4–15.

Cimbala, S. J., & S. R. Waldman, eds. *Controlling and Ending Conflict: Issues Before and After the Cold War.* Westport, CT: Greenwood, 1992.

Clifford, J. G. "History and the End of the Cold War: A Whole New Ball Game?" *Organization of American Historians: Magazine of History* 7, no. 2 (1992): 26ff.

Clough, M. *Free at Last?: US Policy Toward Africa and the End of the Cold War.* New York: Council on Foreign Relations Press, 1992.

Cohen, S. F., & K. vanden Heuvel. *Voices of Glasnost: Interviews with Gorbachev's Reformers.* New York: W. W. Norton, 1989.

Coker, C. "Post-modernity and the End of the Cold War: How War Has Been Disinvented." *Review of International Studies* 18, no. 3 (1992): 189ff.

Cortright, D. *Peace Works: The Citizen's Role in Ending the Cold War.* Boulder, CO: Westview, Press, 1993.

Cullen, R. *Twilight of Empire: Inside the Crumbling Soviet Bloc.* London: Bodley Head, 1991.

Denitch, B. *The End of the Cold War: European Unity, Socialism, and the Shift in Global Power.* Minneapolis: University of Minnesota Press, 1990.

Deudney, D., & G. J. Ikenberry. "Who Won the Cold War?" *Foreign Policy* 87 (summer 1992): 123–38.

"An End to the Cold War." *New Times* 52 (December 26, 1989): 8ff.

Enloe, C. H. *The Morning After: Sexual Politics at the End of the Cold War.* Berkeley: University of California Press, 1993.

Freedman, L., ed. *Europe Transformed: Documents on the End of the Cold War.* New York: St. Martin's Press, 1990.

Fukuyama, F. "The End of History?" *The National Interest* 16 (summer 1989): 3–18.

——— . *The End of History and the Last Man.* New York: Free Press, 1992.

Gaddis, J. L. "International Relations Theory and the End of the Cold War." *International Security* 17, no. 3 (1992–93): 5–58.

——— . "Tectonics, History, and the End of the Cold War." Occasional Paper (Mershon Center for Education in National Security. Columbus, OH: Ohio State University, Mershon Center, 1992.

——— . *The United States and the End of the Cold War: Implications, Reconsiderations, Provocations.* New York: Oxford University Press, 1992.

Garthoff, R. L. "Why Did the Cold War Arise, and Why Did It End?" *Diplomatic History* 16, no. 2 (1992): 287ff.

Gorbachev, M. *The August Coup: The Truth and the Lessons.* London: HarperCollins, 1991.

——— . "The River of Time." *Bulletin of the Atomic Scientists* 48, no. 6 (1992): 22–27.

Halliday, F. "The Ends of the Cold War." *New Left Review* 180 (March-April 1990): 5–24.

Harries, O. "Is the Cold War Really Over?" *National Review* 41, no. 21 (1989): 40ff.

Harris, S., & J. Cotton, eds. *The End of the Cold War in Northeast Asia.* Boulder, CO: Lynne Rienner, 1991.

Hauss, C. "The End of the Cold War? Challenges for Peace Education." *Peace and Change* 15, no. 3 (1990): 223ff.

Hawkes, N. "The Dawn of a New Age." *The Observer* (London) March 5, 1989.

Hogan, M. "The End of the Cold War: A Symposium." *Diplomatic History* 16, no. 2 (1992): 223ff.

Hogan, M., ed. *The End of the Cold War: Its Meanings and Implications.* Cambridge: Cambridge University Press, 1992.

Hopf, T., & J. L. Gaddis. "Getting the End of the Cold War Wrong." *International Security* 18, no. 2 (1993): 202–10.

Hunter, R. E. "Starting at Zero: U.S. Foreign Policy for the 1990s." *Washington Quarterly* 15, no. 1 (winter 1992): 42ff.

Huntington, S. P. "The End of History?" *Quadrant* 33, no. 10 (1989): 27–32.

Hyland, W. *The Cold War Is Over.* New York: Times Books, Random House, 1990.

Ilukhina, R. "A. Sakharov and M. Gorbachev: Russian Nobel Peace Prize Winners." Paper presented at an international conference on the Meaning and Acceptance of the Nobel Peace Prizes in the Prize-Winners' Countries. Oslo, Norway, 1992.

Joseph, P. *Peace Politics: The United States Between the Old and New World Orders.* Philadelphia: Temple University Press, 1993.

Kaiser, R. G. *Why Gorbachev Happened.* New York: Touchstone, 1991.

Kaldor, M. "After the Cold War." *New Left Review* 180 (March-April 1990): 25–40.

Kanet, R. E. "Mikhail Gorbachev and the End of the Cold War." *Soviet Union* 16, no. 2–3 (1989): 193ff.

Keithly, D. M. *The Collapse of East German Communism: The Year the Wall Came Down, 1989.* Westport, CT: Greenwood, 1992.

Kiyofuku, C. "An End to the Cold War?" *Japan Quarterly* 37, no. 3 (1990): 270ff.

Kriesberg, L. "Explaining the End of the Cold War." *New Views of International Security*, Occasional Paper Series No. 2 (Syracuse, NY: Syracuse University Press, 1990).

LaFeber, W. *America, Russia and the Cold War, 1945–1992.* 7th ed. New York: McGraw-Hill, 1993.

———. "An End to Which Cold War?" *Diplomatic History* 16, no. 1 (1992): 61ff.

Lesourne, J., & B. Lecomte. *After Communism: From the Atlantic to the Urals.* Philadelphia: Harwood Academic Publishers, 1992.

Lynch, A. *The Cold War Is Over—Again.* Boulder, CO: Westview, 1992.

Lynn-Jones, S. M., & S. E. Miller, eds. *The Cold War and After: Prospects for Peace.* Cambridge, MA: MIT Press, 1991.

Mandlebaum, M. "Ending the Cold War." *Foreign Affairs* 68, no. 2 (1989): 16–36.

Mann, Paul. "Reflections on the Cold War: End of the Game, or End of an Inning?" *Aviation Week and Space Technology* 131, no. 25 (1989): 18ff.

Meese, E. "The Man Who Won the Cold War." *Policy Review* 61 (summer 1992): 36–39.

Meyer, D. S. "How We Helped End the Cold War (and Let Someone Else Take All the Credit)." *Nuclear Times* 8, no. 4 (1990): 9ff.

———. "International Change from Below: Activism and the End of the Cold War." *Sociological Practice Review* 3, no. 4 (1992): 189ff.

———. *The Winter of Discontent.* Westport, CT: Praeger, 1993.

Nation, R. C. *Black Earth, Red Star: A History of Soviet Security Policy, 1917–1991.* Ithaca, NY: Cornell University Press, 1992.

Nissani, M. *Lives in the Balance: The Cold War and American Politics, 1945–1991.* Wakefield, NH: Hollowbrook Publishing, 1992.

Nixon, R. M. "A War about Peace: The Victory of Freedom." *Vital Speeches of the Day* 57, no. 12 (1991): 357–60.

Petersen, E. "The End of the Cold War: A Review of Recent Literature." *The History Teacher* 26, no. 4 (1993): 471ff.

Quester, G. H. "The 'End' of the Cold War." *Fletcher Forum of World Affairs* 15, no. 2 (1991): 1ff.

Renger, N. J. "Arms Control, International Society, and the End of the Cold War." *Arms Control* 13, no. 1 (1992): 32–57.

Risse-Kappen, T. "Did 'Peace Through Strength' End the Cold War?" *International Security* 16, no. 1 (1991): 162–88.

Roberts, A. *Civil Resistance in the East European and Soviet Revolutions.* Monograph Series No. 4. Cambridge, MA: Albert Einstein Institution, 1991.

Roberts, B. "Arms Control and the End of the Cold War." *Washington Quarterly* 15, no. 4 (1992): 39–56.

Rossi, G. "Africa Facing the End of the Cold War." *Rivista di Studi Politici Internazionale* 59, no. 3 (1992): 384–92.

Rusi, A. M. *After the Cold War: Europe's New Political Architecture.* New York: St. Martin's Press, 1991.

Shultz, G. P. *Turmoil and Triumph: My Years as Secretary of State.* New York: Charles Scribner's Sons, 1993.

Simons, T. W. *The End of the Cold War?* Basingstoke, England: Macmillan, 1990.

Soley, L. "Clandestine Radio and the End of the Cold War." *Media Studies Journal* 7, no. 3 (1993): 129ff.

Sturua, M. "The Real Coup." *Foreign Policy* 85 (winter 1992): 63–72.

Stutzle, W. "1987—The Turning-Point?" in *SIPRI Yearbook 1988: World Armaments and Disarmament,* 3–6. Oxford: Oxford University Press, 1988.

Suter, K. *Global Change: Armageddon and the New World Order.* Sydney: Albatross, 1992.

Thompson, E. "Comment—The Ends of Cold War." *New Left Review* 182 (July-August 1990): 139–46.

Thorne, C. "American Political Culture and the End of the Cold War." *Journal of American Studies* 26, no. 3 (1992): 303–30.

Trofimenko, H. "The End of the Cold War, Not History." *Washington Quarterly* 13, no. 2 (1990): 21ff.

Tuathail, G. O. "The Bush Administration and the 'End' of the Cold War: A Critical Geopolitics of US Foreign Policy in 1989." *Geoforum* 23, no. 4 (1992): 437ff.

Venturelli, S. "The End of the Cold War: European Unity, Socialism, and the Shift in Global Power" (Review Essay). *The Cresset* 55 (January 1992): 14–16.

Wheaton, B., & Z. Kavan. *The Velvet Revolution.* Boulder, CO: Westview, 1992.

Wicke, P. "The Times They Are A-Changin'." *Peace Review* 5, no. 2 (1993): 199–208.

Williams, P. "US-Soviet Relations: Beyond the Cold War?" *International Affairs* 65 (spring 1989): 278ff.

Wolfson, M. *Essays on the Cold War.* Basingstoke, England: Macmillan, 1992.

Index

About the Contributors

JOHN W. BURTON was a Distinguished Jennings Randolph Fellow at the United States Institute of Peace. He was an Australian delegate to the United Nations Charter Conference in 1945 and was appointed Permanent Head of the Australian Foreign Office in 1947. He is the author of many books, including *International Relations: A General Theory; World Society, Global Conflict: The Domestic Sources of International Crisis;* and *Conflict: Resolution and Provention.*

JOSEPH A. CAMILLERI is a Reader in Politics at La Trobe University, where he teaches international relations. Among his many books in the areas of strategic studies, peace research, and Australia's external relations has been the best-selling text *An Introduction to Australian Foreign Policy and Australian-American Relations: The Web of Dependence.*

APRIL F. CARTER was a Fellow of Somerville College, Oxford, from 1976 to 1984 and is now a Senior Lecturer in Political Science at the University of Queensland. Her most recent books are *Success and Failure in Arms Control Negotiations* and *Peace Movements: International Protests and World Politics since 1945.* Her theoretical interests relate primarily to democracy, the state, and militarism.

C. L. CHIOU is a Reader in Political Science at the University of Queensland whose major interest centers on Chinese politics. He has a secondary interest in the political development of postwar Japan. His publications include

Maoism in Action: The Cultural Revolution; Democracy and the Future of Taiwan; and *Political Cultures of Asia: Japan, Taiwan, and China.*

KEVIN P. CLEMENTS is Professor of Conflict Resolution and Director of the Institute for Conflict Analysis and Resolution at George Mason University. He is also President of the International Peace Research Association. His publications include *From Right to Left in Development Theory.* He recently was involved in the editing of three books: *Peace and Security in the Asia Pacific Region, UN Peacekeeping at the Crossroads,* and *Building International Community: Cooperating for Peace Case Studies.*

DAVID CORTRIGHT was the Executive Director of the National Committee for a Sane Nuclear Policy (SANE) from 1977 to 1988. Currently, he is the President of the Fourth Freedom Forum in Goshen, Indiana, and a visiting faculty fellow at the Joan B. Kroc Institute for International Peace Studies, University of Notre Dame. He is the author of *Peace Works: The Citizen's Role in Ending the Cold War.*

GEOFF DOW is a Senior Lecturer in Political Economy at the University of Queensland. He has taught and researched comparative political economy in Australia, the United Kingdom, Sweden, and Denmark. Some of his research appears in the jointly authored book *Class, Politics, and the Economy*, and in the jointly edited *The State, Class, and the Recession.*

ROBERT ELIAS is an Associate Professor of Politics and Chair of Peace and Justice Studies at the University of San Francisco. He is also the editor of *Peace Review* and on the editorial board of *New Political Science*. His books include *The Politics of Victimization: Victims, Victimology, and Human Rights,* and *New Culture, Less Crime.* In 1994, he coedited *Rethinking Peace* with Jennifer Turpin.

JOHAN GALTUNG founded both the International Peace Research Institute, Oslo (PRIO) and the *Journal of Peace Research*. He is the author of the six-volume *Essays in Peace Research* and many other books and articles. He has held numerous professorial posts around the world and is currently Professor of Peace Studies at the University of Hawaii and Professor at the Universitat Witten-Herdecke. In 1987 he received the Right Livelihood Award, and he has been a nominee for the Nobel Peace Prize for his contribution to peace research and peace studies.

RICK KUHN is a Lecturer in Political Science at the Australian National University. His scholarly interests, which are reflected in his publications, are political economy, labor party and movement politics, and Australian and New Zealand politics generally.

DAVID LANGE was Prime Minister of New Zealand from 1984 to 1989. During his administration, he banned all nuclear facilities, including visits to his country by nuclear-armed or nuclear-powered naval vessels. He strongly opposed France's testing of nuclear weapons in the Pacific, and prosecuted the French agents responsible for the bombing of the nuclear protest vessel, the *Rainbow Warrior*. His strong antinuclear stance was highlighted in a televised debate with American evangelist, Jerry Falwell, at Oxford University.

DENNIS PHILLIPS is a Senior Lecturer in History at Macquarie University, lecturing in American history and politics. He also coordinates the Peace Studies course. Among his many books are *Ambivalent Allies: Myth and Reality in the Australian-American Relationship*, and *Cold War 2 and Australia*.

MICHAEL E. SALLA is an Associate Lecturer in Political Science at the Australian National University. His scholarly interests are in the areas of nonviolence, international relations, peace studies, and ethnic/religious conflict. He is the author of *Islamic Radicalism: Muslim Nations and the West* (1993) and coeditor of *Essays on Peace: Paradigms for Global Order* (1995).

RALPH SUMMY is a Senior Lecturer in Political Science at the University of Queensland. He also coordinates the Peace and Conflict Studies program. He cofounded and continues to serve on the editorial collective of *Social Alternatives*. His research interests focus on nonviolent politics and the Australian peace movement. Among his many publications is the jointly authored *The Australian Peace Movement: A Short History*.

ULF SUNDHAUSSEN is a Reader in Political Science at the University of Queensland. His research and publishing interests center on political culture, civil-military relations, Third World politics (especially Indonesia), and politics in Western Europe. Among his many publications are *The Road to Power: Indonesian Military Politics, 1945–1967*, and the jointly authored work *A .H. Nasution, A Political Biography*.

KEITH SUTER has lectured in politics at the University of Sydney and directed an Australian-based national goals think tank. He has held executive positions in the United Nations Association of Australia and Friends of the

Earth and is a member of the Club of Rome. He is a prolific writer whose latest book is *Global Change: Armageddon and the New World Order.*

JENNIFER TURPIN is an Associate Professor of Sociology at the University of San Francisco. She also is the senior editor of *Peace Review.* Among her publications is the book *Reinventing the Soviet Self: Media and Social Change in the Former Soviet Union.* She coedited *Rethinking Peace* with Robert Elias.

JOANNE WRIGHT is a Lecturer in International Relations at the University of Queensland. Her research interests include nuclear strategy, terrorism, and West European politics. Among her publications is the book *Terrorist Propaganda: The Red Army Faction and the Provisional IRA, 1968–86.*

ISBN 0-313-29569-7

90000>

EAN

9 780313 295690

HARDCOVER BAR CODE